The ESSENCE *of* CATALONIA

The Comarques of Catalonia

PICTURE CREDITS

Albert A. Aubeyzon Fotògraf (Barcelona): pp. 42–3, 63, 73, 83, 113, 115, 117, 147, 172, 182; Ampliaciones y Reproducciones Mas (Barcelona): p. 205; Barceló Fotos (Barcelona): p. 66; F. Català-Roca (Barcelona): pp. 47, 69, 178, 247, 250–1; Departement de Comerç, Consum i Turisme (Barcelona): p. 100; Jordi Gumí Fotògraf (Barcelona): pp. 26, 60, 74, 91–2, 98, 160, 246, 268, 270–1, 273, 274; Eugenio Repòrter Fotògraf (Barcelona): p. 227; Museu d'Art de Catalunya (Barcelona): pp. 203–4; Museu d'Art Modern (Barcelona): pp. 256–60; Museu d'Història de la Ciutat (Barcelona): p. 32; Museu Nacional Arqueològic (Tarragona): p. 164; Spanish National Tourist Office (London): pp. 34–5, 37, 39, 50, 97, 101–2, 106, 161, 167, 184, 199.

All other photographs were taken by the author.

TEXT CREDITS

The extract from *Homage to Catalonia* by George Orwell is reproduced courtesy of the Estate of the late Sonia Brownell Orwell and Secker and Warburg Ltd; extracts from *Modern Architecture in Barcelona (1854–1939)* by David Mackay are reproduced courtesy of the author.

Introduction

The name Catalonia has a certain resonance in English. Most people know that Barcelona is the capital. Millions have used this city as the gateway to the Costa Brava or the Costa Daurada. Many will recall its prominent and ultimately tragic role in the Spanish Civil War. Orwell's *Homage to Catalonia* probably hovers somewhere in the minds even of those who have not read it. Some who are a bit closer to the subject will recall Professor Allison Peers's *Catalonia Infelix* and may have read Josep Trueta's *The Spirit of Catalonia*. Others will know that Gerald Brenan's *The Spanish Labyrinth* contains important Catalan sections. John Langdon-Davies's *Dancing Catalans* was published back in 1929, followed after the Second World War by his *Gatherings from Catalonia*. Earlier still, there were several eighteenth- and nineteenth-century British travellers who recorded their impressions of Catalonia. Henry Swinburne made a journey in 1775–6 in search of Roman and Moorish remains. Joseph Townsend followed him in 1786–7, paying particular attention to 'the Agriculture, Manufactures, Commerce, Population, Taxes and Revenue' of a region widely known for its manufacturing skills and commercial flair.

Further interest was stimulated by the Peninsular War and the heroic defence of Girona against the French: Robert Southey travelled in Catalonia while writing his history of the Peninsular War; his friend Edward Hawke Locker made a journey in 1813 with Lord John Russell, an account of which was published in *Views in Spain* (1824). The indefatigable Richard Ford included Catalonia in his famous *Handbook for Travellers in Spain* (1st ed., 1845) without disguising his preference for the more southerly lands of Moors, bandits and gypsies. And his view, if more pronounced than others, is not exceptional. For it has to be said that most British travellers, whether in more remote or more recent times, after describing the antiquities of the two or three principal cities of Catalonia, have tended to head south for 'romantic' Spain without paying too much attention to the Catalan interior. It is one of the purposes of this book to show that this is to deprive oneself of a whole spectrum of enjoyable and instructive experiences.

1

At one stage I thought this book should cover Greater Catalonia, which came about through the federal union of Aragon and Catalonia in 1137 and the subsequent incorporation of the Balearics and Valencia. This would have had the virtue of including the homelands of all Spaniards who speak Catalan – Valencian and Majorcan are essentially the same language as Catalan – and would certainly have pleased those of my Catalan friends who wish to see the historic confederation restored. But the reasons against this course were equally strong: it would have been impossible to carry it out within the scope of a single book without either skimping or making it inordinately long. And the present-day reality is that Aragon, Valencia and the Balearics all have their own statutes of autonomy and a separate relationship with central government. Besides, it would be hard to know where to stop: Catalan is also spoken in Perpignan, Roussillon and the French Cerdagne, which as far as I know have no intention of seceding from France. The Catalonia described here is, therefore, the autonomous region of that name arising out of the new Spanish constitution of 1978 and the Catalan statute of autonomy of 1979 derived from it.

The area I cover has two very positive attractions which are worth stressing at the outset. The first is that Barcelona belongs to the select club of great cosmopolitan Mediterranean cities which have managed to retain a human scale. With one and three-quarter million inhabitants it has virtually all the services and features – grand architecture, museums, theatre, music, art, good public transport, high and low life – that tend to be associated with a national capital but without the inconveniences of great size. It is a city you can come to grips with and enjoy within a relatively short time without feeling lost or bewildered or over-whelmed. It is open, informative, comprehensible, efficient and on the whole well planned. Yet it is more than an individual city like Marseilles, Naples or Seville, for it is also the capital of a nation of six million people, using this word now not in its nation-state connotation but to define a geographical and historical area whose inhabitants share a common language and a common culture. The second great attraction is that within this small nation there is great variety. There is a major mountain range with many subsidiary spurs and protuberances. There is a seacoast some 580 kilometres in length which is itself very variegated: there is a world of difference, for example, between Cape Creus and the Ebro delta. Moving inland, there are few similarities between the Vall d'Aran and the plain of Urgell or between the fruit plantations of Lleida and the cork forests of La Selva. I am not writing a brochure for the Catalan government but these things are true and should be stated.

Catalonia is subdivided into thirty-eight districts or *comarques* (sing. *comarca*), which are the same as those recognized by the earlier statute of autonomy of 1932. At the same time, and rather confusingly, the provinces of Girona, Lleida and Tarragona, as well as that of Barcelona, are still in existence. Dating from the French-inspired territorial reform of the 1830s and based on a centralist vision of the state, the latter were the administrative organs of General Franco's régime and there is an obvious tension between them and the *comarques* aspiring to replace them as the natural organic cells of the region. There is a further subdivision into something like a thousand municipalities, ranging from Barcelona to remote villages with under a hundred souls.

Sharing as it does the same peninsula, Catalonia naturally has some common characteristics with the rest of Spain: the most obvious are the Mediterranean climate, flora and fauna and the amount of land devoted to the almond, the vine and the olive. In other respects it is more remarkable for its differences. Although occasional waves of Europeanism were generated from Madrid, the Europeanism of Catalonia has never been much in doubt. The only real geographical interface between Iberia and the rest of Europe is to be found at the eastern end of the Pyrenean system, which has always been more permeable, and more permeated, than the higher central and western sectors, whose more difficult passes have been jealously defended by combative Basques, forming a sort of permanent buffer between Spain and Europe. To the south of the mountains much of Catalonia is extremely hilly and densely wooded – forty-three per cent of the landmass is occupied by wood or forest. But there are a central plain and narrow coastal plains which, together with the basins of the five main rivers – the Fluvià, the Ter, the Llobregat, the Francolí and above all the mighty Ebro – attracted settlers from very early times. Trueta considers that the Ebro was more of a natural boundary in those days than the Pyrenees; certainly it became the boundary between the Romans and Carthaginians and later between the Christian states and the Moors.

As a number of excellent archaeological museums demonstrate (Solsona is one of the best), the lowlands of Catalonia were popular from the Mesolithic period and positively crowded by the end of the Neolithic in about 2000 BC. Bronze and Iron Age cultures followed. In about 700 BC the Ter and Llobregat valleys were occupied by Indo-European tribes and between 700 and 500 BC Celts crossed the Pyrenees by the upland valleys of the Cerdagne and penetrated the valley of the river Segre. Iberians then began to spread upwards from their settlements around Alicante and Elche, bringing with them their culture, as exemplified by such sculptural masterpieces as the *Dama de Elche* (Museo Arqueológico, Madrid). Intermarriage with the Celts produced the Celtiberian stock, which is proverbial in the rest of Spain for hard-headed obstinacy and independence. Meanwhile, on the coastal flank, Phocaean Greeks established trading colonies at Roses and Empúries (Ampurias), through which at first Hellenic and then Roman influences flowed into the Catalan amalgam.

The Carthaginians conquered Spain between 239 and 228 BC. When the Romans arrived, they concluded a pact with their rivals in 226, establishing the frontier along the Ebro. They then set up the province of Septimania, which included much of Catalonia and was ruled from Béziers. During the second Punic War (218–201 BC), the Carthaginians were expelled from the mainland and forced to take refuge in Ibiza and Minorca, and the Roman centre of gravity shifted southwards to Tarragona (Tarraco), which became the most important Roman city in the peninsula; Augustus later further enhanced its status and it became the capital of the imperial province of Tarraconensis, controlling not only Catalonia but most of the rest of the peninsula as well. Barcelona was of much less account in Roman times, not acquiring adequate walls until the fourth century when Roman domination was nearing its end.

After the sack of Rome (AD 410) and the collapse of the empire, the vacuum was filled in a transient fashion by successive waves of Vandals, Cimbri, Teutons and Ambrones. This flux was not really halted until the Visigoths began to push south from their first capital of Toulouse in the fifth century. Euric set up his capital at Narbonne and then moved it to Barcelona. His successors continued the southward drive, ultimately selecting Toledo as their imperial capital. I always find the Visigothic civilization rather opaque, perhaps because there were relatively few of them, possibly some two hundred thousand, controlling an indigenous population of Romanized Iberians who were the real repositories of the spirit of the country. Although the best collections of Visigothic artefacts are to be found in the Museo Arqueológico in Madrid and the Museo Visigótico in Toledo, nonetheless there are some interesting Visigothic remains in

Catalonia, notably at Terrassa just outside Barcelona and in the capital itself, which help to shed some light on their somewhat inscrutable culture.

The Moorish invasion of 711 sliced like a gleaming sickle across the peninsula, reaching Catalonia in 717 and penetrating far up into France until arrested by Charles Martel at Poitiers in 732. The Moors attained no firm footing either on the northern or southern flanks of the Pyrenees. Charlemagne then established the Spanish march, which comprised the feudal counties of Roussillon, Cerdagne, Urgell, Besalú, Barcelona, Girona, Osona and Empúries. These became the southern bastions of the Frankish empire. Gradually the counties of the march weakened their links with that empire in its decline and went their own ways until a number of them were gathered in by Wilfred, count of Cerdanya-Urgell, who in 878 founded the house of Barcelona, which was to rule Catalonia for more than five hundred years. Guifré el Pilós, as he was known, is variously rendered into English as Wilfred the Shaggy, the Hairy or the Hirsute, but in order to avoid choosing between the uninviting English versions of his sobriquet I shall simply call him Count Wilfred. A deeply rooted legend is attached to his name which runs that, after his valiant support of Charles the Bald at the gates of Paris, the Frankish king dipped his fingers in the blood flowing from Wilfred's wounds and drew them across the Catalan warrior's unblazoned golden shield, thus creating the four red bars on a yellow ground which form the scutcheon and flag of Catalonia. There are other versions of a similar stamp – it was obviously desirable from a popular point of view to attribute the coat of arms and the national emblem to the first independent count of Barcelona – but in fact neither the arms nor the flag was formally adopted until 1082; even so the Catalan national flag is the oldest in Europe, antedating that of Denmark by more than a century.

Count Wilfred founded a line that lasted until the Compromise of Caspe in 1412 brought a Castilian, Ferdinand of Antequera, to the throne of Aragon-Catalonia. Wilfred was by all accounts a warrior who also had some feeling for the arts of peace. The writ of Christian rulers was already well enough established in what is now northern Catalonia to permit the foundation during the ninth century of a number of mainly small and mainly Benedictine monasteries. Wilfred reinforced and extended this civilizing process by himself founding in about 880 the famous abbey of Ripoll and its feminine counterpart Sant Joan de les Abadesses in 885, of which his daughter Emma was to be the first abbess.

As well as consolidating their domains south of the Pyrenees Count Wilfred's successors, in more or less constant enmity with the counts of Toulouse, retained their Provençal possessions and attempted to underpin them by marriage, as in the case of Ramon Berenguer III, who in 1113 married the heiress of the county of Provence. These dynastic marriages, claims and counterclaims with their attendant squabbles over who owed allegiance to whom are extremely complex and difficult to follow and not perhaps of vast interest except to specialists. But there are some crucial dates coming up. In 1137 the counts of Barcelona became rulers of the much poorer kingdom of Aragon through the marriage of Ramon Berenguer IV to Petronella, heiress of Aragon. Though this union was federal in the sense that each state preserved its own parliament and customs, there were far-reaching consequences which will emerge shortly. During the reign of Alfons the Chaste (1162–96), Roussillon was formally incorporated under the crown of Aragon, but otherwise some very damaging deals were struck with Castile from the point of view of future Aragonese-Catalan influence in the peninsula. The reconquest of Cuenca by Alfonso VIII of Castile in 1177 was achieved with the collaboration of the federation but without any *quid pro quo* and, more seriously, by the treaty of Cazorla in 1179 the Aragonese crown renounced in favour of Castile any right to or interest in the reconquest of Murcia, thus effectively limiting for ever its possibilities of southerly expansion and leaving to Castile an open field for a leisurely – extremely leisurely – completion of the reconquest of the rest of the Spanish mainland over the next three centuries.

These self-denying ordinances by Count Wilfred's successors were clearly due to preoccupations in other areas, not all of which had successful outcomes. The next important date is 1213, when King Peter the Catholic, only one year after helping the Castilians to win the crucial battle of Las Navas de Tolosa, which opened up the whole of the Guadalquivir valley, was himself killed in the battle of Muret, effectively putting an end to the Provençal ambitions that had formed the cornerstone of the policy of the later counts of Barcelona and the first count-kings of the federation. The trans-Pyrenean zone of influence (to pitch it a bit lower than 'empire' in those rather confused times), which had stretched as far as Nice and up to Albi, began to shrink drastically until virtually extinguished by the treaty of Corbeil in 1258, whereby the French king renounced his almost worthless paper rights as Charlemagne's successor to a number of patently Catalan counties, while James I renounced all the rather more substantial Catalan claims north of the Pyrenees with the exception of his right to Montpellier.

James I was king from 1213 to 1276, and his long reign is remembered less for his failure in France than for his successes in other directions. He took Valencia and Majorca and thus became Jaume el Conqueridor (James the Conqueror), after whom so many streets and squares are named. This made sense in terms of consolidating his peninsular and offshore positions (within the limits of the agreement signed with Castile), but even more importantly it was during his reign that Catalan Mediterranean ambitions escalated, partly I think as a result of frustration north of the Pyrenees, partly because of the restrictions on further reconquest to the south and partly, but not least, because the mercantile class – it is a bit early to talk of the bourgeoisie – that had grown up under the wing of the house of Barcelona actively demanded an expansion of trade which could, in the circumstances, only be secured by colonization beyond the peninsula.

After the conquest of Majorca in 1229 the next major step was the establishment of a bridgehead, so to speak; this was achieved by Peter the Great, who took advantage of the rising in Sicily in 1282 (known as the Sicilian Vespers) against Charles of Anjou to assert his right to that crown through his wife Constance, daughter of the late King Manfred. Sicily was successfully invaded and then served as a base for the capture of Athens and Neopatria (1302–11) by Roger de Flor with his mercenaries, the famous Almogàvers; next Corsica was taken (1323), followed by Sardinia (1324) and eventually Naples (1423), making Catalonia the greatest power in the Mediterranean in the fourteenth and early fifteenth centuries with consulates in no less than fifty-four towns and cities. This phase of Catalan history set the scene for the colourful exploits of the great corsairs, not only Roger de Flor but also Roger de Llúria (or Lauria), who had earlier defeated the Angevin fleet at Malta (1283) and in the bay of Naples (1284). Often denigrated as pirates, like Drake after them, these mercenary leaders were highly valued by their royal employers, it being cheaper to engage their services than to maintain a regular fleet. It is their patriotism that is stressed in popular legend and these two in particular rank high in the league of Catalan heroes. The exploits of the former and of the Almogàvers are the subject of murals in Barcelona city hall and many historical paintings; the latter is buried next to his master, Peter the Great, in Santes Creus.

All this was very fine and splendid, but it was a distraction from the peninsula. It has been suggested to me that the essence of Castile was warlike and that its whole culture and ethos were based on campaigns against the Moors, whereas the more commercially minded Catalonia was bound to seek trading outlets wherever it could find them. And, in effect, while the Catalans were absorbed by their Mediterranean interests, Castile had ambled its way southwards – it took two and a half centuries to carry the reconquest from Seville to Granada alone – establishing forms of government and institutions that were really rather alien to those of freedom-loving Catalans. I cannot help but wonder what might not have happened if Aragon-Catalonia had pressed on southwards, outflanked Castile, taken Córdoba and Seville and established the confederation as the main political force in the peninsula. It might of course have led to the overextension and collapse of a relatively small kingdom, but it might equally have succeeded, for Castile was deeply divided by civil wars in the fourteenth century. The question, though hypothetical, is not entirely frivolous: when the moral and political bankruptcy of Spain culminated in the loss of Cuba, Puerto Rico and the Philippines in 1898, Catalonia did not have the geographical base in the peninsula or the national clout to assume the role of leadership into the twentieth century to which some of its politicians aspired.

But that is to jump the gun. Returning to chronological tracks, the death of Martin the Humane without issue in 1410 brought Count Wilfred's line to an end and put the throne into the hands of an electoral college, from which, after much intrigue by supporters of all six claimants, a most Castilian prince, Ferdinand of Antequera, emerged the victor. He only reigned for four years but with the change of dynasty the history of Aragon-Catalonia altered course. Alfons the Magnanimous, a most cultivated man, abandoned Barcelona in 1443 to establish himself in Naples. In his absence, the Generalitat, the highest organ of government under the crown, began to act in a sovereign capacity to the extent of carrying on a war against Alfons's brother and successor John II, whom it formally deposed. The loyalty of Catalonia to its royal house was seriously weakened and the interests of that house were in any case no longer one and the same as the interests of the Catalan people.

During the course of the fifteenth century, attacks on the Jews, who had been favoured and protected by the monarchs of the Aragonese-Catalan confederation as bankers and bureaucrats,

8

increased markedly. In 1469 the future Ferdinand the Catholic, that most Machiavellian prince, married Isabel of Castile. The Castilian throne came to her after a short civil war in 1474, the Aragonese throne to him on the death of his father John II in 1479. The Inquisition, which had existed since the thirteenth century, had traditionally been applied rather lightly in Aragon-Catalonia. All this changed. Dominican inquisitors (*domini canes* – dogs of the Lord, as one wag put it) were appointed as elsewhere. Their yoke was firmly set on Aragonese and Catalan necks. In 1492 the Jews were expelled. It was in 1492 likewise that Granada finally fell to Ferdinand and Isabel and that Columbus returned from his first voyage. I have always disliked 1492: it was such a triumphal year for Castile and I have an aversion to triumphalism. Also, it shifted the world's centre of gravity from the Mediterranean to the Atlantic – much to the detriment of Catalonia. Barcelona, Marseille, Genoa and Naples all lost weight. The cities of the future were to be São Paolo, Buenos Aires, New York, Mexico, which were to develop on an altogether different scale. The immediate Spanish beneficiaries were Cádiz and Seville.

After the union of the crowns of Aragon and Castile, Aragonese and Catalan customs and institutions remained intact on paper but power shifted to the Supreme Council of Aragon, increasingly dominated by Castilian viceroys. Isabel's strong absolutist tendencies, shared by her husband, ensured that there would be no further development of separate institutional rights in Catalonia: the long erosion had set in. This was accompanied by severe discrimination in trade whereby Barcelona was debarred from participation in the fruits of the discovery of the New World. The Aragonese patrimony of the Spanish crown became merely another source of soldiers and revenue. Things came to a head in the War of the Reapers (1640–52), when the people rose against demands by Philip IV's favourite, the Count-Duke of Olivares, for money, men and quarters for his mercenary army in the war against France. They declared a republic and placed it under the protection of the French king, Louis XIII. Their litany of grievances was turned into a marching song, *Els Segadors* ('The Reapers'); which was later to become the Catalan national anthem. None of this was of much avail. Barcelona surrendered in 1652. By the treaty of the Pyrenees of 1659 (at which the painter Velázquez was one of the commissioners) Philip IV ceded to France, Roussillon, Vallespir, Conflent and part of the Cerdagne. The Catalans had achieved nothing but the severance of their remaining brethren north of the Pyrenees, though ironically their rising on their own behalf contributed to the liberation of Portugal on the other side of the peninsula by drawing off the royal army, which could not cope with two rebellions at once.

The death of Charles II without issue in 1700 led to the War of the Spanish Succession, in which Catalonia, along with England and Genoa, espoused the cause of the Austrian claimant against the dauphin's son, the future Philip V. The Genoese motive was financial: they had acted as bankers to the Spanish Habsburgs, a source of profit they would lose with a Bourbon on the throne. The English could not contemplate with equanimity such a distortion of the balance of power. The Catalans wanted to recover their liberties and break the Castilian monopoly on the American trade. It is noteworthy that at the time of the pact of Genoa of 1704 Catalonia still maintained an ambassador in London, Pau Ignasi de Dalmases, a well-known figure at the court of Queen Anne. In 1705 Lord Peterborough stormed and took the fortress of Montjuïc overlooking Barcelona, which was occupied by Bourbon troops, an action described by Ford as 'one of the most brilliant feats of that chivalrous commander, the Don Quixote of History'. However, the conclusion of the war with the confirmation of the first Bourbon on the throne of Spain led to severe repression. Catalan laws and institutions were suspended. A fortress, La Ciutadella, was built on the site of the present park of that name, to control 'the rebel subjects of His Majesty'. The universities of Barcelona and Lleida were closed and in 1718 a new university was opened at Cervera (which had supported the Bourbon cause), designed to teach the new orthodoxy. The language was proscribed for official purposes, though it survived on the farms and among the artisans, clergy, lawyers and minor nobility. This loss of ancient liberties is commemorated every year on 11 September – known as the *Diada*, which simply means momentous day – when Philip V's troops entered and sacked Barcelona after a thirteen-month siege. The *Diada* is still used as an occasion for launching current Catalan complaints.

Whether all this was quite as dire as it sounds is open to question. Political failure drove Catalonia in on itself but also stimulated private initiative and social institutions outside the framework of the state. The Catalan people dug in, tilled their land, developed their craft-based industries, built their modest but solid churches, preserved their language – and survived. A distinguished historian told me he was once asked by Josep Tarradellas, head of the Catalan government in exile and first president of the restored Generalitat after Franco's death, to sum up the spirit of Catalonia in a single image. The historian offered the red bars of the national flag, but Tarradellas scornfully rejected this: No, he said, Catalonia is like a dry-stone wall which is washed away by a flood and no sooner has the flood subsided than the people come out to rebuild it.

There were also factors favourable not only to survival but to economic growth. The population doubled in the eighteenth century, more land was brought under cultivation, productivity improved, profits were invested in commerce and industry, the surplus labour from the countryside moved to the cities where it found employment. At the same time there was some official alleviation of Catalonia's subordinate condition. The suburb of Barceloneta was built to replace the district that Philip V had demolished to make way for his citadel. Charles III founded what was intended to be a great fishing port at Sant Carles de la Ràpita. In 1778 the embargo on trade with the New World was finally lifted and this provided a stimulus to shipbuilding and the export of textiles. My historian friend shed few tears over Catalonia's long exclusion from the Atlantic, which he felt had served to internalize and concentrate its energies, which might otherwise have been overextended and dissipated.

Before these energies could be unleashed, however, the French Revolution and the Peninsular War (1808–14) intervened (it should be remembered that the latter was *la Guerra de la Independencia* – the War of Independence – as far as the peninsula itself is concerned and you never hear much mention of Wellington). Although most members of the upper classes in Madrid belonged to the French party and accepted Napoleon's appointment of his brother Joseph as King of Spain, the lower classes did not (cf. Goya's canvases, the *Second* and *Third of May 1808*, Museo del Prado, Madrid) and on this occasion the Catalans too were vehemently anti-French. There were several heroic actions in Catalonia, notably the long defence of Girona against a vastly superior besieging army (1809). Also Montserrat, the shrine and symbol of all that is Catalan, was seized and sacked – though it should be recalled when talking of the indisputable outrages performed by the French soldiery upon the monks that Montserrat was not only a monastery but also a fortress and defended as such.

During the war the national *cortes* in exile in Cádiz proclaimed a liberal constitution in 1812, which was promptly repudiated by the Bourbon Ferdinand VII, resettled on the throne of Spain by the treaty of Versailles. Spanish liberalism has from time to time raised hopes in Catalonia which have not been fulfilled. The constitution of 1837 was accompanied by Mendizábal's tardy reformation when monastic lands were sold off to pay the national debt and to provide the government with some working capital; however, the purchasers were often lawyers who simply formed a new landowning class and the liberal administrations remained fundamentally centralist. From this period dates the division of the country into fifty provinces on the French model with governors appointed from Madrid, the creation of a national police force (the Guardia Civil) and the reimposition of Castilian on Catalan schools. Catalans played a leading role in the so-called 'revolutionary period' of 1868–74. It was General Prim who sent Queen Isabel II packing and went abroad for a new monarch, the reluctant Amadeo of Savoy. But Prim was assassinated while Amadeo was on his way and the imported king abdicated shortly afterwards. The short-lived First Republic (1873–4) was presided over first by another Catalan, Pi i Margall, but he survived only a matter of months. None of these ephemeral régimes was capable of creating the modern industrial society for which the Catalan bourgeoisie yearned. Catalonia never became (and is still not) liberal territory; the Bourbon restoration of 1874 in the person of Alfonso XII was strongly supported by Catalan conservatives.

Of far more importance to Catalonia than the seesaw of national politics was a native phenomenon that came to be called the *Renaixença* (Renaissance). This should not be thought of as a political *risorgimento* of the Italian type because it did not initially formulate any political goals and did not, in the event, succeed in modernizing the south from the north. Its first stirrings in the 1830s were linguistic and literary but as it developed it percolated and irrigated not only the cultural but also the economic and political fields. It should not be assumed from its first emergence in poetic and philosophical garb that it was entirely exclusive or élitist. The language had endured through several centuries of repression and nonrecognition and was revived simply in the sense that it once again became of interest to literary people and was then taken up by intellectuals and politicians to make intellectual and political points. Jacint Verdaguer and Joan Maragall wrote Catalan poems; Valentí Almirall used Catalan in an influential daily newspaper. But they did not invent the language and could have done none of this if it had not been there to hand in the first place. Business interests at first treated the Catalan renaissance as a purely cultural development but later sought to exploit the pervasive *catalanisme* that sprang from it, although this did not happen until their disillusion with the restored Bourbon monarchy and the Madrid politicians was far advanced.

Catalonia resumed economic growth after the Napoleonic wars. This growth was based in the early stages on water-powered mills and forges situated along the river valleys. With the invention of steam power the pace of expansion quickened. The first railway in Spain was the local line from Barcelona to Mataró further up the coast (1848) and this was shortly followed by a much wider network to Zaragoza, Valencia, Tarragona, Girona and the French border. But it was not only manufacturing industries and infrastructure that developed: Reus near Tarragona became a world centre of trade in almonds, hazelnuts and dried fruits, while the cork forests did well from the growing popularity of champagne. The major exercise in commercial public relations of the century was the great Universal Exhibition of 1888, strongly promoted by the mayor and corporation of Barcelona. This was the beginning of the city's reputation as an international trade-fair centre, which it maintains and exploits to this day.

It is desirable here, I think, to attempt a sketch of the Catalan bourgeoisie who were behind all these activities. There had been a very strong craft and guild system in the Middle Ages and Ford remarks that many of the tombstones in Barcelona's cathedral cloister bear the trademarks of master craftsmen who had themselves founded chapels and paid for works of art, rather than the more usual armorial bearings of penniless gentry. The Mediterranean conquests of the kings of Aragon were enthusiastically supported by merchants in search of markets. The important Jewish communities in Barcelona, Girona, Besalú, Lleida and Tortosa certainly contributed to early notions of capitalism; as they were not bound by the Church's prohibition of usury they were able to arrange loan capital for the crown and nobility and even after the expulsion of the Jews in 1492 not a few remained as *conversos* or nominal apostates, so their expertise in financial services was not lost. The system of tenure of relatively small farms based on primogeniture undoubtedly encouraged younger sons to move into the towns and start up small businesses. By the same token, farming units remained intact and were enabled to improve and specialize. All these factors contributed to the growth and strength of the bourgeoisie and made Catalonia a ready recipient for the early inventions of the industrial revolution.

All this appears very fine and progressive. There can be little doubt that Catalonia is as different as it is from the rest of Spain – 'high-bred indolent Spain' in Ford's approving words – because it was the only zone of the peninsula, with the exception of the slightly later Basque equivalent, to possess an active entrepreneurial bourgeoisie. But there were difficulties on the way. The Catalan industrialists wanted special treatment; in 1885 they presented King Alfonso XII with a document demanding protection for their industries. They did not want free trade. When Cuba, the Philippines and Puerto Rico were lost in 1898 and these tied markets wiped out at a stroke, their exasperation with the incompetent militarism of Madrid reached a high point. Any notion they might have entertained of leading the country as a whole into the twentieth century was dropped and they became late converts to the idea of Catalan nationalism – that is, of going it alone. But however legitimate their complaints against Madrid, their own performance left a great deal to be desired. Apart from their protectionism, their labour relations were extremely primitive; for example, laws limiting the daily hours of female labour to eleven and prohibiting the employment of children under the age of ten did not come into effect until 1907 and in the event had to be foisted on them by Madrid. Eduardo Moreno and Francisco Martí in *Catalunya para españoles* (1979) are very critical of the bourgeois position, which they see as 'closer through its reactionary conservatism to industrial feudalism than to economic liberalism . . .' and anchored to 'the purest type of Manchester capitalism sprinkled with clerical paternalism'. Whether you share the centre-left viewpoint of that book or not, it is clear that Catalan employers were determined not to recognize working-class organizations. This put them in the inconsistent position of resenting and despising central government yet depending on it for the preservation of law and order. It is therefore hardly surprising that when they adopted *catalanisme* as a last resort, they were unable to build a solid Catalan nationalist movement across all classes and this produced violent polarizations.

On the credit side, the bourgeoisie were essential to the cultural flowering of the *Renaixença*, particularly in architecture, the visual and graphic arts, music and the theatre. These are the aspects of Catalan life best known and most accessible to the outsider. The main movement to emerge from the renaissance was Modernisme, whose architectural expression is often simply seen as a Catalan version of Art Nouveau, though it had greater force and thrust and caught on more extensively with all sectors

14

of society. The Catalan architects and designers knew all about Ruskin and Morris but had the good fortune to coincide with a strong political trend towards Catalan nationalism which required outward and visible expression. Although Modernisme may appear, as in a sense it was, avant-garde, most of its leading lights were on the right politically, including Antoni Gaudí. His is the most famous name but he should not be regarded either as the leader or as typical of the movement. It is true he shares with his fellow practitioners the incorporation into his buildings of a wide range of craft materials, but he was more imaginative and inventive and plain eccentric than his fellows and achieved more fluid effects with steel, concrete and brick; in later life he became obsessed with religious symbolism and slave to a gigantic folly, the church of the Sagrada Família. It was a period in which Ibsen, Nietzsche and Wagner were popular and it has been said that the great bourgeois family houses and mansion flats along the Passeig de Gràcia rose to the strains of *Der Ring des Nibelungen*.

Modernisme was succeeded by Noucentisme. The former had received a great boost from the Exhibition of 1888; the latter, a leaner and less extravagant movement, brought a more rationalist and ultimately more classical solution to architectural problems. Le Corbusier was its hero, and in Barcelona Josep Lluís Sert, who was later to build the Miró Foundation, was one of its principal exponents before his emigration to Harvard. The new classicism was the dominant mode in the great Exhibition of 1929, which was set up on the Montjuïc hill as part of a great scheme of urban reclamation. The enormous Palau Nacional is totally lacking in originality but is now home to the Museu d'Art de Catalunya, one of the great museums of the world.

Modernisme and Noucentisme were bridges, if frail ones, to modern art. Though Picasso is now institutionalized in his own museum, stocked mainly with the Jaume Sabartés collection and the artist's own later gifts, Picasso was a bird of passage: he moved permanently to France in 1904 and never returned to Barcelona after 1934. Miró, on the other hand, was and still is symbolically very important to Catalonia. His status as grand old man and mentor is suitably recognized by Sert's splendidly clean spare building housing the foundation. His murals greet you at the airport, his designs form the cover of tourist brochures. Miró belongs: Miró is *cosa nostra*. Dalí is also very Catalan, exhibiting extraordinary qualities as showman, entrepreneur and humourist; in some respects he is not unlike Gaudí, a great eccentric. But he does not enjoy the same elevated place within the pantheon of *catalanisme* as Miró: during the Civil War he supported General Franco.

This brings me back to politics, regrettably perhaps, but some familiarity with the political map of Catalonia is unavoidable if the region is to be understood today. As I have already suggested, some of the progressive elements in the nineteenth century were distinctly right-wing; there was little political liberalism in our sense of the word, and the leading working-class movement to emerge was anarchism. But these political configurations are of more than local interest – if only because of the close scrutiny given them by British writers such as George Orwell, Franz Borkenau and Gerald Brenan, and the continuing magnetism of the Spanish Civil War. For these reasons I have attempted a more detailed analysis in 'Political Life and Institutions'.

Here I will limit myself to a rapid sketch of the scene. A helpful distinction is made by Moreno and Martí between *catalanitat* and *catalanisme*. The former is a concept based on language and culture and is innate among all Catalan speakers. The latter, springing from the nineteenth-century renaissance, was eventually taken up by the commercial and political classes as a weapon against Madrid; it was in the main a bourgeois autonomist movement from which the industrial workers were absent. Basically *catalanisme* has limited its aspirations to some form of federal status rather than thoroughgoing separatism, in which it differs from Basque nationalism. Nor in modern times has it given birth to terrorism. Barcelona's reputation at the turn of the century as a city of bombs and anarchist excesses (partly fomented by the right as an excuse for repression) cannot be attributed to Catalan nationalism but to working-class movements which could find no legitimate outlets. An attempt was made in 1907 under the banner of *Solidaritat Catalana* and the leadership of Francesc Cambó, president of the Lliga (League), to unite all Catalan political interests in a common cause but the attempt was brief. In 1909 the people rose against conscription for the war in Morocco, which led to mob rule, violence, church-burning and considerable loss of life in the *Setmana Tràgica* (Tragic Week). The employers insisted on reprisals and executions followed, further fuelling the anti-political anarchism of the working class. In this climate of class conflict it is easy to understand how *catalanitat* failed to translate into widespread *catalanisme*. It was not entirely through sinister outside forces that Barcelona became the capital of world anarchism until 1939 – the bourgeoisie must bear a substantial share of the blame.

There was, however, an interlude in which the Lliga, the party of business and industry, did manage to play a more positive political role. After several years of patient negotiation with Madrid, permission was secured for a voluntary union of the assemblies of the four Catalan provinces, which came into being in 1914 as the Mancomunitat. Under the leadership of the energetic conservative Prat de la Riba, it successfully harnessed most of the creative and progressive forces of the time. Prat died young and was succeeded by Puig i Cadafalch, the architect, who remained president until the abolition of the Mancomunitat after General Primo de Rivera's coup d'état in 1923. Primo was very popular in the south (he was an Andalusian) and a programme of public works was embarked on, culminating in the simultaneous Barcelona and Seville Exhibitions of 1929 (in the teeth of the Wall Street crash and world recession). The general fell in 1930 and in 1931 the municipal elections turned into a referendum on the monarch and sent Alfonso XIII into exile. None of the political parties ever forgave the king for his espousal of Primo's dictatorship. (In a moment of joviality he once introduced the general as *'mi Mussolini'*. Primo was certainly no Mussolini but the comment did not impress the politicians.) In an eccess of enthusiasm after these elections Colonel Francesc Macià proclaimed the republic of Catalunya within a future Iberian confederation, but he soon had to climb down from this semi-mystical position and settle for the restoration of the Generalitat.

The rest, as they say, is history – on the wide screen. The national elections of 1932 returned a popular front government. The Generalitat was reconstituted with a new Catalan statute. But the national government failed to get to grips with the most burning issue of the time, agrarian reform, and there were notable outbreaks of violence, particularly in Andalusia. This led to a right-wing government in 1934, which ushered in the famous *bienni negre* (black biennium); the left remained in the ascendancy in Barcelona. Nineteen thirty-six produced a new popular front, shortly followed by the assassination of Calvo Sotelo and the orchestrated military rising of 17–18 July, which formally inaugurated the Spanish Civil War of 1936–9. When Orwell arrived in December

> Barcelona was something startling and overwhelming. It was the first time I had ever been in a town where the working class was in the saddle. . . Servile and ceremonial forms of speech had temporarily disappeared. Nobody said 'Señor' or 'Don' or even 'Usted';

everyone called everyone else 'Comrade' and 'Thou' . . . Tipping
was forbidden. . . There were no private motor cars. . . The revolutionary posters were everywhere, flaming from the walls in clean
reds and blues that made the few remaining advertisements look
like daubs of mud. Down the Ramblas. . . the loudspeakers were
bellowing revolutionary songs all day and far into the night. And it
was the aspect of the crowds that was the queerest thing of all.
Except for a small number of women and foreigners there were no
'well-dressed' people at all. Practically everyone wore rough
working-class clothes or blue overalls or some variant of the militia
uniform. All this was queer and moving. There was much in it I did
not understand, in some ways I did not even like it, but I recognized
it immediately as a state of affairs worth fighting for.

(Homage to Catalonia, 1938)

Orwell, who was despatched to the Aragon front without adequate training or weapons, was shortly to be very critical of the
interfaction feuding, the poor supplies and the bad organization:
it is a miracle that he ever survived to die at a relatively early age
from tuberculosis. The war continued its well-documented
course. Madrid resisted a long siege but the government evacuated to Valencia. Catalonia was the scene of the great battle of the
Ebro, when Republican troops crossing the river to relieve
pressure on Valencia were pinned down for several months,
unable to continue their advance for lack of air cover, with huge
loss of life. There was open Italian and German intervention
despite the nonintervention pact; British, French and American
idealists joined up as private citizens. The Aragon front offensive
failed. Guernica was destroyed. Bilbao fell. Valencia was in its
turn evacuated. Then the *chute* began: early in 1939 four or five
hundred thousand refugees straggled into France through the
frontier posts north of Barcelona. Among them was the poet
Antonio Machado, the Sevillian who so superbly interpreted
Castile in *Campos de Castilla* (1912); he died just across the border
at Collioure. Lluís Companys, president of the Generalitat, is
reputed to have said on abandoning Catalonia, 'We will fight
again; we will suffer again; we will return victorious.' He was
later captured by the Gestapo in France and returned to Spain
where he was shot. But his valedictory words were not wholly
unprophetic.

During the Franco years the old central-state apparatus was
reimposed on Catalonia with great rigour and there were severe
reprisals, including executions. The Catalan language was banned in the schools, the churches, the media, the press and

commercial documents. Obviously it could not be stamped out of private use, any more than Basque could be. But it was certainly discouraged to the maximum and parish priests were reported for saying mass in Catalan. The monasteries were a bit more independent and Montserrat became a centre not exactly of resistance (the Benedictines stressed reconciliation) but at least a repository of *catalanitat* in hard times; the abbots were not, like bishops, appointed by the central state and could not be bullied. For this reason the abbot of Montserrat to this day enjoys enormous prestige among all Catalans. Economically the government did everything it could to build up its power base in Madrid: most of the investment went to this poorly located industrial centre with no port or river and an inefficient road network. This continued even after the *apertura* of 1959, when industrialists told Franco he had to modernize the economy, as government investment per head of the population in Catalonia remained relatively low. Culturally there was always a certain independence among painters, whose medium enabled them to be more enigmatic than writers. The student movement of 1968 caused some ripples in Spain and the régime quite cynically allowed a little breathing space, a sort of safety valve, to university and other small literary magazines of very limited circulation. The theatre as a public spectacle was more of a threat and attracted greater censure. Even as late as 1978, after Franco's death, the leading actors of the Catalan group Els Joglars, who were held to have insulted the army in one of their productions, were tried by a military court and sent to prison. The Franco years are extraordinarily well evoked in Pere Gimferrer's long poem *L'espai desert* (*The Empty Space*, 1976).

When General Franco finally died at the end of 1975, a great hush fell over the whole country. No one quite knew what was going to happen. But unlike most dictators he left a mechanism for succession in his Organic Law of the State (1966). The council of the kingdom met. A king in the person of Juan Carlos de Borbón, son of the count of Barcelona and grandson of Alfonso XIII, was waiting in the wings and was speedily sworn in. A constituent parliament was called and a draft constitution was elaborated, and approved by the first proper general election in 1978. This may be a bland account of a quietly traumatic period, but Spain was determined to put its violent past behind it.

The new constitution provided for a measure of devolution within a unitary state. The principal ethnic and cultural minorities latched on to this immediately with Catalonia first in the queue, headed by the almost legendary figure of Josep Tarradellas, who had formed part of Companys' administration and acted as head of the government of Catalonia in exile from 1954 until his return in 1977. However, the new statute of autonomy was something less than active Catalan nationalists would have liked. The constitution, which is rather vaguely drafted (no doubt deliberately), is open to various constructions in the chapter on regional autonomies and the Generalitat is already at loggerheads with central government over questions of legality, interpretation and so forth. But the Catalans are good at making much out of little: *El catalán*, runs the old Castilian proverb, *de las piedras saca pan*. (The Catalan can turn stones into bread.) And there is another equally potent element in the Catalan character – *seny*. This is largely untranslatable but lies somewhere in the area of good sense, judgement, wisdom, a sense of proportion. It may seem less immediately attractive than the Andalusian *duende*, also untranslatable but roughly flair, inspired improvisation, unpremeditated grace. Both are needed, but *seny* is particularly necessary for rebuilding Spain.

Trying to bring the complexities of Catalan history into a single and reasonably clear focus, I am drawn back to the modern sculptor Josep Maria Subirachs' wall relief in the Generalitat, in which Liberty, the Eclipses, Ariadne, the Labyrinth, Saint George, Theseus, the Minotaur, Art and Death are all symbolically represented. The Labyrinth is perhaps the most important of these symbols, because it embraces Catalonia's arduous and difficult past. But to pick up Ariadne's thread is to find a way into a world of great riches in terms of art and the human spirit – that will be my attempt throughout the rest of this book.

P A R T
ONE

1

Barcelona

'Barcelona, one of the finest and certainly the most manufacturing city in Spain, is a better placed and handsomer city than Madrid,' wrote Richard Ford in the mid-nineteenth century. This remains true today. 'It is', he continued, 'the Manchester of Catalonia, which is the Lancashire of the peninsula.' A connection can certainly be traced between Britain and Catalonia, which was an early convert to the industrial revolution, but the contemporary traveller will find little resemblance between the north-west of England and present-day Barcelona and its environs. On the contrary, the ambition of Puig i Cadafalch, the Modernist architect and politician, was to make 'Greater Barcelona the Paris of the Midi'.

In fact, neither Manchester nor Paris spring to mind when you embark on **Las Ramblas.** Comprising five articulated sections – Rambla de Canalete, Rambla dels Estudis, Rambla de Sant Josep, Rambla dels Caputxins and Rambla de Santa Mònica – running in that order from the Plaça de Catalunya down to the Columbus column at the lower end, they combine to form one of the great streets of Mediterranean Europe. Las Ramblas should be sampled on the day of arrival; they are at their best between early evening and one or two in the morning. The number of large bookstalls open at that time is striking; a casual glance reveals Nietzsche, Ibsen, Keynes, Joyce, Lowry, Neruda, E.H. Carr – did you know he was Edward Hallett Carr? The people of Barcelona do. All nine

23

BARCELONA

Within the Roman Wall
1 Cathedral
2 Museu d'Història de la Ciutat and royal chapel of Santa Agata
3 Plaça del Rei/Saló del Tinell
4 Museu Frederic Marès
5 Ajuntament
6 Sants Just i Pastor
7 Palau de la Generalitat
8 Pía Almoina
9 Archdeacon's house
10 Arxiú de la Corona d'Aragó
11 Roman temple

Within the First Mediaeval Enlargement
12 Santa Maria del Pi
13 Santa Maria del Mar
14 Santa Anna
*15 Palau de la Música
16 Sant Pere de les Puelles
17 Museu Picasso

Within the Second Mediaeval Enlargement
18 Museu Marítim (Drassanes)
*19 Palau Güell
20 Teatre del Liceu
21 Sant Pau del Camp
22 Hospital de la Santa Creu
23 Palau de la Virreina (Cambó collection)

Montjuïc
24 Museu d'Art de Catalunya
25 Museu Etnològic
26 Museu Arqueològic
27 Fundació Miró
28 Museu Militar
29 Poble Espanyol
30 Avinguda de la Reina Maria Cristina (with conference and exhibition buildings)

Parc de la Ciutadella
31 Museu d'Art Modern
32 Parlament de Catalunya
33 Zoo
34 Museu de Geologia
*35 Museu de Zoologia
36 Born Market (exhibition centre)
*37 Arc de Triomf

Eixample
*38 Loewe shop
*39 Casa Amatller
*40 Casa Battló
*41 Editorial Montaner i Simon
*42 Casa Milà
*43 Casa Terrades
*44 Casa Fuster
*45 Casa Viçens
*46 Sagrada Família
*47 Hospital de Sant Pau
*48 Parc Güell

Asterisks denote key examples of Modernist architecture.

• Roman wall   ▪ Mediaeval wall

Las Ramblas with pavement mosaic by Miró, and the Liceu in the background.

sheets of the Firestone 1:500,000 maps of the peninsula are available from one stall: you are lucky to find anything more than the local sheet elsewhere. Every conceivable Italian paper is on sale and most German, French, American and British papers as well. Then there is the Catalan press led by *Avui* (*Today*). And there is plenty of Catalan literature: the *Renaixença* poets Jacint Verdaguer and Joan Maragall, the novelist Mercè Rodoreda, the post-war poets Salvador Espriu and Pere Gimferrer. People read a lot: the receptionist in my hotel was deep in Bertrand Russell's *La conquista de la felicidad* (*The Conquest of Happiness*) and was shocked to learn I hadn't read it nor could recall on the spur of the moment the exact title in English.

On the wide central promenade glass- and fire-swallowers have their pitches; a pavement artist on the grand scale has just abandoned a not unworthy version of El Greco's *Rending of Christ's Garment*. Street portraitists and caricaturists deftly delineate American tourists and sailors in five-minute sittings. A medical student will take your blood pressure – you pay what you please. Numerous sex shops and peep shows add a touch of the Tottenham Court Road, though the similarity ends there. The nearby Plaça Reial, haunt of students and pushers and troubadours of many races, has more of the flavour of Marrakesh. In McDonalds you can have beer with your *McPollo* (McChicken). The draught beer in Barcelona is very good, a darkish strong lager, which beefy young exhibitionists swallow in quart jars. At Nó. 41 is La Castellana, a grocery doubling as a bar, which serves drinks and snacks and watermelons into the small hours. In the middle of Las Ramblas is the Boqueria market, described by Ford as Barcelona's Covent Garden – it too rose upon the garden of a vanished convent – and the grand Lyceum theatre, the Liceu, the Covent Garden of the city in the other sense. Honours are distributed between Calderón and Mozart, Rossini and Moratín, who are represented by busts on the façade. Municipal posters announce forthcoming visits from foreign companies to the open-air theatre in the Plaça del Rei: the acrobatic circus of Peking, a month's festival of Greek music, dance and song and so forth. The Romea theatre offers *The Tempest* in Catalan. There is always something on.

But the greatest show of all is simply the *paseo*, the endless flux of mashers, molls, respectable couples, beggars, tobacco vendors, weirdos, smart liberated girls challenging the world with their eyes and poise, all, or nearly all, revelling in the subtle combination of anonymity and community conferred on them by a great promenade. The prostitutes still hover as they always have and will on the corner of the Hotel Oriente with the Carrer de la Unió. A black-haired, twenty-year-old member of the sisterhood in a gold-lamé miniskirt is fleetingly beautiful. The *pensión* door to which they hold the keys and through which they whisk their catches is next door to an aseptic branch of the Banco Atlántico. All this is the 'gape-seed' beloved by Ford. But if you would gape on Las Ramblas, perhaps from the Terraza del Oriente, any drink will cost you five or six times what it does across a zinc counter in a side street. The Catalans know the value of their great spontaneous spectacle. Next, a stroll down to the bottom reveals Columbus on his great Corinthian column, a wholly inappropriate hero for a city whose commercial decline dated from his discoveries and the subsequent monopoly of the American trade by Seville. But Barcelona will yield to no city its pre-eminence in the peninsula. *Barcelona més que mai!* (Barcelona more than ever!) proclaim hundreds of posters slapped round street lamps. This is the municipality's answer to Madrid's slogan *Madrid, claro que sí!* (Madrid, but of course!) The rivalry between the capital of Spain and the capital of Catalonia is longstanding, deep-seated and ineradicable.

The draw of Las Ramblas is such that you start willy-nilly at the popular end of Barcelona's life, but theatres and books have already come to the fore as important interests to Catalans and I think there is solid foundation for saying that they are more cultured than other Spaniards. I realize the word 'culture' is a bit of a chameleon, taking on different hues according to whether it is used by archaeologists, sociologists or literary people, but I use it here in its widely accepted sense of applying to a society that attaches importance to literature, the arts, architecture, crafts, museums and the theatre – accompanied by a considerable investment of private or public funds (or both) in these activities. Private subscription was for a long time the cultural mainstay of Barcelona, particularly during times of political repression; the proportion of public investment has risen since the re-establishment of regional autonomy. Also, many of the present public buildings devoted to these purposes, or serving now as museums, were put up at public expense for one or other of the international Exhibitions of 1888 and 1929. Yet private patronage of the arts is by no means dead and there is said to be a literary competition held in almost every village. Barcelona is kind as well to wandering minstrels – or buskers, call them what you will – many of whom are foreign. Whether they make their pitches in a romantic corner of the old quarter or in a pedestrian link between metro lines, they are not moved on (the hub of the metro system beneath the Plaça de Catalunya is often extremely difficult to negotiate because of underground concerts attracting several hundred people) – it is accepted that these musicians have come to try their luck and are at least paying their way in what Ford called the 'Athens of the Troubadour'. He was referring to the thirteenth century, but there are signs that the description may be apposite again today.

There are other manifestations of this general culture. Whenever they dig up a street in Barcelona, the municipal archaeologists are there, sifting each skip full of earth and rubble in case any precious pieces from the past have been thrown up. Cleanliness is another facet of a civilized approach to life and this is particularly noticeable in Catalonia. The local trains are sprayed and cleaned frequently between their relatively short journeys. Squads of young street-cleaners in orange boiler suits are active throughout the day and well into the night. All this might be explained by the region's proximity to France. These northern Spaniards, the visitor might be tempted to speculate, have been blessed by certain airs wafted across the border from *la douce France* and the rough edges characteristic of the south and the Castiles have been rubbed off them. The Catalan, recalling that his empire before 1213 embraced Toulouse, Albi and Nice, may be inclined to say the boot is on the other foot. To my mind there is a peculiarly rich Catalan culture which can only in small measure be attributed to the French connection. Barcelona beats Marseilles in my estimation (and I know both). Marseilles has the splendid Provençal hinterland, it is true; it has Nîmes, Arles, Avignon, Orange, Aix. But Barcelona is a more agreeable city and has no mean hinterland, as I shall endeavour to show.

Before immersing yourself in Barcelona you may like to get a bird's eye view of the place. This is easily done. The city's public transport services – subterranean, terrestrial and aerial – are excellent and it requires only a short journey, albeit in three stages, to reach the commanding height of **Tibidabo** (532 m). The Plaça de Catalunya is not only the hub of the metro system but also the terminal (likewise underground) of the local railway network, the Ferrocarril de Catalunya. Trains leave very frequently for Avinguda del Tibidabo (be careful not to get on to the Terrassa/Sabadell line). Then a charming old tram continues the ascent between bourgeois villas with conical spires to the funicular station, attached to which is a very pleasant café, La Venta, where you can refresh yourself before the final stage (funiculars leave every fifteen minutes) up the pine-clad slope to the top. From here there is a tremendous view of the port and the city spreading upwards from its *pla* or coastal plain, climbing the lower eminence of Montjuïc with its Exhibition buildings, and filling the whole amphitheatre of hills to the base of Tibidabo itself. To the north-east is the jagged ridge of Montserrat, the magic mountain of Catalonia. To the immediate north are the hills of the Serra del Montseny and beyond them the great southerly spur of the Pyrenees formed by Mount Canigó and the Serra del Cadí. On a clear day Majorca can just be discerned far out to sea.

Barri Gòtic

Let us now take possession of the city. As the old quarter, the Barri Gòtic (Barrio Gótico), is the core from which everything else sprang, it seems sensible to start there, *sur place*. The Hotel Gótico in Jaume I is excellently placed, as is the more expensive Hotel Colón just across the Plaça Nova from the cathedral. The Barri Gòtic has much that is pre-Gothic, for it stands on the site of several previous layers of civilization and is located within the fourth-century late Roman wall, substantial stretches of which are exposed – notably above the Plaça de Berenguer el Gran, where it incorporates the royal chapel of Santa Agata, before running into the Plaça Nova, where it is broken by the wide flights of steps leading up to the cathedral's west front.

Barcelona's cathedral is not one of the grandest or largest of the peninsula but it is a compact and well-designed Gothic church begun in 1298, whose façade was not completed until 1892. Ford complained in the 1840s that 'the principal façade is unfinished, with a bold front, poorly painted in stucco, although the rich chapter have for three centuries received a fee on every marriage for this very purpose of completing it. . .' Whatever the canons actually did with the marriage fees, eventually it was done and the late Victorian work is perfectly acceptable – it might have been worse if completed in the eighteenth century, witness Hawksmoor's rather inappropriate towers for Westminster Abbey. The features to note inside are the huge bosses of the vault, the blind triforium with little rose windows above, and the elegant colonnade which forms the ambulatory behind the high altar. There is nothing of great interest in the apsidal chapels but the crypt chapel is a place of great local veneration, containing as it does the remains of Saint Eulalia, co-patroness of the city: her sarcophagus with scenes from her martyrdom is raised on a harlequin set of antique columns. Her chapel was completed in 1339 and the precious corpse installed in the presence of two kings, three queens and other notabilities, whose heads are carved on the elliptical arch above the entrance. On the right-hand wall of the ambulatory are the wooden coffins of Count Ramon Berenguer I and his wife Almodis. In the first chapel on the right inside the west door is the smoke-darkened Christ of Lepanto, the crucifix carried by Don John of Austria on the prow of his flagship *La Real* at the battle of Lepanto (1571), to which the Catalans contributed an important contingent including the vice-admiral.

The enclosed choir is of some interest as it was here that Charles V (*Invictissimus Carolus*) celebrated in 1519 the first and last chapter of the order of the Golden Fleece: among the knights' coats of arms are those of the kings of England, Portugal, France, Hungary, Denmark and Poland. Henry VIII's stall is in the top row immediately to the right of the emperor and facing the high altar. The cloister is pleasant but not especially peaceful as, apart from the daily throng of tourists, it is also home to a flock of geese, who live in a pool called the Font de les Oques (the Fountain of Geese). According to Ford, these sacred geese were installed by the canons in imitation of those on the Roman capitol and as a reminder of

Barcelona's Roman greatness (though the city was in fact eclipsed by Tarragona). Be that as it may, these capitoline geese emit the most unholy shrieks every few minutes. The practical and commercial character of the Catalans is evidenced by the dedication of the first chapel on the left, as you emerge from the transept, to the Virgin of Light, patroness of electricians and plumbers, and by the burial stones in the cloister floor of bootmakers, tailors and members of other guilds marked with the signs of their trades. The shoemakers' guild was apparently an important benefactor of the cathedral. Ford remarks, 'Trade was never held to be a degradation, as among the Castilians; accordingly, heraldic decorations are much less frequent on the houses here, where the merchant's *mark* was preferred to the armorial *charge*.' The rather small chapter house opens off the cloister. It contains the central panel of the retable of the guild of esparto workers by Jaume Huguet (1415–92) and a pietà (1490) by Bartolomé Bermejo with the stamped gold background and thick raised gold *estofado* haloes and garment hems so characteristic of Aragonese and Catalan Gothic art (see 'Gothic Art and Architecture').

Before going any further afield it is, I think, sensible to visit the **Museu d'Història de la Ciutat**, which is to be found in the Carrer Veguer, a mere step from the cathedral apse. Here the models, maps and plans enable you to get your bearings and plot the development of the city. Founded by the Carthaginian Hamilcar Barca (hence the early name Barcino) in about 230 BC, it passed shortly into the hands of the Romans in which it remained for some six centuries, though it did not acquire its substantial wall until the fourth century in response to increasing raids by the Franks; it was later occupied by the Visigoths and the Moors and had to wait until mediaeval times for its great commercial expansion. The museum firmly reminds the visitor of the importance of the guild system and its associated religious brotherhoods in that period, not least in the establishment of an early and crucial connection between commerce and the commissioning of works of art such as retables and sculptures for the guilds' churches and chapels and the processional crosses and other impedimenta carried through the streets on the great feast days. This connection between commerce and art has survived into more recent times and is responsible for much of the cultural and artistic vitality of Barcelona today, as evidenced by the private sponsorship of the Liceu theatre, the Orfeo Català and the Institut d'Estudis Catalans.

Barcelona's first set of mediaeval walls enclosed an area eight or nine times as large as the Roman enceinte, with its southern flank running along the present northern side of Las Ramblas. A further extension southwards was then required, encircling the shipbuilding yards down on the port and the district of the old hospital, which now houses the Library of Catalonia. But perhaps the most important plans displayed are those for the great nineteenth-century project called the Eixample or Ensanche

Barcelona's preferred option for expansion on radial lines was rejected by Madrid in favour of Cerdà's rectangular grid with diagonal arteries

(Enlargement), whereby the city was to break out of its twice-extended fortifications and expand up into the salubrious hills, leaving behind the cramped streets and ancient districts each named after its mediaeval trade.

The radial plan of Antoni Rovira, which won the municipal prize of 1859, would have endowed the city with a great central *plaça*, bringing together the old and new quarters and opening up the cathedral façade. But this award was nullified by the ministry of public works in Madrid and royal approval was given to the strictly rectangular plan of the engineer Ildefons Cerdà, which left the central focus unresolved and has led to several remodellings of the Plaça de Catalunya. Spanish centralism thus robbed Barcelona of an imaginative development plan which would have provided more and better routes of access than Cerdà's crude diagonal gash across his grid. Also, the transverse streets, which do not run seawards, are now hot and airless in summer – an effect that would have been mitigated by Rovira's plan. Still, Cerdà's design has some pleasing features: he insisted on wide boulevards with trees and the Passeig de Gràcia in particular is very ample and agreeable; he also provided for interior gardens within each block, though most of these were absorbed by land speculation. But on the whole this is a superior piece of urbanization to the bleak Barrio de Salamanca in Madrid. It also preserves some of the old core of the village of Gràcia, which it incorporated.

Apart from its intrinsic interest, the museum also gives access to the royal chapel of **Santa Agata**, built on top of the Roman wall. The chapel features a pointed wooden coffered ceiling and a stone pulpit reached by steps within the inner wall; its bareness is relieved by the great Jaume Huguet's retable of the Epiphany (1465). Through the chapel you enter the great hall of the counts of Barcelona with its huge rounded arches and fragments of battle frescoes. It was here, in the Saló del Tinell, that Ferdinand and Isabel received Columbus on his first return from the New World, which eventually spelt the ruin of Catalan trade.

These great chambers surround the **Plaça del Rei**, the courtyard of the royal palace. This is dominated by the impressive five-stage tower of Martin the Humane (1396–1410) and is now used by the municipality as an open-air theatre during festivals and fairs. There is another branch of the historical museum which should not be neglected and which is accessible only through the adjacent Museu Frederic Marès, from whose patio a staircase leads beneath street level. Running partly under the present

*Statue of Ramon Berenguer III
below the royal chapel of Santa Agata.*

cathedral are the remains of a paleo-Christian basilica with columns and some frescoes; there are also Roman mosaics and stretches of apparently Visigothic masonry. There is quite an arsenal of Visigothic capitals, which suggests the existence of an intermediate building after the destruction of the early Christian basilica and before the Romanesque cathedral (superseded in its turn by the present structure). There would thus appear to be four layers to this rich archaeological cake.

Returning to the surface, the **Museu Frederic Marès** is of considerable interest for its anthology of Romanesque and Gothic art, though this is less specifically regional than the collections of the great Museu d'Art de Catalunya. Marès was the sculptor who reconstructed the royal tombs at Poblet (see p.180), but he was also a zealous traveller and collector. The crypt has some rich detritus, mainly in stone, including capitals from the caliphate of Córdoba. The fine Romanesque church entrance of Anzano (Huesca) has been reconstituted. The ground floor is devoted to

*Plaça del Rei, the courtyard of the mediaeval palace
of the counts of Barcelona, by night.*

early church sculpture in painted or plain wood. The twelfth-century crucifixes and some of the thirteenth retain the Romanesque separation of the nailed feet; then the more artistic impalement of one foot on the other with a single nail comes into fashion. The Christ child ranges from a tiny bundle in swaddling clothes to a precocious teenager delivering a lecture with his dexter hand raised in benediction. Robust Romanesque mothers and solid children give way to the poetic sweetness of the fourteenth century; in the fifteenth century the Virgin seems to coarsen again. The first floor offers examples of the waxwork realism which began in the sixteenth century. The cult of the Immaculate Conception begins to inspire some work, though this never reached the fever pitch in Catalonia that was to characterize it further south. The pietà becomes popular too for its expressive possibilities. Next come the tableaux vivants of the seventeenth century, with their glass eyes and real nails and hair. There are three small figures attributed to Pedro de Mena and a few busts ascribed to him or to Alonso Cano. Much of this work would not be out of place in the Museo Nacional de Escultura in Valladolid. There is little of local interest until the nineteenth-century bas-reliefs in terracotta and the room devoted to prints, rosaries, medallions and similar items associated with the Virgin of Montserrat.

It is on the top floor that the Marès magpie quality really emerges. From fifty years of foreign travels he brought back – mostly in the small label-encrusted suitcase on display – an astounding variety of objects: dolls, terracotta animals and figurines for cribs, hatpins, garters, scissors, shawls, parasols, amulets, combs, pinboxes, handbags, purses, pipes and pipe cases, pouches, cigar labels, cigarette cases, cigarette cards, matchboxes, tarot cards, early cameras, clocks, watches, walking sticks, snuff boxes, embroidered braces, eyeglasses, apothecaries' jars, inkwells, lustre jugs, minor church utensils and regalia – in short, everything to delight the collector of trivia or the addict of nostalgia. The small ceramics collection has some good fourteenth- to seventeenth-century pieces from Manises, but these again serve mainly to whet your appetite for the ceramics museum within the Museu d'Art de Catalunya.

While still in the district bounded by the Roman wall, it is well worth looking in on the two principal organs of local administration, the Ajuntament (Ayuntamiento), home of the city council of Barcelona, and the Palau de la Generalitat (Palacio de la Generalidad), seat of the regional government of Catalonia. They face each other across the Plaça de Sant Jaume at the heart of the old quarter. The city hall at the time of writing is socialist and the regional government centre-right and this gives rise to certain tensions, as might be expected. According to a local joke you cover the greatest distance in Barcelona when crossing the Plaça de Sant Jaume from one to the other. (See also 'Political Life and Institutions'.)

The **Ajuntament de Barcelona**, which runs most of the museums and promotes numerous cultural activities in addition to its more practical responsibilities, is open to tourists every day. Behind the nineteenth-century neo-classical façade lies the patio, from which a grand Renaissance staircase on one side and a Gothic staircase on the other both lead to a first-floor gallery. The main chamber was built in 1369–73 to house the Consell de Cent, the hundred worthies who governed the city. The Renaissance entrance has swirling Solomonic columns and the roof is supported on great rounded arches designed along the same lines as those of the Saló del Tinell. Opening off this is the present-day city council chamber with seats of dark shiny oak in the form of a

Mediaeval entrance of the Ajuntament in the side street Carrer de la Ciutat.

hemicycle. Dating from the reign of Isabel II (1833–68), the chamber is solemn and glossy enough to delight the heart of the most ardent municipalist. You are also shown the Sala de les Cròniques with Josep Maria Sert's large ochre, sepia and gold murals of the extraordinary expedition of Roger de Flor and his Catalan mercenaries, who were hired by Constantinople to defend the Byzantine empire against the Turks (1302–11) and later went on to take Athens and Neopatria for Catalonia. The guide delights to demonstrate and extol the tricks of perspective but the whole effect is pretentious; this artist should not be confused with Josep Lluís Sert, architect of the splendidly spare Fundació Miró. The building's old façade with its great Gothic portal of radiating voussoirs is located in the side street Carrer de la Ciutat, off which the short Carrer Sant Just leads to the church of that name (1345–60), which features a broad aisleless nave, tall windows above the string course and solid buttresses sustaining the wide vault – all are characteristic of the fourteenth-century Catalan Gothic style (see 'Gothic Art and Architecture'). This is a favourite church for fashionable weddings. Carrer de la Ciutat continues downwards towards the port and past the headquarters of the central committee of the Marxist PSUC (Partit Sociàlista Unificat de Catalunya), whose flagpoles carry both the red flag and the red bars on a yellow ground of Count Wilfred and his successors. In Catalonia even communism is regionalist.

The **Palau de la Generalitat**, immediately across the *plaça* from the Ajuntament has the more distinguished of the two façades; it is by Pere Blai (1597–1600). This is the seat of the autonomous government of Catalonia, trustee of the Catalan statute of 1979, which sets out the powers devolved to the region by the Spanish constitution. Perhaps to reflect its superior status and wider jurisdiction, the Generalitat can only be visited other than on business on Sunday mornings. The building has some interesting architectural features. The grand staircase leads to a gallery with slender clusters of columns supporting a Gothic arcade. The front room on the first floor is the classical Saló de Sant Jordi (Saint George is the patron saint of Catalonia and you meet him at almost every step – see 'Popular Culture'). The large historical murals are clearly captioned and include the concession by Peter III of '*el gloriós Consolat de Mar*', which laid down the maritime and commercial rights of the citizens. Otherwise the subjects depicted rather curiously tend to emphasize Castilian supremacy: the battle of Las Navas de Tolosa in 1212, which opened the way for Castile into Andalusia; the Compromise of Caspe, which in 1412 brought the Castilian Ferdinand of Antequera to the throne of Aragon; the marriage in 1469 of Ferdinand of Aragon to Isabel of Castile, which brought about the absorption of the former crown by the latter; and the celebration by Charles V in

1519 of the first and only chapter of the Golden Fleece, held in the cathedral of Barcelona, an act of imperial oneupmanship if ever there was one. There are portraits of local heroes and worthies up on the ceiling but they are less visible and make a correspondingly lesser impact.

The Generalitat has an attractive first-floor courtyard with orange trees. Off this is a relatively small Sala de Sessions, which is still, rather confusingly, the council chamber of the Diputació, a provincial body under the previous régime and not yet abolished.

Gallery of front courtyard of the Generalitat with the patio of orange trees beyond the grille.

The deputies' chairs are arranged in adversarial manner, twenty-five or so on each side of the aisle. Over the presidential table is a modern portrait of the king and queen looking extremely young and vulnerable. The Generalitat itself does not perform here; it has to give account of itself to the Catalan parliament in the Parc de la Ciutadella.

On this level there is a small chapel with a decorated (or what the French refer to as flamboyant) entrance, opening into a domical chancel with columnettes hanging oddly in the air. There are some Flemish tapestries and an altar frontal depicting Sant Jordi, to whom the chapel is dedicated. Off the orange courtyard on the opposite side to the council chamber lies a passage containing the modern wall relief by Subirachs which I mentioned in the Introduction. This includes a key to the symbols which represent respectively *Catalunya, la Llibertat, l'Eclipsi, Ariadna, el Laberint, Sant Jordi, Teseu, el Minotaure, l'Art, la Mort*. It is pretty clear that Saint George and the dragon have merged with Theseus and the Minotaur and that these themes are intimately connected with Catalonia, past and present.

The streets of the Barri Gòtic contain some handsome examples of Gothic and Renaissance domestic architecture. The most characteristic feature is the round-arched entrance with large radial slabs or voussoirs. Most of the grander buildings feature an imposing staircase leading from the patio to the first-floor gallery with an arcade of pointed arches on clusters of slender columnettes. The prime examples are Pia Almoina (the House of Charity), on the north side of the cathedral steps, the archdeacon's house on the opposite side of the same flight of steps and the Arxiu de la Corona d'Aragó (the Archive of the Crown of Aragon) with its great round-headed door leading into a Renaissance courtyard; sited between the cathedral and the Plaça del Rei, this was formerly the seat of the viceroy after the union of Aragon and Castile. In the Carrer del Paradís there are more old houses and at No. 10, rather unusually enclosed by the thriving Centre Excursionista de Catalunya, are the remaining columns of a Roman temple dedicated to Augustus and destroyed (presumably by Franks) before the fourth-century wall was built.

The Mediaeval Enlargements

The first mediaeval wall extended the city as far as Las Ramblas on one side and out to Portal Nou (the New Gate), which stood not far from the present Arc de Triomf erected for the 1888 Exhibition. The streets throughout this whole area are very similar to those of the older core. From the Plaça Nova in front of the cathedral the Carrer de la Palla describes a curve and emerges in the Plaça Josep Oriol under the flank of the fine church of **Santa Maria del Pi** (1320–1400). This has a single wide nave with no aisles and rather deeper side chapels than the cathedral. In addition to the main characteristics of Catalan Gothic already noted at Sant Just, there is a large rose window in the flat façade and a slim octagonal tower round the corner in the Placeta del Pi – features also common to many churches of the period. The main Plaça del Pi in front of the church is a favourite stage for roving entertainers – dancers, guitarists, mountebanks, puppeteers – who abound in

Roman and Mediaeval Barcelona

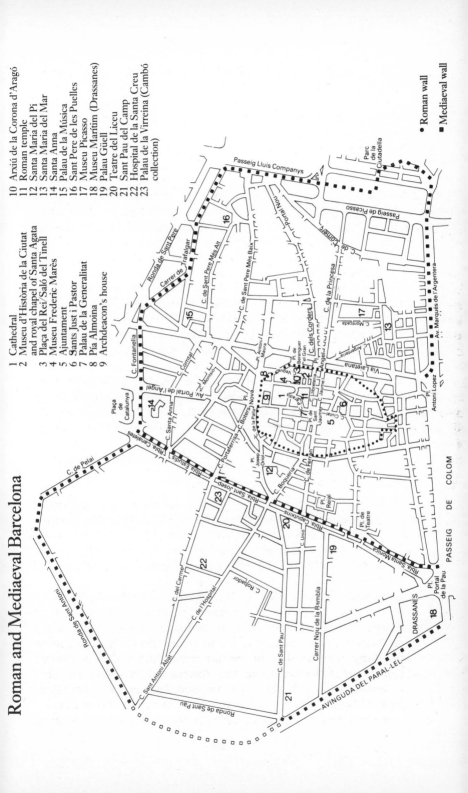

1 Cathedral
2 Museu d'Història de la Ciutat
  and royal chapel of Santa Agata
3 Plaça del Rei/Saló del Tinell
4 Museu Frederic Marès
5 Ajuntament
6 Sants Just i Pastor
7 Palau de la Generalitat
8 Pia Almoina
9 Archdeacon's house

10 Arxiu de la Corona d'Aragó
11 Roman temple
12 Santa Maria del Pi
13 Santa Maria del Mar
14 Santa Anna
15 Palau de la Música
16 Sant Pere de les Puelles
17 Museu Picasso
18 Museu Marítim (Drassanes)
19 Palau Güell
20 Teatre del Liceu
21 Sant Pau del Camp
22 Hospital de la Santa Creu
23 Palau de la Virreina (Cambó
  collection)

● Roman wall
■ Mediaeval wall

Barcelona at all times and especially during fairs.

But the queen of Barcelona churches, barring none in my opinion, is **Santa Maria del Mar.** From the lower end of Jaume I you cross the Via Laietana, the great gash cut through this quarter

West front and rose window of Santa Maria del Mar.

in the early part of this century to link the port to the new centre, and take the downhill diagonal street called Argenteria, from which the church's openwork spires are quickly visible. It was built between 1329 and 1383, probably by Jaume Fabre, second architect of the cathedral, who seems to have profited from lessons learned in that slightly earlier construction. Slender octagonal columns launch the main vault; the vestigial and pointless triforium has been suppressed in favour of tall luminous windows above the string course; the side aisles are not quite as tall as the nave as there are rose windows at aisle level, but the overwhelming impression is of a great hall church. The ambulatory, however, is the real glory of the place; it is very similar in ground plan to the cathedral's but the narrow arches above the cornices of the columns are much taller and more elegant. Also, because most of the church's fixtures and fittings were destroyed

Columns and vault of Santa Maria del Mar's superb ambulatory.

by fire in 1936, there is no central choir compartment to obstruct the view; the few images are dwarfed by the commanding architectonic lines of the building. This does not mean that it is frigid – far from it. Evening mass with a boy's solo voice is not to be missed. Weddings, which also take place in the evenings, often give rise to stunning visual effects, as the natural refulgence is filtered by the stained glass and the very low-hung lamps make haloes of light just above the heads of the congregation.

There are two other churches within the first mediaeval enlargement – both older than those discussed so far – which should be seen. **Santa Anna** with its small cloister is tucked away just off the Plaça de Catalunya and is reached via the Portal de l'Àngel which runs up from the cathedral district into the hub of the modern city. Near the top on the left is the Carrer Santa Anna, off which an archway opens into a little square where the church stands. There is a flower stall just inside the arch. The church is very cool and dark and features squinches supporting a cupola. This is a good place to take refuge from the big department stores, the Galerías Preciados and El Corte Inglés, which are only a stone's throw away. **Sant Pere de les Puelles** can be reached by crossing the Via Laietana into Carrer Sant Pere Mès Alt and following this (passing the Palau de la Música on the left) to the *plaça* of the same name, where the church stands. Enclosed in later accretions of buildings is a fine twelfth-century nave; the east end was built in 1498.

In trying to describe a large and complex city coherently I inevitably found myself torn between a chronological and a zonal approach. My chronological imperative usually wins, but for practicality's sake it seems only sensible to describe in this section the **Museu Picasso.** This is not very suitably housed in a gloomy Gothic palace with later titivations in the Carrer Montcada, which runs down from the Carrer de la Princesa to Santa Maria del Mar and was the centre of the fashionable quarter in the sixteenth century. This is not to say that the museum is not interesting and important to an understanding of this great magician of modern art. It is both. Picasso clearly plunged into the *fin de siècle* ferment like many of his companions. This is the period of charming little oil sketches on board; of his portraits of his sister, his mother, his father; of charcoal drawings of fellow artists in emulation of Casas; of his retreat to Horta de Sant Joan; of his portrait of the doomed Casagemas; of his designs for a social-security advertisement, for a carnival poster and for the menu of the bohemian tavern Els Quatre Gats. Shapes and

outlines are reminiscent now of Arles, now of Münch. The breakthrough came before the blue period with the Paris trip of 1900,
which sparked off the potent red figures of Margot (1900) and La
Nana, the dwarf (1901). There is a superficial resemblance to
Toulouse-Lautrec at this time but the French aristocrat was *au
fond* a dilettante, while Picasso had the drive, energy and
determination to take the world by storm. (See also 'Modern Art'.)

The museum is patchy. It began life with the collection of
drawings, paintings, etchings and lithographs donated in 1960
by the artist's lifelong friend Jaume Sabartés, who became his
secretary in 1935. The blue period is well represented, then there
is nothing more until 1917, the year in which Picasso returned to
Barcelona in triumph with Diaghilev's *Parade*, for which he had
designed the costumes and décor. There are a few works of this
period, notably *The Harlequin* (1917). This is followed by a very
long gap which ended in 1957 when an extraordinary outburst of
energy (even for Picasso) produced some fifty or sixty variations
on the theme of *Las Meninas* by Velázquez presented by the artist
in 1968. The little Princess Margarita and her lady-in-waiting
Isabel de Velasco, the pert page Nicolasito Pertusato, the dwarf
María Borbolla and the dog undergo all sorts of transformations
while somehow remaining themselves. Some of the larger canvases are *sense* Velázquez, ie. without the painter, who is a major
protagonist in the original, while Picasso plays with his creatures
and explores a wide range of different colour combinations. The
painting of the whole scene with Velázquez restored is tonal: it is
composed of whites, greys and blacks across an even narrower
colour range than *Guernica*. The top floor of the museum is
devoted to Picasso's graphic work, from which the fauns of 1948,
several versions of *Jacqueline* and the doves of peace stand out.
Picasso also designed the giant thumbnail frieze running round
the front and side elevations of the architects' college in the Plaça
Nova almost opposite the cathedral (and there are other designs
by him inside the building). Here he seems to be cocking a cheerful
snook at all the solemn masonry piled up across the way. There
are a couple of minor Modernist buildings in this area, the
headquarters of the hydroelectric company, virtually next door to
the architects' college, and the gas and electricity company's head
office with its Egyptianized façade in the Portal de l'Àngel.

The area enclosed by the second mediaeval wall is also noteworthy. Perhaps the best place to start is at the Drassanes, or royal
shipyards, erected in the thirteenth century and now containing
the **Museu Maritim**. Rather poor pictures of battles at sea are

usual in naval museums but these are frequently compensated for by excellent models and this is very much the case here. The largest exhibit is a life-sized reproduction of Don John of Austria's flagship *La Real* at the battle of Lepanto. Also, moored in the port not far from the museum is a full-scale replica of Columbus's flagship *Santa María*, looking incredibly small for the distance it covered and the feat it performed. It is incidentally a rather curious feature of Barcelona life that a people with such a long and distinguished maritime history use their portside promenade so little, preferring the thronged urban axis formed by Las Ramblas, the Plaça de Catalunya and the Passeig de Gràcia, running inland towards the hills.

Walking from the port up Las Ramblas, you reach, a third of the way up on the left, an intersection with the Carrer Nou de la Rambla. A few doors down this street, again on the left, is Gaudí's Palau Güell, the forbidding townhouse built for his patron. It is now occupied by the **Museu de les Arts de l'Espectacle**, or the theatre museum, which puts on rotating exhibitions devoted to individual actors, actresses and designers or to other theatrical topics. Its architectural significance is discussed within the context of the Modernist movement as a whole (see 'Modernisme').

Continuing upwards, the second turning on the left, Carrer Sant Pau, forms a corner with the Liceu theatre and traverses a not too salubrious but lively red-light district for five hundred yards before leading you to the mini-basilica of **Sant Pau del Camp**. This was founded before 977 and is said to be the oldest standing church in Barcelona. At the time of its foundation it stood well outside the walls. It is best to arrive about seven in the evening when there may be a mass in progress; otherwise there is no chance of getting in. The symbols of the Evangelists (Saint Matthew – man; Saint Mark – lion; Saint Luke – ox; Saint John – eagle) are carved over the entrance and there is a curious dexter hand in benediction set sideways in the stonework. The decoration of the lintel below the tympanum appears to be Visigothic. The octagonal tower over the crossing is supported on sturdy squinches inside. Various grace notes have been added, including a little barbican over the façade and a rustic baroque belfry. But this is essentially a well-designed little church featuring an attractive triple apse with Lombard bands, which has survived all Barcelona's vicissitudes.

Retracing your steps for a couple of hundred yards and turning left up Carrer Robador you emerge on to Carrer de l'Hospital

Sant Pau del Camp, the oldest standing church in Barcelona.

almost in front of the large old complex of buildings which
constituted the Hospital de la Santa Creu. This now houses two
very important bodies in the history of *catalanitat*, the **Institut
d'Estudis Catalans** and the **Biblioteca de Catalunya**. Walking
through the courtyards, a favourite haunt of pensioners and
students alike, you emerge in the Carrer del Carme, by which you
can regain Las Ramblas on the corner with the Carme church. On
the other side of this junction is the Palau de la Virreina, housing
the **Museu d'Arts Decoratives** and the Cambó collection of
paintings. The former is not of great interest, though it contains
some good neo-classical beds, and must yield here to the Museo de
Artes Decorativos in Madrid, which offers a fine survey of all
periods.

Francesc Cambó's collection, however, deserves some attention. He was one of the founders and later leader of the Lliga, a
political party representing Catalan business interests which
played a crucial part in Catalan politics between 1901 and the
First World War (see 'Political Life and Institutions'). His collection is of the statutory rich man's type. It has a bit of everything,
with some good items but nothing outstanding, and was assembled – I would guess – by a dealer wishing to ensure that his client
had a respectable collection of expensive art. There are some
perfectly acceptable but not major works from the studios of
Correggio, Tintoretto, Titian and Veronese. A *Saint John the
Baptist* is attributed to Botticelli and a *Portrait of a Lady* to
Raphael. Gainsborough's *Margaret, Countess Spencer* is the most
impressive painting. There are also some agreeable frolics by
Tiepolo and Fragonard. I was most struck by the usually pedestrian Pantoja's portrait of Philip III as a young man, looking
singularly inept for government, which sheds some light on his
subsequent dependence on the unscrupulous duke of Lerma.

Montjuïc

It is only on grounds of distance from the old core that I have so far
refrained from visiting the very impressive **Museu d'Art de
Catalunya**. This is up on the flank of the Montjuïc hill and is
housed in the vast Palau Nacional erected for the 1929 Exhibition,
which the city council admits is of '*discutible qualitat arquitec-
tònic*' ('debatable architectural quality'). It can be reached by
taking the metro from the Plaça de Catalunya or from the next
stop, Liceu, on Las Ramblas (*direcció* Zona Univèrsitaria) and
alighting at Paral.lel, thence by funicular to Avinguda de Mir-
amar and a short walk following the signs. Alternatively you can
justify a taxi up by walking down, which is easily done by
descending the grand steps immediately in front of the museum
to the international fair centre below and thus to the Plaça
d'Espanya.

The story of the assembling and preservation of the superb
Romanesque section is quite dramatic. The inauguration of the
episcopal museum of Vic in 1891 (see pp.84–6) fostered a new
appreciation of the value of Romanesque painting on wooden
panels. In 1902 a commission of municipal museums was created
in Barcelona and the altar frontals of Tavèrnoles and Isil were
acquired. In 1907 the prestigious Institut d'Estudis Catalans
initiated a campaign to copy, photograph and publish the

Romanesque murals in remote Pyrenean village churches. However, as a result of all this activity antique dealers became interested and started to buy up everything they could lay their hands on for sale abroad; for the delicate task of the removal of the frescoes they relied on Italian technicians. Following the exportation to Boston of paintings from the main apse of the church of Mur, the Barcelona commission woke up to what was going on, secured a ban on exports, moved in themselves and – employing the same Italian experts – acquired between 1921 and 1923 most of the splendid murals which form the core of the collection today. During the Civil War some of the most important items were sent to Paris, where they formed part of an exhibition of tenth- to fifteenth-century Catalan art, which took place in the Jeu de Paume in 1937 before their transfer into safekeeping in the country. They were returned to Spain in 1939.

The museum now has thirty-three rooms of Romanesque art. Anyone who fears that the murals may have been removed unnecessarily from their natural setting by greedy curators may rest assured that, given the condition of the original churches, many of these paintings would have otherwise perished. The frescoes and paintings on board have been cleverly installed and are beautifully displayed along with helpful wall maps of the main sources of both the wooden panels and great murals. So well is all this presented that a newcomer can grasp the essentials of this Catalan Romanesque world in little more than an hour. I shall not attempt to describe the rooms – they simply have to be seen – but some remarks on the development of Romanesque painting will be found in 'Romanesque Art and Architecture'. I was personally moved by the fresco of the stoning of Saint Stephen in room 3, the marvellous wooden figures from a Descent from the Cross in room 16 from Santa Maria de Taüll, and the miniature figures of the Virgin and Saint John nailed to the arms of a crucifix in room 19 (this is not unique but I have not seen it outside Catalonia).

The Gothic section has some splendid exhibits but is more fussily arranged and more didactic. There are maps of the mediaeval Aragonese-Catalan empire in its various phases. In room 42 the technical process of the stamped and gilded *esgrafiado* backgrounds, so fundamental to Catalan painting, is explained. A large room attempts conscientiously to interpret arts and artefacts of the period in terms of social conditions and daily life. Utensils, sanitation, trade signs, guilds and the condition of tolerated minorities such as the Jews and Moriscos (converted

*Museu d'Art de Catalunya: fresco of the pantocrator saved from
Sant Climent de Taüll.*

Moors) are all covered. The collection of painted panels, carved
figures and retables which follows is extensive and of high
quality. It leads up to the celebrated retable of the Virgin of the
Councillors (1445) by Lluís Dalmau and to many of the best works
of the magisterial Jaume Huguet, whose exhibits 6, 7, 8, 9 and 25
should be dwelt on. What is most distinctive within the various

streams of peninsular art of the fifteenth century is the extraordinary persistence in Catalan and Aragonese painting of raised
gilt *estofado* haloes and garment trimmings, and also of the gilded
esgrafiado backgrounds not unlike sumptuous wallpaper. These
were superseded even in Castilian art – which was relatively
backward vis-à-vis the rest of Europe – by the middle of the
century. This may be due simply to the artistic conservatism of
the Catalans, who tended to stick to what they liked in defiance of
new fashions; although the inclination of the guilds, who often
commissioned these works, for good solid craftsmanlike work
produced by their own members may also have played a part. The
result is curious, however. Sensitive faces in Renaissance garb
peer out of an archaic formalized decorative framework – and we
are well into the lifetime of Raphael. There are as always some
exceptions, in particular the small *Annunciation* and *Saint Jerome*
in room 61 by the Mestre de la Seu d'Urgell. (See also 'Gothic Art
and Architecture'.)

The first floor of the same building houses a good ceramics
museum. The collection is not quite as extensive as that of the
Museo Arqueológico in Madrid but should certainly be seen if
your appetite has been whetted by the Museu Frederic Marès or
your interests lie in this direction. Salas II and III are the most
impressive. The former has very striking designs from Paterna
(fourteenth to fifteenth centuries), and also from Teruel and
Catalonia. Sala III is devoted mainly to Manises, Muel and Reus
(fifteenth to eighteenth centuries). The lustre technique passed
down by the Mudéjares (Spanish Muslims) is explained. There
are some splendid great platters with blue animal figures on a
lustre background belonging to the fifteenth century. The lustre-
ware acquires a coarser, ruddier tone in the seventeenth and
eighteenth centuries after the expulsion of the original craftsmen
by Philip III in 1609. The remaining rooms include seventeenth-
century ware from Talavera and Puente del Arzobispo, tiles with
hunting scenes from Seville, kitchen and larder tiles from Catalonia, tiled series of the Stations of the Cross, holy water stoups,
and eighteenth-and nineteenth-century wall tiles from Barcelona
depicting various arts and crafts, grotesque scenes and regional
costumes.

In contrast with Picasso, Joan Miró (1893–1983) has a superb
custom-built setting for his work not far from the Museu d'Art de
Catalunya. Though he lived mainly in Paris from 1920 to 1932, he
spent most of these summers at Mont-roig near Tarragona and
never became a real expatriate; in 1940 he settled in Majorca. He

is now the posthumous doyen of Catalan culture. The **Fundació Miró** is perfectly laid out for relaxed viewing and in fact there is not too much on show. The architect was Josep Lluís Sert, a disciple of Le Corbusier and lifelong friend of the artist, who succeeded Walter Gropius in the chair of architecture at Harvard. Constructed of shuttered concrete, the foundation is the sort of building that works marvellously well in a Mediterranean climate, where strong sun and shadow bring the surfaces alive, but is less to be recommended for lands of rains and mists and subtly diffused light.

Miró's calligraphic strain is evident in many works but he is much more than a purveyor of elegant doodles and arabesques. There is a brutal self-portrait of 1934. The Barcelona series of 1939–44 consists of fifty lithographs in which all the repression and frustration of the years immediately following the defeat of the republic are expressed. Black, large areas of it, is a potent force with Miró. There are black suns; No. 97 (1973) uses savage strokes of black which bring to mind the stabbing beak of a bird of prey. The large *Tapis de la Fundació* (1979) is a great tapestry with a bulky surface that is almost sculptural; it is interesting that a number of young contemporaries are now working in a similar vein with woven materials or making collages of cloth. Whether this is attributable to Miró's influence or to the long tradition of the Catalan textile industry I do not know – probably to a bit of both. Miró seems to have discovered plastic form in the 1930s through ceramics and sculpture but his sculptural climax is not reached until the mid-1960s; there are important examples here of his work in that period. The foundation is so well organized that the sculpture section even has labels in braille. The upper floor is devoted to rotating exhibitions of current artists. (For further comments on Miró see 'Modern Art'.)

In the immediate vicinity of the Fundació Miró, there are two museums which deserve a short visit. The first is the **Museu Etnològic**, which features interesting exhibits from pre-Hispanic America and a wide collection of objects from other religions and cultures. The other, just below, is the **Museu Arqueològic** with important Greek sculpture from Empúries; the Roman, early Christian and Visigothic exhibits are also noteworthy.

Lunch may be had cheaply at the café-bar a couple of hundred yards from the Fundació Miró – between the *telefèric* and the Funicular de Montjuïc – or a little more expensively at the adjacent restaurant. The transport system on Jove's Mount should be explained. If you want to climb to the amusement park (first stop) or the castle (second stop) you take the *teleféric*, an aerial cable car. The castle affords a fine view of both the passenger terminal and the commercial port. It also houses the **Museu Militar** with its extensive collection of arms of all periods, including some very elegant Persian helmets with chainmail neckcloths. There are plans and models of the main castles of Catalonia, while several rooms are devoted to the history of the fortress itself during the War of the Spanish Succession and the Peninsular and Carlist Wars. After Barcelona fell to the Nationalists in the Civil War it was used as a prison, and it was here that Lluís Companys, president of the Generalitat, was shot in 1940.

The funicular, whose terminal is almost next door to the *teleféric*, is a train carriage on a hawser which takes you back down to city level at Paral.lel, whence the metro (*direcció* Lesseps) will put you down at Liceu or Placa de Catalunya. About five hundred yards downhill by road is a restaurant called L'Ast, which also provides a good view of the port, though this is no longer 'felucca-crowded' as in Ford's day. But there is a yacht-basin and cruise liners put in from time to time, and the Balearic ferries ply in and out daily. From here the intrepid may take a different *teleféric*, the Transbordador Aèri, which swoops down in two stages: the first lands on a steel tower in the middle of the port area; the second comes to rest on a similar construction in the maritime suburb of Barceloneta, celebrated for its fish restaurants.

While still up on Montjuïc, it is a pity not to visit the **Poble Espanyol** (Pueblo Español). This lies beyond the Palau Nacional, home of the Museu d'Art de Catalunya, and may be reached either by skirting this by road or by walking under its façade. The *poble* was another flourish of the international Exhibition of 1929 and sets out to illustrate the regional architecture of the whole of Spain. You enter by the Puerta de Avila. The Plaza Mayor, overlooked from one corner by a crazily paved Romanesque belfry, reproduces sections of various types of porticoed arcade from rounded, pointed or flattened arches to the simple wooden lintels and pillars of El Burgo de Osma. The renaissance town hall of Valderobres, being Catalan, is reproduced in its entirety. The steps of Santiago lead immediately to Medinaceli and Alcañiz, whose brick church front with Solomonic columns surprisingly gives birth to a very elaborate Mudéjar tower. There is of course a *barrio andaluz* (Andalusian quarter) and, if you know the peninsula at all well, you will come across a number of old friends, for example about one half of the facade of the Palacio de Peñaflor in Ecija. A round-headed doorway from Tàrrega presides over the fountain from the village square of Prades. Montblanc and Besalú likewise represent Catalonia, while a number of buildings speak for the old Castilian towns of the Duero. It is an amusing and lavish anthology of Spanish styles and well worth a visit if you don't mind rubbing shoulders with other tourists, for it is – as intended – a popular place. There is a little information centre just inside the entrance with a graphic plan of the layout, from which you can pick out your favourite region or town and make for it. The complex must have cost the earth to construct and was perhaps intended to put Seville's nose out of joint, for the Andalusian partner in the great exhibition year certainly produced nothing like it.

If you walk downwards from the Poble Espanyol, the Palau Nacional rises on the right, looking from below almost as large as the Escorial and bringing home the gigantic scale on which Barcelona's contribution to the exhibition year was conceived. Also, the natural fall of the land permitted the achievement of effects unobtainable in flat Seville. On balance I think it is fair to say that Barcelona wins the title of master fairground of Spain from its longstanding rival in the south, and it is clear from the fountains splashing along the Avinguda de la Reina Maria Cristina, flanked by later conference buildings and exhibition facilities, that it is determined to maintain this supremacy.

Parc de la Ciutadella

After Montjuïc the largest expanse of green in downtown Barcelona is provided by the Ciutadella park. Originally the site of a fortress erected by Philip V to keep his rebellious subjects in order, it became the stage for the great Exhibition of 1888. Most of the Exhibition buildings have been dismantled, but there are older buildings of the Bourbon period, one of which houses the **Museu d'Art Modern.** This museum is strictly for Hispanophiles with a strong Catalanophile streak. There are of course a number of *tours de force* such as Fortuny's *Battle of Tetuan* (1863), but there is much poor stuff, saved neither by the facile Sorolla nor by Josep Maria Sert (who seems to have studied Giovanni Battista Tiepolo to ill effect). Ramon Casas shows himself in the charcoal and ochre portraits of his contemporaries to have been the Rothenstein of Spain; his oil sketch of Alfonso XIII is a rather interesting study of that headstrong and ultimately friendless monarch. Santiago Rusiñol's tasteful portraits are surprisingly reminiscent of Sir William Nicholson. Joaquim Sunyer has studied Cézanne and acquits himself creditably in several canvases. Gargallo's stone head of Picasso with a squashed nose like a prize-fighter's is amusing; his restless work is always talented. Ultimately, however, I found that the museum generated a sense of ennui. Perhaps that is its most important achievement, for it was out of this self-conscious bourgeois bohemia that Picasso and Miró sprang gasping for air into the twentieth century.

It is worth remarking here that the Museu d'Art Modern at present shares the same building with the Parlament de Catalunya, a body of 135 deputies to which the Generalitat is responsible. But parliaments are always avid for yet more space for offices and committee rooms and this one is no exception. The museum will therefore be moved over the next few years to the Palau Nacional on the Montjuïc hill, where the Museu d'Art de Catalunya is already installed.

The Parc de la Ciutadella also contains the **Museu de Geologia** and the **Museu de Zoologia.** The latter is housed in the café-restaurant built by the Modernist architect Domènech i Montaner for the 1888 Exhibition and was later to become an arts and crafts centre popularly known as the Castell dels Tres Dragons (the Castle of the Three Dragons). In the same area are a boat pond and a monumental cascade, where *La Dama del Paraigua*, a popular piece of sculpture, protects herself from the spray with an umbrella. There are also a curious stone mastodon, an 1899 locomotive on a plinth and, near the parliament, a small zoo. The park is very much Barcelona's answer to the Buen Retiro in Madrid, with an appropriate industrial touch. Just outside it, in the direction of the port, is the **Born Market** (1873–6), an iron and glass structure by the engineer Josep Cornet and now one of the city's main exhibition centres. Going inland from the park, you enter a promenade called the Saló Víctor Pradera, at the end of which is Vilaseca's rather splendid **Arc de Triomf**, another brick building put up especially for the great Exhibition.

Modernisme and the Eixample

It is now time to focus on the architecture of the late nineteenth and early twentieth centuries for which Barcelona is famous. This is discussed at greater length in 'Modernisme', where the affinities with the international Art Nouveau movement are also explored. Most of the principal Modernist buildings are to be found in the Eixample, but – as we have just seen – some are located in the Parc de la Ciutadella, while there are others in the old city and the Parc Güell. There are also some examples outside these zones, notably the Hospital de Sant Pau.

The finest boulevard of the Eixample is the Passeig de Gràcia, which is derived from the village it led to rather than the quality of grace which it also possesses. Several well-known Modernist buildings are to be found here. Starting from the Plaça de Catalunya, No. 35 on the left is an interesting example of the work of Domènech i Montaner with prominent circular balconies (1905); the ground floor is occupied by Loewe's leather shop. A little higher up on the same side is Puig i Cadafalch's **Casa Amatller** (1898–1900) in a Dutch gabled style with a tiled and pargeted exterior; this is followed immediately by Gaudí's **Casa Batlló** (1905–7), whose iridescent mosaic tiles and undulating gallery create a much more mobile front. The two houses manage to co-exist, however, because Gaudí demolished a room in his building in order not to spoil Puig's skyline – 'an extraordinary example of good manners in urban architecture', to quote David Mackay's excellent monograph, *Modern Architecture in Barcelona (1854–1939)*. At No. 74, next to the Hotel Majèstic, is a house with a Modernist tribune gallery and balconies. Further up on the same side at No. 92 is Gaudí's La Pedrera, officially **Casa Milà** (1905–11). Whereas Casa Batlló was actually a remodelling of a family home, this is an early version of a mansion block of flats with a stone surface hung on a steel frame and adorned with iron balconies that resemble seaweed; the pale tiled roof was designed to merge into the sky and thus de-emphasize the roofline, which is higher than those in the rest of the street. It is worth penetrating the porte-cochère to see the circular inner court from which a ramp descends to the underground parking area, one of the first of its kind.

The Passeig de Gràcia continues across the great gash of the Diagonal. The last house on the right before the road narrows, No. 132, is the imposing **Casa Fuster** (1908–10) by Domènech i Montaner. Its most notable features are the use of squat columns with bulbous capitals to support the tribune galleries and the ultra-semicircular windows used to turn the building's corner in which the front door is set. Here the promenade gives way to the Carrer Gran de Gràcia and you enter a more modest area of small shops which was once the core of a village of pronounced artisan character. Almost at the top of this long street on the left is the Carrer de les Carolines containing an early work by Gaudí, the **Casa Viçens** (1883–5), built for a tile manufacturer. Here there are Mudéjar references in the interplay of tile and brick, and there is a distinctive Gaudí feature in the double façade along the second floor where the windows lie in a second plane behind the columned gallery.

The strict grid of the Eixample contains a number of other significant Modernist buildings. On the Carrer d'Aragó is Domènech i Montaner's early work for the publishing house of Montaner i Simon (1880), and at the intersection of Carrer de Majorca with the Laietana stands the Palau Montaner, begun by another architect and completed by Domènech in 1893 – this sumptuous bourgeois mansion is now the seat of the central government's delegate to Catalonia. Also in this area, on a triangular site between the Diagonal and Carrer Rosselló, is Puig i Cadafalch's **Casa Terrades** (1903–5), popularly known from its spires as Casa de les Punxes. Of pronounced mediaeval tendency, it is highly eclectic in detail with both ogival and Renaissance windows and stunted columns at ground level featuring wide-spreading foliage-laden capitals, reminiscent of both Domènech and Gaudí. The quest for original forms of column and capital shape is common to the whole movement. Domènech's **Hospital de Sant Pau**, interesting for its Mudéjar features and for the layout of the wards as individual pavilions surrounded by gardens, is some way out of the centre on the Carrer de Cartagena. It is probably best combined with a visit to Gaudí's Sagrada Família, with which it is linked by the Avinguda Gaudí.

Returning to our original axis, the Carrer Mayor de Gràcia culminates in the Plaça Lesseps, not far from Gaudí's **Parc Güell**, but the intervening ring road makes access difficult, so a taxi is advisable from this point onwards. Coming from the centre by car, take the Carrer de Sardenya and follow the signs. This unusual hillside park was intended as a garden suburb with some sixty villas. The general layout was traced and the grounds were threaded with grotto-like arcades, where Gaudí could safely indulge his passion for tilted columns; all the paths eventually lead to a great *mirador* with a long undulating serpentine bench-cum-parapet decorated with a mosaic of broken tiles and supported on a dark forest of fluted temple-like columns. From here, and even better from the higher walk, there is a panoramic view of the whole city including the petrified rocket spires of the Sagrada Família. But apart from the two fairy-tale icing and gingerbread lodges of the main entrance, only two of the projected houses were ever built. The failure of the original project has been of some benefit to the general public, however, for the park is popular with locals and tourists alike. I even came across some strapping Catalan women playing boule with their menfolk on a patch of sand – a rough and ready version of the mixed doubles on the bowling greens of Parliament Hill Fields.

I shall surely be asked at this point why I have so far avoided the **Sagrada Família**, probably the most famous sight in Barcelona. The answer is that it is without doubt the most misconceived building in Christendom. A local joke runs that it is officially called the Temple Expiatori de la Sagrada Família and that, as it will never be finished, the sins of the human race – or at any rate of the Barcelona branch – will never be expiated. Of course they won't, Sagrada Família or no, but it is rather nice to be able to pin the blame on this overambitious building.

Gaudí inherited the project in 1883 from an architect called Villar, whose original design was much more traditional. You may well wonder why the local worthies allowed Gaudí to get away with so extravagant a project and David Mackay offers a possible explanation:

> The creative imagination of Antoni Gaudí (1852–1926) provided an extreme baroque formulation of the effervescence generated by Modernisme. Extending the analogy we can see in Gaudí's exuberant Modernisme a sort of collective Orphism of the Catalan community seeking to recover its Eurydice across the centuries of decadence when the full experience (social and cultural) of the baroque was denied to them. This may be one explanation for the patent contradiction between the normal sobriety of Catalan architecture and the public acceptance of the 'exorbitance', as Nikolaus Pevsner puts it, of Gaudí's work. . .

Sobriety is certainly the keynote of most Catalan architecture and 'baroque' is clearly the right word here (though the style is, if anything, Gothic) because baroque buildings are conceived as grand pieces of sculpture in themselves, to which all parts are subordinate. The trouble with Gaudí's conception is that it was too grand for a parish church or for any reasonable hope of completion within his lifetime. I have great admiration for some of Gaudí's works, notably the bishop's palace at Astorga, but the Sagrada Família was largely the product of his diseased imagination in his later years. As Mackay points out,

> His abundant imagination, private wit and public self-confidence finally became mortgaged to a consuming and reactionary religiosity that grew up around him through his work on the Sagrada Família temple. He misread his brief, and it destroyed him. His architecture became subjected to a religion of symbols. . .

Few people realize that the four-pronged Façana del Naixement and the spires copied from them on the Façana de la Pasió are simply those of the transepts and that a great central tower of some five hundred feet (equalling Cologne cathedral and much exceeding St Paul's, London and St Peter's, Rome) was envisaged. The west front, not even begun, was to have been approached by a great flight of steps spanning the present Carrer Majorca. The actual entrance for the public is by the Porta de la Pasió, with its splayed buttress-arcade still under construction. The Sagrada Família museum contains plans of Villar's earlier conventional project and photographs of the massed crowds following Gaudí's coffin. As far as the details of the building are concerned, there are, as you would expect, some amusing touches such as the tortoise bases of the columns on the Naixement front and the animal kingdom represented bottom left and the giant snails on the spires. But the later carving of the magi is extremely academic and the pure white harpist perched aloft above the portal is a tiresome distraction from the baroque concept of the whole.

Nineteen eighty-two marked a century since work first began on the building. This may not be long in mediaeval terms, but it is quite out of step with rational expectations of completion today. Also, mediaeval cathedrals were usually begun from the east end, which made it possible to consecrate a viable liturgical sanctuary within twenty or thirty years. Here the ambitious design has merely produced an incomplete shell. As Gaudí left no detailed plans, the sensible thing to do would be to desist from work as from the completion of the Porta de la Pasió and leave the admittedly amazing shell with the air blowing through the unglazed windows; it would then be possible to take down the ugly hoardings that surround the building works and put the centre down to grass, as a playground perhaps, or a quiet retreat with fountains, taking advantage of the walls and spires as shelter from the brutal summer sun. It might then become one of the most agreeable places in Barcelona rather than nightmarish and

Antoni Gaudí's church of the Sagrada Família,
still overshadowed by its brooding crane a century after work
first started on the building.

oppressive – as it threatens to become if the great gantry crane
remains in place and the skyscraper tower is ever built.

The Environs

Moving further outwards from the city centre, there are several
places that deserve a visit. The first and nearest is the **Monestir de
Pedralbes** founded in 1326 by Elisenda of Montcada, wife of
James II. The church is open daily (though the cloister may only

be seen on Sundays between 12 and 2 p.m.) and is a good example of the Catalan Gothic style. There is a wide vault and a semi-circular apse of seven ribbed compartments with tall windows; the wall is quite plain below the nave windows without any string course or other distractions; the glass is original and in good condition; the nuns' choir is enclosed by a grille at the rear and it is always occupied, so you cannot be slovenly in your devotions. In the grand three-storeyed cloister there is a *sala didàctica,* or graphic display, which tells you a great deal about the royal house of Aragon-Catalonia, where everyone of importance is buried, where the principal monasteries in Catalonia are located and which order they belonged to. A diligent student with a pen and pad can save buying several books.

The cloister has the usual dependencies. The refectory has place settings with real bread, which reminded me of that marvellous little Zurbarán still life in the Prado; the kitchen has a grand armorial sink; the dormitories are divided into discreet compartments by curtains, as in a sanatorium, each with its chamberpot; the market garden is sadly uncultivated; the museum in the chapter house has some interesting pieces, notably the little chests the nuns were allowed for their personal possessions. Queen Elisenda's monastery is most agreeably situated above the hurly-burly of the town. You can walk back down to the Diagonal by the Avinguda de Pedralbes, where, towards the bottom on the right, there is a lodge by Gaudí with a wrought-iron gate in the shape of a dragon against which visitors, myself included, love to be photographed. You may be moved to visit the nearby **Palau de Pedralbes**, given to Alfonso XIII by the haute bourgeoisie of Catalonia to encourage him to spend more time in this corner of his kingdom. The palace is filled with very standard Bourbon fixtures and fittings, but the grounds are pleasant and contain a carriage museum.

For forays further afield, the Ferrocarril de Catalunya can be recommended. It starts underground from the Plaça de Catalunya and connects with the metro system at certain points but is separate and more far-reaching. It offers second and third class (even the latter has arm rests). The network is a good example of Catalan efficiency, perhaps not the most exciting of human characteristics but certainly very welcome when you are trying to see a lot in too little time. There is an excellent day's excursion which can be made on this railway to **Sant Cugat del Vallès** and then to Terrassa (do not take the Tibidabo branch line).

The ex-Benedictine monastery at Sant Cugat is about fifteen

minutes' walk from the station (taxis are also available). The foundation is very ancient, dating from 878 to be precise. There is a fine great rose window over the church entrance; the east end is triapsidal and decorated with Lombard bands. Beyond this end of the building there is a leafy glade in which the locals play boule, a sign that you are still within the French zone of influence, though you are in fact near the southern fringe of the great Benedictine expansion which followed Charlemagne's establishment of the Spanish march; a little further south you enter reformed Cistercian territory (see 'Monasticism'). The large cloister, founded in about 1190, is extremely pleasant and restful and is used in summer for contemporary art exhibitions (there are no longer any monks, only a parish priest). A good cheap lunch can be had in the Bar Catalunya. This faces the station, through which the Terrassa-bound train passes every half hour.

Terrassa is a large industrial town of some 160,000 inhabitants with a long history of textile manufacture. The Museu Provincial Tèxtil, comprising the private collections of a number of barons of the trade, is wide-ranging and includes examples of Egyptian, Coptic, Persian, Turkish, Byzantine, Indian, Chinese, Japanese, Hispano-Arabic, Inca, Aztec and Mexican cloths and clothes. In fact, the clothing section, both civil and religious, is considerably superior to·that of the Museu Tèxtil i de la Indumentària, which virtually faces the Museu Picasso in Barcelona.

But Terrassa has other claims on the traveller's attention. Although well within the radius of the powerful rays emanating from Montserrat, which is visible from the upper town, it has honoured older gods, and their temples are to be found on a site that was probably an Iberian settlement and was certainly occupied by the main buildings of the Roman *municipium* of Egara. This is reached on foot by walking up the traffic-free Carrer de Sant Pere from the town hall until the traffic begins again and then veering half-right along the Carrer de la Creu Vella and across an old bridge to a walled enceinte which contains three important, not to say unique, buildings: the *conjunt*, or ensemble, is known as Les Esglésies de Sant Pere. You can also drive round the edge of the town. Ask for directions.

The lower of the three buildings was the cathedral of Santa Maria, a bishopric from the year 450. The early basilica was larger than the present church which, however, still preserves the original domical apse framed by a Visigothic horseshoe arch. The nave is eleventh-century, though the old font, let into the floor for total immersion, dates from the fifth century. In a little apse off the nave are some traces of a mural devoted to the martyrdom of Thomas à Becket (d. 1170), to whom quite a number of churches in the peninsula were dedicated following the marriage of Eleanor, daughter of Henry II of England, to Alfonso VIII of Castile. Santa Maria also rather incongruously contains some important Gothic paintings, notably the magnificent retable by Jaume Huguet of the deaths of Saints Abdon and Sennen, who appear in the central panel as two mournful youths full of sweetness and resignation. This is as good an example of this artist's work as can be found in

The octagonal baptistry of Sant Miquel in the magical Visigothic complex of Terrassa.

the Barcelona museum. The present forecourt of the church has remnants of a fourth- or fifth-century mosaic floor, which would have lain within the walls of the earlier building.

The middle of the three structures in this exceptional complex is called Sant Miquel; it was the main baptistry. Its splendid octagonal bath is covered by a lantern on narrow heightened arches, supported by eight columns of different girths; some of the capitals are Roman, some Visigothic. This building, restored by the Modernist architect and politician Puig i Cadafalch, is thought to date originally from the sixth century. There is a little crypt with three apses in the form of a trefoil. The upper church, Sant Pere, is barrel-vaulted and dates in the main from the twelfth century. Yet it too preserves part of the Visigothic triapsidal east end, though the central apse has been truncated to make way for a curious blind tenth-century arcade with traces of painting – a sort of primitive retable.

This brief inventory does little to convey the extraordinary *genius loci* of this holy precinct on the edge of a rather busy, brash, manufacturing town; it not only breathes antiquity but has the shrine-like quality of a haven where the lamp of Christian civilization flickered and survived in the desert of the Dark Ages.

Another variant of this excursion would be to combine Sant Cugat with **Sabadell**, which can be done by simply resuming the journey from Sant Cugat on a Sabadell-line train. This is another large industrial town, proudly claiming the title *la Manchester catalana*, which Ford awarded to Barcelona itself. Like all industrial centres in Catalonia it prides itself on its cultural associations and has an important Institut de Paleontologia; there is also an interesting collection of agricultural tools in the Masia de Can Déu (God's Farmhouse). The town is graced by a number of Modernist buildings.

Whichever bifurcation you choose from Sant Cugat, the return to Barcelona is accomplished in comfort and a spirit of relaxation: this is much better than trying to ensure that you get into the right lane on to and off the motorway. On alighting at the Plaça de Catalunya, it is not unnatural that the magnetism of Las Ramblas should once again make itself felt and that you should succumb to it. It was said of Córdoba in the heyday of the caliphate that there was nothing available to man that could not be obtained there, including the milk of birds of paradise. I am not sure Las Ramblas are as exotic as that but you can certainly buy a parrot, orchids, succulent seafood, *The Times* (for about one pound) and much of the world's literature, while a table on the admittedly pricey Terraza del Oriente is an excellent place from which to review your impressions of Barcelona and its environs with a drink in hand – not gin, which is out of tune with the place, not wine, which does not sufficiently fire the imagination, but perhaps a well-iced pastis or a glass of the excellent local champagne (when the Catalans started selling corks to the French, they also learned to make the stuff themselves).

Within the peninsula Barcelona jostles with Madrid for both cultural and economic supremacy. The resulting tension has sometimes spiralled into hatred and is unlikely to disappear: for the Catalans Madrid will always be an upstart overgrown village, populated with idle and incompetent bureaucrats; for Madrid Catalonia and its capital will remain a 'question' and a 'problem'. Steps have been taken to ameliorate this through the limited statute of autonomy, but Catalan aspirations and *amour-propre* will continue to exert constant pressure on the centre. Outside the peninsula, Barcelona ranks not with London, Paris or Rome (nor really does Madrid) but with Marseille, Genoa, Naples, Alexandria, Beirut (before its tragic destruction) and Trieste, in which league it scores high, perhaps the highest.

To start with practical considerations, it is an efficient city, certainly the most efficient in Spain. Things work. Local trains run on time (the national network is another matter). Internal communications – metro, buses, funiculars and cable cars (for those who can stomach them) – are good. Although the design of the nineteenth-century enlargement of the city, the Eixample, leaves something to be desired, it is on the whole a better attempt at urbanization than the equivalent expansion of Madrid at about the same time. You are seldom stuck in a traffic jam except when there is a carnival or a political demonstration. Museums open and close at their advertised times (the current Michelin is the best guide in this respect). Churches, other than the cathedral and Santa Maria del Mar, are less reliable but are usually open in the early morning and from about seven in the evening. Food is rather good (see 'Food and Drink'); pastries are a great feature and there are *pastisseries* everywhere which also sell champagne. Exhibitions, fairs, theatre, concerts and art shows are held frequently and maintain a high standard. Barcelona is a great shop window both for commerce and the arts, which have always been intimately linked in its history.

Nowhere, however, is the spirit of Barcelona better evoked than in the **Palau de la Música**, where you should endeavour to spend at least one evening during the season, which runs from October to early summer. This extraordinary concert hall was put up by

*The exuberant stage, proscenium and organ loft
under the mysteriously glowing stained-glass ceiling of the
Palau de la Música.*

Domènech i Montaner and completed in 1908 for a private society of music lovers, the Orfeó Català. Around the stage bas-reliefs of damsels with dulcimers and other instruments burgeon out of the tiled walls. The proscenium arch sprouts, on the left, a huge moustachioed bust of Anselm Clavé, founder of the society; he is so dominant I thought at first he could only be Wagner. On the other side of the stage is an amazing confection that features a bust of Beethoven between two columns of a classical temple, from which a cloud of smoke whirls upwards metamorphosing into Wagner's cavalcade of the Walkyrie, complete with real reins and lances. In the auditorium, around the tiled columns of the upper gallery, are slightly slanted chandeliers like Visigothic crowns; the lightly pointed arcade launches a tiled fan-vault; the tiled ceiling i encrusted with ceramic roses; the centrepiece is a luminous mosaic bowl of stained glass which glows mysteriously like a prop from a science-fiction film. Whatever the concert (they are usually good), the eye can roam for a long time over all these architectural reminiscences and decorative pleasantries.

The Palau de la Música is tremendously expressive of the predilections of the Catalan bourgeoisie at the beginning of the century; it hovers close to the bad taste which always lurked in the wings of Modernisme and was to be severely repressed by Noucentisme. But it also tells you quite a lot about Barcelona as a whole, now as well as then. Despite its extravagances it is on a more domestic scale than the Liceu of 1844 and pleasanter to be in. The musicians of the city orchestra mingle in the bar with the public. It has something of the atmosphere of a club – which of course it is for regular subscribers. It is the favourite resort of a commercial bourgeoisie that still loves pastries and champagne and Wagner and a bit of a show. These are the people who make Barcelona tick.

2

The Beacon of Montserrat

I must confess I had been rather dreading Montserrat ever since reaching Barcelona. I knew 'the great Diana of the Mountain', to use Ford's phrase, was important to Catalonia, but I recalled Fatima and Lourdes and expected a similarly commercialized cult. But I was told firmly by a Catalan friend that I was wrong, that Montserrat was a living place, not merely another centre of the world pilgrimage industry, and belonged to the people of Catalonia, who had held its mistress in special affection for many centuries. I also learned that Montserrat's religious tone was ecumenical and that the abbot was deeply respected as a champion of Catalan liberties.

I went accordingly in a humble spirit, leaving Barcelona by the Diagonal on to the autoroute and taking exit 25. The massif of Montserrat is indeed extraordinary, like a weird combination of Arizona and Bavaria. The monastic complex looks from below like a great cantilevered barracks on the mountainside. The whole place was sacked by Marshal Suchet in 1811 and what was left fell into total ruin when the monks were forced to abandon it in 1835 and the holy image was removed to Esparreguera. The modern installations, designed to receive large contingents of pilgrims, are standard of their kind and not particularly offensive. There is a pleasant remnant of the earlier buildings on the left as you cross the forecourt towards the basilica. The church is a late Renaissance structure of no great distinction, but the grandeur of the setting compensates, while the lack of buildings of vast interest helps to concentrate the mind on the Virgin herself.

The black goddess reigns aloft in the wall behind the high altar. She is said to have been made by Saint Luke and brought to Barcelona by Saint Peter in AD 50, then to have been hidden during the Moorish occupation and rediscovered by shepherds; on hearing that she had been found the bishop of Vic claimed her, but she could not be forced beyond a certain cave on the mountainside – La Santa Cova (the Holy Cave) – where a shrine was immediately built. The widespread Spanish tradition of the hiding and rediscovery of images probably has some basis in fact and was recently revived in the Civil War, when the present Virgin was hidden by the monks and replaced in the church by a replica,

La Mare de Déu de Montserrat, Ford's
'Great Diana of the Mountain'.

knowledge of the substitution being confined to the abbot and a few senior brethren. Whatever images preceded her, the incumbent was actually carved in the twelfth century. The artist has endowed her with a face whose long nose, slightly receding chin and warm smile are those of a real mother, not an idealized doll.

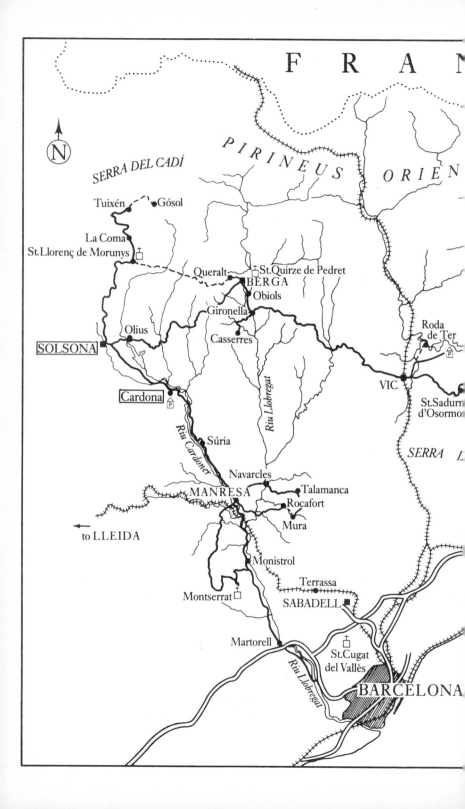

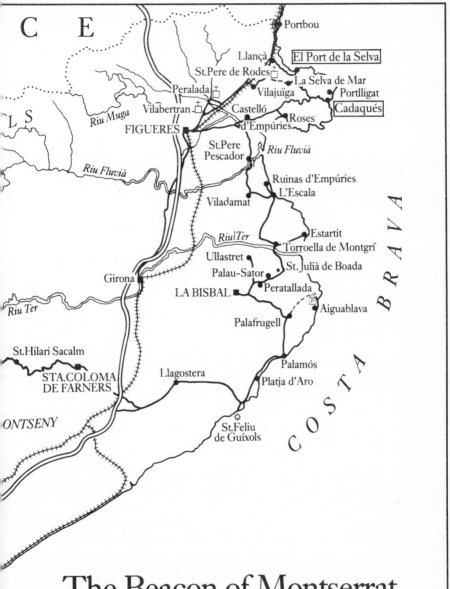

C E

L S

Portbou

Llançà

St.Pere de Rodes

El Port de la Selva

La Selva de Mar

Peralada

Vilajuïga

Portlligat

Vilabertran

Castelló
d'Empúries

Cadaqués

Riu Muga

FIGUERES

Roses

St.Pere
Pescador

Riu Fluvià

Riu Fluvià

Ruinas d'Empúries
L'Escala

Viladamat

Riu Ter

Estartit

Torroella de Montgrí

Ullastret

Palau-Sator

St. Julià de Boada

Girona

LA BISBAL

Peratallada

Aiguablava

Palafrugell

B R A V A

Riu Ter

St.Hilari Sacalm

STA.COLOMA
DE FARNERS

Llagostera

Palamós

Platja d'Aro

ONTSENY

St.Feliu
de Guíxols

C O S T A

The Beacon of Montserrat

0   5   10   15   20   25 km

SCALE

Here it is worth remembering that her official title is La Mare de Déu (Mother of God), highlighting the importance attached by the Catalans to maternity as opposed to virginity, which obsessed the Sevillians and led to the cult of the Immaculate Conception – of little importance in these parts.

There are, of course, a number of celebrated black Virgins, of whom Our Lady of Guadalupe, patroness of the Hispanic world, is the most widely known. The darkening of the features is generally attributed to centuries of candle smoke, day and night, in a confined space and sometimes behind glass. Our Lady of Montserrat is often referred to affectionately as La Moreneta (The Dusky One). And despite her elevated position in the church, she is not at all remote. On the contrary, she receives a daily stream of visitors. You may enter her *cambril* (small chamber), climb the few steps leading up to her and kiss her extended hand, which holds the orb of the world. This, incidentally, is often interpreted by artists as an apple, a pear, a pine cone or even a bird, but they mislead the observer in their pursuit of decorative effect for the original symbolism is undoubtedly that she holds the world in her hand.

After visiting the Virgin there are various hermitages and shrines on offer, while Ford suggests that a morning should be spent scrambling about the mountain and examining its geology, botany and picturesque scenery. The walks are certainly very pleasant. I personally jibbed at taking the funicular to La Santa Cova but the walk up to the modern hermitage of Sant Miquel affords fine views over the river Llobregat (said to divide upper French Catalonia from the lower 'Moorish' zone) and over the pine-clad sierras northwards as far as the Pyrenees. On this route you pass statues of Pau (Pablo) Casals and Saint Francis. There is also a monumental slab with a roll call of religious and political figures who have professed a special devotion to Montserrat – there can be no doubt of this monastery's importance to the Catalan sense of national identity. In times of political repression, when local representative bodies were banned, the Catalans always turned to their religious leaders and communities. As the abbots of Montserrat have traditionally been elected to office by the monks (whereas until recently bishops were appointed by the central state), the monastery managed to preserve a certain independence even under Franco. In December 1970 the monks opened their doors to several hundred intellectuals who assembled in protest against the régime. After Franco's death Montserrat celebrated the first service of reconciliation in Spain. Neither the symbolic nor the real role of this place in Catalan national life should ever be underestimated. (See 'Monasticism'.)

Having paid my respects to the Virgin of Montserrat, I decided to sample the Catalan interior which lies between the larger cities and off the main routes that join them. If you look at the small-scale map of the peninsula – or even at the Firestone 1:500,000 (sheet 3) – you will see that there is a sort of empty quarter within the circuit of red roads linking Barcelona to Lleida, Lleida to La Seu d'Urgell, La Seu to Puigcerdà and Puigcerdà to Barcelona via Vic. This trip describes a loop within this hinterland, stretching out to Solsona before curving back via Berga to Vic, whence I descend to the lusher pastures and popular beaches of the Costa Brava. To make straight for the coast would be to neglect the core of Catalonia.

From Montserrat you can either return to Monistrol and cross the Llobregat by a mediaeval bridge, or descend on the road which hugs the mountain, passing the little Romanesque church

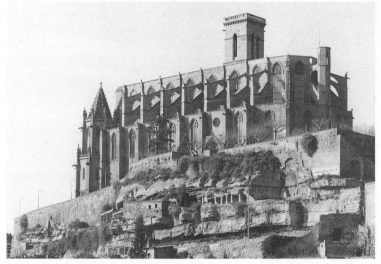

La Seu, the great parish church of Manresa.

of Santa Cecília and turning right at the first junction, for **Manresa**. This is a hillocky, windswept, dusty town, a bit abrasive and not obviously attractive on first sight. But you should persevere and proceed to the Plaça de l'Ajuntament. The joint hardware store and pharmacy with its old apothecaries' jars should be seen. But La Seu is the jewel of the place, a superb Gothic church built in the main between 1328 and the mid-sixteenth century. It has a fine example of the characteristic Catalan wide nave vault sustained by two-tier buttresses on the outside. The stained glass, though damaged by the French in the Peninsular War, is still most effective, particularly the rose window. The most interesting interior fitting is the retable of the Holy Ghost (1393–4) by Pere Serra for the tanners' guild. It is an outstanding piece of Catalan art of the period. It features the typical stamped gilt backgrounds and haloes but is unusual in that the dove of the Holy Spirit descends directly on to the Virgin in the central panel while the dead Christ is shown in a horizontal rather than the usual recumbent position in the predella. It is difficult to get inside this church as gypsies are said to roam and steal; the best times are early in the morning or about seven in the evening.

Before leaving Manresa it is worth seeking out Saint Ignatius Loyola's *cova santa*, in which the founder of the Jesuits spent some months in 1522 and where he is said to have written his *Spiritual Exercises* (1548). A not very pleasing church now rises over the

The spine of the Serra de Montserrat as it would have been contemplated by Saint Ignatius Loyola from la cova santa.

grotto – an example of what Ford calls 'the bad period of 1660, with Ionic decorations, clumsy angels and corrupt architecture'. But there is a very fine view of the whole saw-toothed spine of the Montserrat massif, from above which the Virgin would smile down on Loyola during his spiritual labours. Inside the church, behind the high altar, there is a grotto chapel under a roof of living rock, where devotees are constantly bowed in prayer. In the nave of the church are statues of other Jesuit saints and personages.

Ford makes a fierce but shrewd attack on the Jesuit order:

As printing, which gave wings to the Bible, was shattering the fabric of the Vatican, the Jesuits monopolizing the lever of *education* became missionaries abroad, tutors and teachers of the rising youth at home, and thus not only disarmed knowledge of its power but made it minister to its own suicidal destruction and became a tool for the carrying on of that implacable exterminating contest, which Rome has ever warred, wars and will war against all civil and religious liberty.

Ford was an Anglican High Tory who revelled in these diatribes but in Catalonia too, despite Loyola's dedication of himself to the Virgin of Montserrat, feelings have been traditionally less warm towards the Jesuits and their militaristic organization than towards the gentler Franciscans, whose civilizing mission to the New World set out from Majorca.

Despite its unpromising exterior the Hotel Pedro III is comfortable and efficient. There is a modest but pleasing circuit that can be made from Manresa by taking the road for Vic, leaving it after a few kilometres at Navarcles and taking the winding hill road BV 1221 to **Talamanca**, an agreeable little summer station with an unpretentious hotel (no sign – look for the yellow letter box on the front) and swimming pool. You then continue for a short distance to the turning marked BV 1223 down to **Mura**, a village tucked into a ravine with a charming little Romanesque church. From Mura an unsurfaced track, perfectly passable with care, follows the river course for five or six kilometres to Rocafort. Here the tarmac starts again, and you descend to Pont de Vilomara, where there is an old bridge over the Llobregat, thence rapidly to Manresa again. It is through expeditions such as these that you discover how extraordinarily rippled is the terrain of much of the Catalan interior. At times it recalls the Basque country with its settlements in river gorges, but it is less dour. At every stop for directions or refreshment the people are most helpful – what is more, in my experience their directions are scrupulously accurate.

Heading from Manresa in the direction of Solsona, you come first to the small industrial town of **Súria**, which very much resembles a Basque hive of industry hemmed in by wooded hills. Next you are rewarded by the sight of **Cardona** rising on its height above the river Cardoner. The place was approved by Ford because it was never taken by the French. It also boasts a huge salt mine, which has been active since Strabo's time. Giant greyish-white slag heaps are piled up across the river, the residue of centuries: you can visit the mine, which now mainly produces potash, and there is a museum of salt artefacts. Both may be missed with equanimity but you should not underestimate the importance of salt in Cardona's history. The town is all ups and downs, like Manresa only more so. It is a harsh place with quaint corners – the main promenade with views over the salt mounds is pleasantly shaded by plane trees. On 8–10 September the towns-people erect an improvised bull ring in front of the town hall, whose balcony is converted into a box for dignitaries. On the first day they run little bulls through the streets Pamplona-style. The crumbling old parish church rises immediately above the scene of these festivities; it is underpinned by an arcade with bars.

The castle of the dukes of Cardona, constables of Aragon once the yoke of Castile had been laid firmly on the necks of the Aragonese and Catalans alike, is the dominant feature of the town. It has become a National Parador and offers the usual high standards of these hostelries. I decided not to stay because my arrival just failed to coincide with the popular festival and because I did not fancy waking up on a hot morning to the glittering escarpments of salt waste across the valley. But the church of Sant Vicenç inside the Parador must be seen. It was used as a prison during the Civil War, when the crypt was converted into a latrine. The building was subsequently whitewashed throughout to purify it. Then, once the policy of stripping to reveal the structural elements of ancient monuments gained ground, official architects stepped in and chipped and scrubbed it back to its bare bones. The result is a splendid unadorned example of early eleventh-century Romanesque building with massive piers, a great barrel vault, brick and rubble vaulted aisles, a dome on squinch arches, three apses (the main one very elegant) and a delicate crypt. There is also a rear gallery for the castle folk. You are shown around by a very earnest guide whose tales of long-dead lords and ladies should be taken – if I may be forgiven – with a pinch of salt.

On to **Solsona**, of which I had heard good reports which were not disappointed. It lies in an agricultural plain – or the nearest thing you can find to a plain in these parts – which is rather a relief after the tortuous little gorges in the foothills of Montserrat; it also opens up the view of the great mountain range to the north and allows you to prepare yourself mentally for its assault. The old city slopes upwards slightly from the cathedral, which occupies the bottom left-hand corner of the old walls, of which some stretches and gateways still remain. When Philip II (1556–98) obtained permission from Clement VIII to establish a new bishopric at Solsona with the object of reinforcing defences against the Huguenot menace, the old church of Santa Maria was extended and given a facelift. It had already acquired a thirteenth-century Gothic nave in the Catalan style (though less impressive than Manresa's), whose buttresses rise above the wall of the primitive church. The Romanesque apses still jut out from the city wall, the windows of the Gothic chancel rising above them. Then an extension with a Renaissance dome and urns and a tall, rather austere bishop's palace were built; the latter later acquired a façade on the Plaça de la Catedral, 'overdone with pilasters and ornaments' in Ford's tetchy view, though it seemed quite tasteful to me – and in any case now provides access to the quite exceptional diocesan museum.

Cathedral museums are often no more than jumbled warehouses indulging in dubious attributions. Solsona's is an outstanding exception. I have already remarked on the excellent layout and informative display technique of the great Museu d'Art de Catalunya in Barcelona. Solsona's museum, though very much smaller, is in the same league and in some respects is perhaps even more advanced. The first room sketches the area, focusing on its geology, topography and local dress, and describes the foundation of the bishopric. There is then a superbly selected series of vitrines with relics and pottery from the Mesolithic and Neolithic periods; the Solsona plain seems to have become extremely popular in about 2000 BC. There are some Iberian painted vases predating the Roman invasion. Then you come quickly to the Romanesque. A plan identifies eighty-six Romanesque churches within the *comarca* of Solsona. A press-button slide-show gives a selection of these: some are very small and humble while the grander churches feature one or more apses adorned with Lombard bands and columns. The style is different in some respects from the Castilian equivalent: there are none of the arcaded porticoes that characterize Segovian Romanesque, for example, and there is less luxury of capital and column than is to be found on the route to Santiago (see also 'Romanesque Art and Architecture'). But there is a beautiful cloister column with elongated figures from the earlier church of Santa Maria (the influence is said to be Toulousian) – observe the delicate naturalism of the female figure's hands. There are frescoes of the thirteenth century from Sant Pau de Casserres and of the twelfth from the Mozarabic church of Sant Quirze de Pedret; the frieze pattern of the latter is of almost Pompeian sophistication (there are other fragments from this church in the Museu d'Art de Catalunya). When the Pedret paintings were peeled off, an even earlier layer was discovered and two fragments from the tenth century are also on display.

All this construction of churches, large and small, with their paintings on walls and wooden panels, escalated with the early repopulation of the southern foothills of the Pyrenees after the Moors abandoned the area in the ninth century. It should be remembered that by the middle of the tenth century the Catalan end of the Christian frontier was well down in the Penedès district to the south of Barcelona and that the county of Castile was only just beginning to form. Thus, if Catalan Romanesque is in some respects more primitive than that of Old Castile, this was largely because the more stable political climate was conducive to an earlier demand for religious architecture. This period also produced some splendid ironwork, while some of the wooden Virgins with faces like those of real country girls are delightful. The Gothic section has some important pieces by Pere Serra (1357–1409), Lluís Borrassà (1380–1424) and Jaume Ferrer II (active 1434–57) which were awaiting fresh installation at the time of my visit. But even without them the museum is a model of intelligent display and should not be missed.

From the Castellvell or old fort above the town there are views round the compass over the undulating plain, revealing a judicious mixture of ancient and modern buildings and some light agro-industries. The typical homestead of the grainlands is the *mas* (or larger *masia*) with pitched roof, open lofts and neatly stacked bales of barley and vetch in the barns. Beyond the cultivable land and the wooded hills crouches the great slumbering flank of the Serra del Cadí, which rises to 2,530 metres. There are two *fondas* in the old town of Solsona, the San Roque and the Vilanova (the latter is located in the little cathedral square and offers beds only). There is also an excellent modern hotel, the Gran Sol, one kilometre out on the Manresa road. The food and service are good and there is a swimming pool.

From Solsona a most spectacular road runs north to **Sant Llorenç de Morunys**. On the left as you climb you are confronted by the grim Serra d'Odèn, though not quite as high as brother Cadí, it obviously means to be taken seriously. The road reaches a junction after twenty-four kilometres: the upward fork leads to the ski station of Port del Comte; the lower descends to Sant

Llorenç, a pleasant hill station in a basin surrounded by steep hills and rock formations reminiscent of Montserrat. Here in the eleventh century the Benedictines built a small monastery, now in the process of being restored. The church, of about the same period as Cardona's, though less grand, is barrel-vaulted and the strippers have again done their work except that they have not dared to meddle with a much prized gilt and gingerbread Churriguresque chapel, one of the few in Catalonia, which was largely bypassed by the baroque style. Another chapel contains a retable of the Holy Spirit by Pere Serra, smaller than that at Manresa but this master's appeal does not diminish. There is also a charming small rustic cloister. There are plenty of lodgings in the town and there is a swimming pool attached to the hostelry one kilometre away on the road to La Coma. The asphalt road continues as far as Tuixén, tucked right into the southern face of the Serra del Cadí; an unsurfaced but motorable road then leads on to Gósol, where Picasso spent the summer of 1906. This is marvellous walking country. From Sant Llorenç you can continue to Berga. Returning to Solsona, the view is again spectacular, in reverse, especially in the evening light, as the rucked-up bull's pelt to which writers from Strabo to Espriu have likened the peninsula is revealed fold upon fold.

Solsona is so pleasant a place that it may entice you to use it as a base for explorations further south, but I decided to defer Calaf, Cervera, Tàrrega and Agramunt for a later trip and to follow through my first plan by heading for Berga, via **Olius**, where there is a Romanesque church in a pleasant setting just off the road. Unfortunately, when I arrived I discovered I should have called the parish priest first on 811 0100 to arrange to see the interior, so I pushed on through a pleasant countryside of pines and carobs to Berga and immediately drove up above the town to the sanctuary of **Queralt**, where an uninteresting church contains a much venerated Virgin of the thirteenth century. This Diana of the Crags has a dove perched on her hand (see my remarks on symbolism at Montserrat), and like her senior sister she lives in a vitrine high above the (hideous) modern altar. You can climb up and visit her too; she is indeed beautiful but wears an extremely enigmatic smile and I personally would be more inclined to put my trust in Our Lady of Montserrat.

Berga is an industrial town, ringed like most others by mountains. It has a long history as a textile centre and there is a core of older buildings. It is now encircled by a rather labyrinthine bypass, but it is well worth asking the way down to **Sant Quirze de**

*Sant Quirze, almost like a natural feature growing
out of the hillside.*

Bridge below Sant Quirze over the ice-cold waters of the Llobregat.

80

Pedret, whose frescoes can be seen both in Barcelona and at Solsona. The motorable road winds down some four kilometres into the valley of the Llobregat. When you reach the river you must leave your vehicle by the old stone bridge and continue on foot. It is about ten minutes' climb upwards and to the left to reach the church, which is Mozarabic, that is to say earlier than either of the layers of painting exhibited in the museums. Its rarity and remoteness and its horseshoe arches make it a very special place, and you have to imagine it as the core of a very small and precarious community before the region was fully secured for Christendom. The condition of the building – it is now covered by a concrete roof – indicates why the frescoes were removed and justifies the role of the museums in preserving what could not be preserved in its natural setting. After scrambling up the hill, try a swim in the pool of the Llobregat below the bridge: it was almost cruelly cold even in warm September.

From Berga I had decided to make for Vic, a cathedral city with another renowned museum. I had marked out two little detours on the way. The first was to the Visigothic church of **Obiols**, a few kilometres south of Berga, just off the road to the right. The approach is tricky, through a semi-abandoned nineteenth-century industrial site, but you arrive by asking. The church is now part of a farmyard and the barn was replete with freshly harvested bales. Only dogs were on guard, so I could not enter the church, but the narrow windows and doorway of crude slabs made the Visigothic attribution seem likely – here was yet another very ancient place of worship, presumably active before the Moorish invasion of 711 (717 in Catalonia). Returning to the road and continuing to Gironella, I disregarded the Vic turning for the moment, crossed the river and took the Casserres road, reaching the really delightful little Romanesque church of Sant Pau de Casserres after four kilometres. The apse is lit by a single elegant window. At the rear of the parochial buildings is an extremely pleasant shady area for an alfresco meal. **Casserres** itself is situated up on a spine and offers the splendid views that are commonplace in these parts. I then returned to Gironella.

Before leaving the towns of the upper Llobregat, it is worth remarking on the local phenomenon of the *colonies industrials* (industrial colonies), which were founded in the late nineteenth century along the course of this river so as to take advantage of hydroelectric power: just north of Gironella is the Colònia Rosal and downstream at Santa Coloma is the Colònia Güell of Gaudí's patron – and there were others. In essence the factory, the workers' housing estate, the church, the school and the owner's mansion were moulded together in a single compound. Though the employers sometimes commissioned well-known Modernist architects like Gaudí or Puig i Cadafalch, the system was highly paternalistic and has been described as semi-feudal (see 'Political Life and Institutions').

The road to Vic from Gironella is well surfaced, which is the

This market in the Plaça Major of Vic takes place every Tuesday and Saturday.

most important consideration in these foothills; curves and hairpin bends are the rule here. Ausa under the Romans and later capital of the Ausetoni, **Vic** is a much larger and livelier cathedral city than somnolent Solsona. Like Solsona, however, it lies in a semi-plain (bishoprics must be nourished by well-stocked granaries). When emerging on to the Barcelona–Puigcerdà road, it is quite easy to miss the crossing into the old city. If this happens, cling to signs reading *Ajuntament, Casc Antic* or *Oficina de Turisme*, which will set you on the ring road round the historical core and lead you eventually into the Plaça Major, a splendid ample square with Gothic houses rising above an arcade which encloses it on all sides. This is the scene of a market on Saturdays and Tuesdays, when it is impossible to enter by car until the afternoon. In general parking is extremely difficult and traffic congestion a real problem. This makes Vic less than ideal as a centre for excursions but it certainly deserves a night for itself. There is a National Parador at seventeen kilometres on the road to Roda de Ter, but this only solves the parking problem at night and on balance it is better to persist until you find a slot and to stay in the centre. There is a comfortable hostel, the Ausa, right on the Plaça Major. Most hotels provide you with a plan of their town

El Cloquer, the handsome Romanesque tower of Vic cathedral.

and Vic's is an exceptionally thorough one. The old quarter is pleasant to wander about in. The reconstructed Roman temple, which emerged from the ruins of an old townhouse, the Palau Montcada and the restored Ajuntament, dating originally from 1358 and occupying a corner of the Plaça Major, should be seen. You are then lured downwards to the cathedral.

The cathedral of Vic is much grander than Solsona's converted parish church. In scale it is more reminiscent of the post-reconquest late Renaissance cathedrals of the south such as Granada or Guadix, but not as pleasing. A harmless neo-classical façade leads into a grandiose neo-Corinthian nave with Escurial-esque piers and fluted pilasters (1781–1803), now all picked out in sepia and gold, presumably to match the pretentious trompe l'oeil murals in those colours by Josep Maria Sert (cf. Ajuntament, Barcelona, pp.37–8). The ambulatory contains a fine alabaster retable of 1420–7 by Pere Oller: the dead Christ and the archangel in the central panel of the predella form an outstanding composition and the whole work, particularly the bony hands and mourning faces, is moving and remarkable. The cloister has two tiers. The elegant upper decorated Gothic arcade rests on an older lower level with rounded arches. But the finest architectural feature of the cathedral complex is undoubtedly the tower, El Cloquer as it is called locally, a restored relic of the earlier Romanesque church. Known to have been under construction in 1064, it rises in six stages (not counting the loft); the window apertures become larger the higher they go. Its only rival as the finest Romanesque tower within the scope of this book is Sant Climent de Taüll (see p.144).

Across the street from El Cloquer and facing the Plaça del Bisbe Oliba stands the diocesan museum. This is not as well presented as Solsona's – there is simply too much on display. But the quality of the main pieces is such that you should buckle down to it for a couple of hours. Less will not do.

The specialities of the museum are Romanesque and Gothic painting and some high-quality carving from both periods. In the first room the importance of Romanesque painting, both mural and on panel, to the message of the Church and the understanding of the flock is amply demonstrated. The twelfth-century apse murals from Sant Sadurní d'Osormort, Sant Martí del Brull and other churches must have been overwhelming in their day, bearing in mind that they filled whole apses of relatively small buildings. The collection of painted altar frontals is also interesting: the early ones are completely flat and iconographic, their purpose being purely symbolic and didactic. As the Spanish art historian Gudiol Ricart points out in *Museo episcopal de Vich* (1954), they were directly influenced by the calligraphic art of the illuminated manuscript.

In the thirteenth century, however, there is a restless search for a third dimension, which then leads into the tender and naturalistic fourteenth century, when in sculpture the Christ child is liberated from his hieratic position balanced on his mother's lap and is raised up into her arms or on to her shoulder – see particularly the *Mare de Déu de Boixadors* (c.1330–60). The narrative element also becomes much more important. The alabaster retable (1341–2) by Bernat Saulet is a good example of this: the representation is treated as a serial on the same principle as a strip cartoon.

Thus we come to the superb collection of Gothic painting. Ferrer Bassa (active 1324–48) produced a lively panel from the life of Saint Benet of Claravall, which depicts a shipwreck being averted; the masters of Rubio and Sixena play a prominent part in the development of the figure. But these narrative and natural-istic advances are hampered by the stamped gilt *esgrafiado* backgrounds and raised gilt *estofado* haloes, as if it were feared that the new-found freedoms might get out of hand without these formalized constraints. Pere Serra, whose work can also be seen at Manresa and Sant Llorenç, offers two splendid panels, Saint Bartholomew with Saint Bernard and Jesus before Pilate. The second room is devoted to a Tarragonese, Ramon de Mur (1402–35). His retable from Guimerà carries the narrative tradition even further: see in particular the extraordinary crossing of the Red Sea, which is literally red and frothing, with the drowning horses and men in pursuit.

Pere Vall still uses very schematic Christ figures. The masters of Glorieta and Fonellosa fully established the technique of raised *estofado* garment hems and borders as part of the design. Lluís Borrassà pushed the limits of what was pictorially permissible a bit further; within the limits of the retable and the traditional symbols of martyrdom he managed to create an extraordinarily rich and lively world. Because of its size the retable of Saint Clara has been split up: its central panels are on the end wall and the upper panels and predella on the adjacent wall. This facilitates the examination of the whole. There is a new exuberance in the swirling robes of the Virgin and Saint Clara and the figures in the predella all seem to be portraits.

You come next to Jaume Ferrer II. The panels of the impressive retable of Verdú are hung separately. Again, two parallel develop-ments are evident here: there is a growing naturalism, especially in the Christ child, but this is accompanied by the extended use of the stamped gilt background and by the raised *estofado* treatment of the robes and gifts. Note especially the Circumcision and the Presentation (and in particular the octagonal haloes for the priests of the temple). In the Pentecost and the Assumption beautiful compositions are achieved with the aid of the raised garment borders and angels' wings. Bernat Martorell (active 1427–52) is represented by one small but fine retable and the great Jaume Huguet (c.1415–92) by some early works: his figures are solid but not overmodelled; muted gold persists in the background. Finally, you reach the Navarrese Joan Gascó (late fifteenth to early sixteenth centuries), whose *Santa Faz*, inspired by the impression of Christ's face on Saint Veronica's handkerchief – Guadix claims to have the genuine article – was formerly attributed to Bermejo. With Gascó the hybrid style of Renaissance naturalism in a rich gold setting reaches its peak after a development lasting two hundred years. (See also 'Gothic Art and Architecture'.)

The museum has a large upper floor which features a magpie collection of Iberian jars, Greek and Roman pottery and burial objects, church vestments, crosses, monstrances, caskets, ironwork, candelabra, swords, plate and ceramics – the latter are well displayed with some good pieces and wall tiles depicting local arts and crafts, but the whole floor does very much fall into the warehouse category and would benefit from greater selectivity as at Solsona.

Leaving Vic for Sant Hilari, heading coastwards now, you are soon back in wooded hills. A few kilometres out of town is the church of Sant Sadurní d'Osormort whose frescoes are in the museum at Vic. On these slopes the pine is king; his courtiers are the ash, the chestnut, the carob and abundant ferns. You come out eventually on to a high pasture with alpine cattle. **Sant Hilari Sacalm** boasts a hundred fountains and is the home of Font Vella, a popular natural, bubble-free mineral water (Vichy Catalan from Caldes de Malavella is naturally sparkling). As you descend towards Santa Coloma de Farners, cork and poplar join the ranks of the forest – indeed cork was the chief export of such little ports as Sant Feliu de Guíxols before the advent of tourism. The timber trade is still clearly important and your chief rivals on these winding wooded roads are timber lorries. Not for nothing is this green *comarca* called La Selva. The lowest slopes are devoted to quite extensive orchards of pears and apples. From Santa Coloma there is a well-signed road, passing under the autoroute and crossing the old main Barcelona–Girona road, to Sant Feliu – a short detour may be made via **Llagostera** whose parish church has an Escurialesque front and buttressed Gothic rear. Its high platform affords a good all-round view of the *comarca* of Baix Empordà.

*Triple apse with Lombard bands of the dilapidated monastery of
Cruïlles, a secluded spot long used as a cemetery.*

Sant Feliu de Guíxols is an old port with some pleasant buildings, but it has been overtaken by beach culture. I am not super-
cilious about beaches: the great breakers off Tenerife and the
rhythmic pounding of the Atlantic surf on the sands between Tarifa
and Cádiz are highly exhilarating; the warm lapping of the Mediterranean into overpopulated coves is less so. Within this framework of personal prejudice I found Sant Feliu a pleasant enough
introduction to the Costa Brava. Going north, Platja d'Aro is like a
mini-Torremolinos. **Palamós** seems to me the best of the lot
because it grew out of an old town and has a good hotel, the Trías
(open March to October). Turning inland, **Palafrugell** also retains
some character in its lively market and handsome parish church
(whose tower was never completed). **La Bisbal**, the comarcal
capital, features a castle belonging to the bishops of Girona. It is
bisected by a dry river bed, a *rambla* in the literal sense. Five
kilometres away is the walled village of **Cruïlles** and on a facing
slope lies the ex-Benedictine monastery of Sant Miquel, which is
presently being reclaimed from its more recent role as a cemetery;
the apses are Lombardic as usual in these parts and there are
remnants of a tenth-century cloister.

The whole of this smiling plain is studded with mediaeval
manor-villages, usually with a semi-fortified principal house,
sometimes with a proper fort. **Ullastret** is one of the latter and

features considerable stretches of hefty wall. Nearby are the remains of an Iberian settlement with a small museum (closed on Mondays). Peratallada is much promoted for its Gothic quarter which is now a hive of restaurants; Palau-Sator has escaped this development. Just beyond Palau, going seawards, is the tiny church of Sant Julià de Boada, said to be Mozarabic, as indeed the horseshoe arches over the entrance and framing the apse seem to confirm, though areas of the stonework and a number of narrow windows suggest it may be of Visigothic origin. What is certain is that this favoured land between the sea and the mountains watered by the Ter and Fluvià rivers, has attracted settlers from very early times, as is borne out by Empúries. I crossed the Ter at Torroella de Montgrí and went down to **Estartit**, where the water is livelier than between Sant Feliu and Palamós. The Illes Medes (Islas Medas) in the bay are said to have been the haunt of pirates.

From Estartit you have to drive inland to reach L'Escala and the ruins of **Empúries**. The large site requires a good hour and a half and is efficiently described in Michelin. You are also handed a plan and description as you drive in. Islands of shade are provided by cypress, olive and umbrella pine, but if you go in the heat of the day take a hat. As you clamber around, you will undoubtedly long for the fiercely blue sea, which is very near but from which you are tantalizingly separated by a wire fence (you must return to L'Escala to satisfy that longing).

There are in fact two towns comprising Empúries, the lower founded by Greek traders in the sixth century BC and the upper dating from the Roman conquest and featuring grand houses, a forum and an amphitheatre. The lower part is one of the cradles of Catalan culture. The museum has some good examples of Attic pottery. The Romans pulled the old Greek and Iberian quarters together and built a great wall to protect their own more imposing structures. 'The Goths', according to Ford, 'used Emporiae kindly and raised it to a bishopric.' There are indeed remnants of a Christian basilica. 'The strong town', Ford continues, 'resisted the invading Moors, and was by them dismantled; it was finally destroyed by the Normans, and the sea, by retiring, has completed the injuries of man.' These injuries are of course irreparable but a long process of excavation, begun at the turn of the century, has revealed the extent and importance of the site, while the models in the museum hazard an informed guess at the appearance of some of the main buildings. It is worth climbing up the hill to the Roman town centre to inspect the two large houses which have been excavated and proceeding at least as far as the forum.

Empúries was the port of entry used by the brothers Scipio at the outset of the second Punic War (218 BC) and subsequently became a colony of veterans. For the following two centuries it was the gateway through which Roman influence spread over the peninsula but the town lost this leading role when it was superseded by the new city of Tarraco (Tarragona), which under Augustus became the capital of the province of Tarraconensis and virtually the whole of Spain.

Driving inland and turning right at Viladamat, you can continue to Sant Pere Pescador, where you cross the Fluvià. Eight kilometres further on is **Castelló d'Empúries**, the seat of one of the counties of Charlemagne's Hispanic march. The large Gothic church, rivalling Manresa's and even Santa Maria del Mar (Barcelona) in scale, has been promoted by local pride to the rank of *catedral*; that is the sign to follow. The vault is wide with slightly lower aisles; it mainly differs from other churches of the period in that its rounded columns replace the more usual octagonal piers. In the apse there is a very unusual, free-standing, pinnacled, alabaster retable (1483–5) by Vicenç Borràs. The carvings of the mourning Magdalen, the Descent and Saint Luke are very fine and remarkably unmutilated either by the 'French' or the anarchists or anyone else – almost a miracle as the lesser scenes at the same level have all been partly hacked away. The magnificent Virgin and Child are also intact but this can perhaps be explained by their height above the ground.

Nearby **Figueres** is the capital of Alt Empordà. It is also the birthplace of Salvador Dalí (b. 1904), whose visual jokes have virtually taken over the old centre of the town. From the pleasant main *rambla* the Carrer Sant Pere leads upwards to the substantial Gothic church of that name with its octagonal lantern-cupola raised on squinch arches across the corners of the crossing. Here in 1701 Philip V – whose claim to the throne led to the War of the Spanish Succession – married María Luisa of Savoy. As you emerge from the church's rather austere and solemn setting and continue into the little *plaça*, you are confronted by three almost identical plaster casts of the French painter Meissonier raised on black columns of different heights and composed of piles of tractor tyres. In front of the entrance to the old theatre, which now houses the Museu Dalí, is the artist's monument to Francesc Pujols, a minor Catalan philosopher: its base is an old tree trunk, to which an assortment of metal, plastic and other objects has been added. The inscription is a quotation from Pujols: *El pensament català rebrota sempre i sobreviu als seus il.lusos enterra-*

dors (Catalan thought will always revive and outlive its deluded gravediggers).*

You are encouraged to start at the top of the museum. On the staircase Dalí's jokes include limbless junk dolls and a coquille shell doing duty as a fig leaf. In the first room his self-portraits with twirled-up waxed moustache seem to parody the great macho painters, Velázquez and Zurbarán. The semi-circular gallery featuring optical tricks in small vitrines is badly designed for circulation. The equivalent gallery on the next floor down is devoted to paintings of the human figure composed of rock, pebbles and rubble; the last one in an El Greco-like stone cave-womb sums up the series. As you go down further the stage for the 'greatest show on earth' begins to unfold. The theatre has been gutted. Shop mannequins of the 1930s fill the embrasures in the wall and look down into the pit. From the stall-space there rises up a great tractor-tyre column, with a felucca on top and an old Cadillac at the base. In the ground-floor salon, under a painted ceiling whose main feature is a huge pair of feet stamping right down on top of the observer, is a bust of Dalí-Velázquez with a miniature version of *Las Meninas* on its forehead. A large photo of the king on one of the walls looks unduly solemn about all the kitsch he is presiding over. In the bedroom is Dalí's dolphin bed and a rather splendid Art Nouveau settee.

Finally, you wend your way on to the stage. A vast backdrop carries a large mural of a bust with a fractured skull against a background of Montserrat crags and Cadaqués cliffs. The beacon of Montserrat truly penetrates every nook and cranny of Catalan life, even the tortuous brain box of Salvador Dalí engaged on weaving a very different kind of spell. Here there is also a whole plaster-of-Paris life-sized orchestra complete with instruments. Visual puns and jocular allusions abound. If you take it lightly, it is rather fun but the pretentious cult element in evidence here is a bit wearisome. There is no early Surrealism in the museum but there are two good Cubist paintings and a wealth of sinuous and seductive drawings. In the adjacent Pujada del Castell Dalí has decorated the whole long façade of a seventeenth-century mansion with a pattern of applied croissants and topped off the parapet with several boiled eggs reminiscent of the Camden Town headquarters of TVAM.

---

* A guide addressing a group of American college students clustered round the base of the monument to Pujols exclaimed: 'Picasso, bah, Picasso can't paint. Dalí is the greatest genius ever to have been produced by the human race.' (For a more balanced assessment see 'Modern Art'.)

From Figueres you can make an enjoyable circuit of the Cap de Creus peninsula. **Roses** has a pleasant esplanade, which is lapped by the sea but offers only small strips of beach. The development round the north end of the bay is unappealing but the southern curve back towards L'Escala is much emptier. The drive from

Cadaqués, a pretty place with intellectual aspirations, where it is respectable to drink pastis before noon.

Roses over a high barren heath to **Cadaqués** is almost obligatory as Dalí was a long-time resident of Portlligat a mile down the road. The comarcal brochure describes it as 'an important centre of painters and plastic artists of the European avante-garde' and goes on to extol 'its artistic and intellectual vitality'. In the hope of immersing myself in this stimulating atmosphere I accordingly found a café whose emaciated patron was indeed drinking pastis before noon, but intellectuals are difficult to distinguish in beach gear and the most intellectual-looking person I saw was reading *Frankfurter Allgemeine Zeitung*. However, Cadaqués is undoubtedly very pretty. Dominated by its church, it consists in fact of several little coves; the Hotel Playa Sol on one of these is good. The Hostal S'Aguarda, one kilometre out on the road to Portlligat, is comfortable and not expensive but you are a bit out of the swim there.

Back up on to the heath and a right turn takes you down to

El Port de la Selva, which is slightly less picturesque than Cadaqués but more open. The sizeable beach and a number of large trawlers give more of a feel of the sea. Parking is also much easier. These two places are the nearest this coast has to offer today to that potent but doomed northern dream of an unspoiled Mediterranean fishing village. El Port de la Selva has the additional advantage of being the nearest point of access to the partly ruined but superbly sited Benedictine monastery of **Sant Pere de Rodes**. From La Selva de Mar, two kilometres above the

El Port de la Selva, the deep-sea fishing village on the northern side of the Cape Creus peninsula.

port, there is a good dirt road that takes you right up to the monastery. Misled on this point, I continued to Llançà, turned inland towards Figueres and turned left again to Vilajuïga, whence a really excellent tarmac road swoops up the western flank of the mountain. This confers the bonus of terrific views inland over much of northern Catalonia and the bay of Roses to the south. Whichever route you take, this is a must. From the top the whole shape of the peninsula is clear, El Port de la Selva lying sharp and precise far below and the indigo sea, almost unnatural in its intensity, stretching to the horizon.

Sant Pere is the decayed but not quite fallen monarch of all this. The monastery is ancient. First documented in 879, it achieved its independence from Sant Esteve de Banyoles in 934. The present church was consecrated in 1022. Aided by the redoubtable Oliba, abbot of Cuixà and Ripoll and bishop of Vic (see pp.111–12), it flourished mightily up to about 1300, when it began a long slow decline until it was abandoned in 1798. The restoration of the structure has now begun and will clearly take many years: the towers are erect but floorless, the dwelling quarters a mere shell. The barrel-vaulted nave and aisles with quadrant vaults and

Sant Pere de Rodes, 'monarch of the indigo sea'.

transverse arches have survived; the nave vault is supported on two stages of columns, themselves raised on a tier of solid masonry. The apse is underpinned by the crypt whose rough columns resemble the roots of a great plant. Some capitals are formalized acanthus, others recall Celtic strapwork. There is a project to carve new capitals for the cloister, though whether this is the right way to go about the restoration is a matter of doubt. What is certain is that Sant Pere will decline no further and will survive as a great monument to the extraordinary energy of the tenth and eleventh centuries in Catalonia. At the time of writing it is the only monument in the whole region not closed on Mondays.

Dropping back down the hillside towards Figueres, it is worth calling in at **Peralada**, whose castle-museum-monastery contains a number of capitals from Sant Pere. This was the birthplace of

Ramon Muntaner (1265–1336), chronicler of the great Catalan expansion in the Mediterranean under Alfons II and James II: the former finally recovered Minorca from the Moors, while the latter added Athens, Neopatria, Corsica and Sardinia to the crown. Visits are accompanied and start strictly at 10.00, 11.00, 12.00, 4.30, 5.30 and 6.30. A little further on is the peaceful monastic church of **Vilabertran** with its fine Romanesque tower. The nave has a barrel vault on round engaged columns. The cloister and dependencies are used for contemporary art exhibitions and music festivals, a secular application to which these semi-redundant religious buildings are increasingly being put throughout Catalonia.

Before abandoning the coast and heading for Girona, it is worth trying to put the Costa Brava in some kind of perspective. Running from Blanes up to Portbou on the border and following the coastlines of the *comarques* of La Selva, Baix Empordà and Alt Empordà, not all of it is equally *brava* or wild; much of it is a bland extension of standard beach culture. But none of it has been quite so brutally developed as the Costa del Sol. Some kind of natural taste seems to have held the Catalans back from the worst excesses of the more exuberant Andalusians. Foreigners are usually sent to Tossa, Lloret or Sant Feliu by their tour operators. Locals prefer Callella de Palafrugell, Llafranc or Begur. The immediate hinterland behind all these resorts with its fortified villages and monuments such as Cruïlles and Ullastret is attractive. The bay of Roses has a fine sweep of sand and L'Escala at the southern end is handy for Empúries. But the congestion on the coastal road in summer reduces traffic to a crawl. In my view, the further north you go the better it becomes: rocky inlets become the norm and beach life gives way to mucking about in boats. The charm of Cadaqués has to be acknowledged, but my own preference is for El Port de la Selva, which offers both deep-sea boats and a beach and lies right beneath the superb Sant Pere de Rodes, monarch of the indigo sea.

3

Lands of the Ter

Girona's river, the Ter, rises in the Pyrenees above Camprodon. Along its upper stretch are situated three famous monasteries, Camprodon itself, Sant Joan de les Abadesses and Ripoll. It then describes an ample curve passing to the north of Vic, which brings it down towards Girona and the sea. Within this curve lie the *comarca* of Garrotxa and its capital Olot, and all the northern part of the *comarca* of Gironès. These are watered by the shorter Fluvià which runs directly inland through the ancient town of Besalú. This is the region that will be explored in this chapter.

Girona – Gerunda under the Romans, later capital of the Ausetani and for three centuries a stronghold of the Moors – is a cathedral city on the high road to France. It demands at least a couple of days. According to Ford it 'boasts to be the first town in which Santiago and St Paul rested when they came to Spain, which neither did'. But he tends to rank cities by their performance under siege, especially in the Peninsular War (1808–14), so all is forgiven – in part for the desperate resistance by 2,000 men in the War of the Spanish Succession (1700–13) against 19,000 troops of Philip V, 'who abolished its university and all its liberties', but even more because of the siege which began in May 1809, when the French with 35,000 men were resisted by the brave and skilful governor Mariano Alvarez, 'well seconded by some English volunteers under the gallant Col. Marshall, who took the lead and was killed in the breaches: Pearson, Nash and Candy also

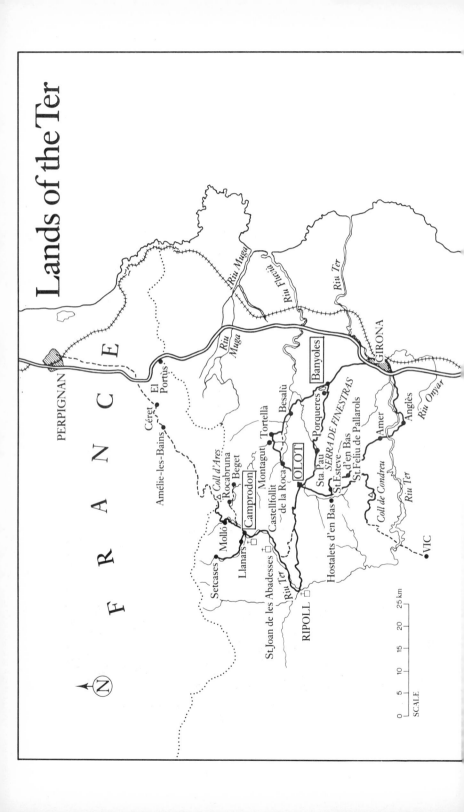

Lands of the Ter

distinguished themselves'. Alvarez became delirious and the town finally fell after a defence of 'seven months and five days, against seven open breaches'. This 'gallant but unavailing' defence has passed like that of Zaragoza from history into Spanish legend.

Although a visit to the Museu d'Història de la Ciutat might do much to arrange your thoughts in the right order, you need not resist a natural urge to visit the cathedral first. A superb triple

The grand flights of steps leading up to the west front of Girona cathedral.

flight of eighty-six steps, erected in 1607, leads up to the west front of 1733, which successfully incorporates a rose window in a baroque framework, an excellent example of architectural 'good

Girona cathedral nave, covered by the widest Gothic vault in Christendom.

manners'. Thus you enter one of the grandest churches in Catalonia, whose breathtakingly wide nave vault, designed by Guillermo Bofill in 1416, does away with the need for aisles altogether and fulfils the Catalan dream of a huge covered space uninterrupted by columns and bounded only by shallow side chapels (see 'Gothic Art and Architecture'). From the width of the earlier ambulatory (which would have dictated the alignment of aisle columns) you can see how much narrower the nave would have been had the great vault not been achieved despite doubts as to its feasibility expressed by the chapter but allayed by a panel of twelve architects. It is, for the record, the widest vault in the whole canon of Gothic architecture, outstretching Albi's by eleven feet. Above the chapels runs a triforium and above this the primary colours of the glass (some still of the fourteenth and fifteenth centuries) make a fine show in the tall windows against the sombre grey walls. The gilt and enamel retable of the high altar is unusual in that these materials were generally reserved for smaller items of church furniture such as crosses and caskets. It is surmounted by a very elegant baldachino. The tomb of Count Ramon Berenguer II (1076–82), known as Towhead, is raised over the doorway of the chapter house and his wife, Ermessenda, lies on the wall facing him across the church. The sarcophagi are of later date.

The museum is a miscellaneous collection of cathedral possessions with a few good items, notably the embroidered altar cloths (exhibits 41 and 42) and, in the end room, a large embroidered wall hanging of the eleventh or twelfth century depicting the Creation with the first creatures emerging from the sea, confidently claimed as 'unique in the world'. The cloister features a twin-columned arcade which has survived from the earlier cathedral and enables the observer to appreciate the massiveness of the buttresses required to sustain the great vault; it also provides a view of the Romanesque north tower, which has been bitten into by the Gothic masonry. This is known locally as the Torre de Carlemany, but old though it is, it was not completed until some three centuries after Charlemagne's death.

On leaving the cathedral, a number of enticing signs compete for your attention. It must be acknowledged that the local tourist board has done a thorough job in promoting its wares and providing facilities such as toilets so that the tour of the *casc antic* (old quarter) should be edifying and unfatiguing. Even so, there is much to be seen and you need to apportion your time selectively. On the façade of the Palau de Justícia at the bottom of the cathedral steps is a plaque to the heroic Alvarez, whose headquarters were located here during the great siege. Going down through the old gate, the Portal de Sobreportes, between two drum-shaped towers, you come on the left to Sant Feliu, a substantial and handsome church whose tower, truncated by lightning in 1581, still makes a considerable impact on the Girona skyline. It has a grand early fourteenth-century nave vault and pointed triforium built up on older rounded arches. The place to head for before it closes for lunch is Sant Pere de Galligants, clearly signposted and not too distant. On the way you pass the neat little rebuilt Romanesque church of Sant Nicolau. The loving care with which it has been reconstructed is evident.

Sant Pere de Galligants is the first really mature Romanesque church I came across. Finished in 1131, it exhibits many of the

Sant Pere de Galligants, one of the finest examples of the mature Catalan Romanesque style.

luxuriant features of a style at its apogee. In the nave there are grand scenic capitals on engaged columns. The main apse is decorated with interior columns and flanked by two minor apses

Capital from Sant Pere de Galligants.

on each side. The capitals of the cloister (1154–90) display a rich variety of treatment. Note also the clusters of five columns in the middle of each arcade. These are all the self-assured grace notes of a style at the peak of its form, to which it clambered from simple rustic places of worship and the sturdy grandeurs of Sant Pere de Rodes (see pp.92–3) to rest for a few decades at most on a plane of excellence before the next technical breakthrough ushered in its successor. Such is this Sant Pere. It also houses an archaeological museum which features a good selection of prehistoric and early historical pieces on the first floor, including a couple of vitrines from the almost impenetrable Dark Ages, when city life collapsed and people were driven back into subsistence farming and self-sufficiency. Also of great interest in the cloister are the steles with Hebrew inscriptions brought down from the Jewish burial ground called Montjuïc as in Barcelona.

The nicely laid out archaeological promenade, the Passeig Arqueològic, under the old walls is very tempting, but the Banys Àrabs (Arab Baths) exert a prior claim. The *sala freda* (cold room) is a delightful chamber with an octagonal tank surmounted by eight columns which feature Romanesque capitals; above them is an arcaded dome rising several feet above roof level to let in air and light. The other rooms show the functioning of the heating system and the tepidarium. All this is a reminder that Girona was not finally wrested from Islam until 1015.

It is now necessary to turn to the museums. The **Museu d'Història de la Ciutat** concentrates on didactic displays with photographs, models, maps and plans. It traces the development of Catalonia from the feudal counties of Charlemagne's Hispanic march to the independent county of Barcelona, founded by Count Wilfred, who inherited Cerdanya-Urgell and gained control of Barcelona, Vic, Girona, Besalú, Peralada and Empúries to the south of the Pyrenees and Roussillon and Vallespir to the north. There is a good model of the city in mediaeval times showing

Elegant octagonal lantern in the frigidarium
of the Banys Àrabs.

where the walls ran (and still run) along the flank skirted by the Passeig Arqueològic. Markets usually developed outside the city walls to avoid taxes and Girona's was set up on the west bank of the river Onyar, whose confluence with the Ter forms the triangle on which the *casc antic* grew up. Eventually the market area, now occupied by the modern town, was also enclosed by a wall. All this information is of interest but if time is short it can be foregone.

What should on no account be missed is the **Museu d'Art** in the bishop's palace off the Plaça dels Apòstols under the southern flank of the cathedral. This begins with a Romanesque section which includes some small objects, among them a little chest (20) from windswept Sant Pere de Rodes, a collection of capitals some of which retain traces of paint (it was not uncommon to paint stone carvings in the Middle Ages, though this may not accord with modern taste) and a fine Virgin and Child (38) from Olot. Room 7 contains three outstanding fourteenth-century carvings of the Mother and Christ child from La Bisbal (140), Santa Maria de Besalú (147) and Pontós (148). There is also an extremely jolly fifteenth-century version of the same theme (116). In room 8 you come to the great retable from Sant Miquel de Cruïlles (172) by Lluís Borrassà (1380–1424), whose work can also be seen at Vic. This is a further example of his restless, vibrant use of colour. It is matched and if anything excelled by his pupil and successor Bernat Martorell's retable from Sant Pere de Púbol (168): Saint Peter occupies the central panel with all the awesome attributes of the papacy, but the scenes of his life and martyrdom and the figures in the predella, particularly that of Saint Catherine, breathe naturalism and life.

At this point the museum thoughtfully provides a rest room with loos and a lift to the other floors. But it is only a step on foot to room 9 where you get your first dose of Italian-inspired mannerism with Joan de Burgunya (1470–1555), who is represented by a major series of panels from the church of Sant Feliu (184–9). In room 11 Joan Gascó and others continue the Catalan tradition of gilded backgrounds well into the first half of the sixteenth century (cf. diocesan museum, Vic, pp.84–6). This tradition was not finally broken until the emergence of Catalan mannerism, as displayed in room 12. Its great exponent is Pere Mates (d. 1558), whose retable from Sant Pere de Montagut uses black-rimmed haloes (still octagonal for the profane), but the backgrounds resembling embossed gold wallpaper, which have been *de rigueur* for two centuries, are replaced by Renaissance architectural motifs and open skies – it is quite a breath of fresh air. Mates, a native of Sant Feliu de Guíxols, seems to have actually observed his animals rather than lifting them from some mediaeval bestiary. The museum has three more floors but it is not strictly necessary to follow Catalan painting through the seventeenth to twentieth centuries. In room 16, however, there are two small and very late Goya drawings of two old crones (1824).

Another area of considerable interest in Girona is the Jewish quarter, *call jueu.* This is bounded by the Carrer de la Força which runs southwards from the Plaça de la Catedral. It centres round the Carrer Sant Llorenç, a steep narrow street that joins la Força at right angles. This district has recently been partly restored. There is not a great deal you can visit because the old houses are being converted privately, but there is a restaurant in the Pati des Rabins and the Museu d'Isaac el Cec consists of a series of catacombs with a small synagogue. Every Friday night in summer there is a recital of Sephardic songs in the patio.

If there is nothing spectacular in the Jewish quarter, this is largely due to the warren-like and unobtrusive nature of mediaeval Jewish buildings. It is nonetheless an ideal place in which to ponder the role of the Jews in Spanish history and the degree of tolerance and protection they managed to obtain. There is some evidence of Jewish settlements in the peninsula in Visigothic times, but the first documented settlement in Girona dates from 889. Jews became useful as treasurers and bureaucrats to the monarchs of the early kingdoms and to the nobility, from whom they received various privileges, including the right of self-government within their small communities. These statutes were guaranteed by the crown and this treatment was roughly on a par with the treatment received by the Jews under Moorish princes: it will be recalled that their philosophers and doctors, among whom Maimonides was pre-eminent in the twelfth century, were accepted and even honoured in Córdoba. The age of tolerance thus extended for a while over both Christian and Islamic Spain: on assuming the throne of Castile and León in 1072 Alfonso VI committed himself to the protection of all his subjects of whatever religion and this policy was reaffirmed by Alfonso VII (the 'Emperor') in 1126. But outbreaks of anti-Judaism had begun as early as the eleventh century and were repeated with mounting intensity in Girona in 1276, 1278, 1285, 1331, 1348, 1391, 1405, and 1418, culminating with their final expulsion in 1492.

Rabble-rousing monks like the Catalan Saint Vincent Ferrer, who threw the Jews out of their synagogue in Toledo (now Santa

María la Blanca) are often seen as the driving force behind this persecution. But in *The Spanish Labyrinth* Gerald Brenan suggests that the underlying reason was economic and that the demagogues were able to harness the mob because of the latter's legitimate grievances. He sees 'the rising against the Jews as indirectly a movement against the nobles who protected them and intermarried with them. . .' The Jews became obvious targets because they were employed by the nobility as stewards and tax collectors. And it is certainly true that intermarriage took place at this social level – Saint Teresa of Avila is said to have had Jewish blood – but whatever popular motive there may have been for anti-Jewish sentiment, there can be no doubt that by the fifteenth century it had become an important instrument of public policy directed towards a unified, orthodox, centralized Spain. Where the earlier Castilian and Aragonese rulers had protected the *aljamas* and *calls* and guaranteed their rights, Ferdinand and Isabel set the yoke of the Castilian Inquisition on the necks of Aragon and Catalonia, where previously it had been hardly felt at all, and in 1492 proceeded to the final act. Some Jews preferred apostasy to expulsion, were converted and intermarried with the native stock. In my view this had a particularly important effect on economic development in Catalonia with its pronounced commercial tradition, but the fact remains that there was no authorized Jewish religious rite in Spain between 1492 and 1966. This may help to explain the zeal behind the rehabilitation of the *call* in Girona. (For a fuller treatment of this topic see 'Catalan Jewry'.)

Continuing downwards towards the river, the lower part of the old town is characterized by wide crypt- or cellar-like arcades on low, rounded arches. These line the whole of La Rambla de la Llibertat, whose plane trees make it a pleasant promenade. The town hall, dating from 1642, is set back from La Rambla in the Plaça del Vi. Sadly the old houses bordering the river Onyar have been unattractively refronted, but there are a number of footbridges over the stream and the Plaça de la Independència on the modern side is a decent nineteenth-century city centre. Yet there is nowhere much to stay and a good deal can be said for making day trips into Girona from the agreeably situated Banyoles only eighteen kilometres away.

Inland from Girona the country rucks up again into the Serra de Finestres, whose slopes are covered with oak scrub and carob. Taking N141 along the valley of the Ter to Anglès, turn right on to C152 and follow its tributary, the Brugent. At **Amer** there is a

Water front on the river Onyar below the old city of Girona.

sixteenth-century arcaded square and an eleventh-century monastic church with an unusual nave of rounded arches raised on sets of four widely spaced columns. Sant Feliu de Pallarols has a pleasant shady square. **Sant Esteve d'en Bas** is an agreeable village with a good church and the beginnings of villa development. It is the centre of the Bas valley and has several hamlets in its domain; the most attractive is **Hostalets d'en Bas** with a street of houses featuring wooden, flower-decked balconies. From Sant Esteve you can turn on to the C153 road for Vic. After climbing for about ten kilometres, you reach the Coll de Condreu with its restaurant and two nearby sanctuaries. This is popular picnic country among the people of the region. You could continue to Vic; equally anyone coming from Vic who already knows Girona and the Costa Brava could link with the present route at Sant Esteve and join me in Olot.

106

Olot has no great antiquities owing to the earthquakes of 1427–8. But it is a civilized town with pleasant leafy walks and promenades. No. 38 on the main promenade is a good provincial example of Modernist architecture, combining Art Nouveau motifs with a traditional pargeted treatment of the façade. The well-stocked bookshop had Robert Graves's *Las aventuras del sargento Lamb* in the window. Anyone who arrives on 11

Modernist window in pargeted façade, Olot.

September, the national day of Catalonia, will be treated to a superlative firework display. The Hostal La Perla at one kilometre on the Vic road is very good value and the restaurant is excellent.

From Olot a circuit can be made taking in Banyoles and Besalú. Leave by the road to Santa Pau and embark according to the signs on the *ruta volcànica de la Garrotxa*. The countryside is green and hushed and, though not even extinct volcanoes are in evidence,

107

Modernist damsel on same façade.

there is a museum in **Santa Pau** devoted to them; this village also qualifies as a *conjunt històric* (historic ensemble) and is built round an attractive porticoed *plaça*. The road continues its bosky way to **Banyoles**, an agreeable town and an excellent place in which to set up base camp for Girona, which can be reached in less than half an hour. The Hostal L'Ast, situated in an avenue of plane trees running down to the lake, is extremely peaceful and has a small swimming pool. The natural reed-fringed lake of Banyoles (this is no hydroelectric reservoir) is very prettily set in a circlet of hills and offers such activities as water-skiing and pleasure cruises; there is also a small zoo and amusement park for children. The old centre has an arcaded square with well-shaded cafés; nearby is the well-restored Gothic church of Santa Maria dels Turers. The town also boasts archaeological and natural history museums. The road circling the lake runs through the hamlet of **Porqueres**, where the little sanctuary of Santa Maria del Tura has some unusual capitals.

Turning back towards Olot on the northerly route, you come shortly to **Besalú**, another *conjunt històric* with a real claim to the label. Unfortunately, all the main churches are kept locked to prevent vandalism and the interiors can only be seen on accompanied visits from the tourist office in the Plaça de la Llibertat, departing roughly every hour between 10.00 and 1.00 and between 4.00 and 7.00. The small city was the centre of one of

Courtyard of the Casa dels Cornellà in Besalú, a rare example of Romanesque domestic architecture.

109

the feudal counties that made up Charlemagne's Hispanic march. With the decline of the Frankish empire it acquired a measure of independence. Though it formed part of Count Wilfred's domains, it was not fully and formally absorbed by the crown of Barcelona until 1111. Following the signs to *Centre Vila*, you arrive in the large Plaça de Sant Pere, which is the best place to park. The monastic church of this name was founded in 1003, but the present building has all the attributes of the assured Romanesque of the twelfth century; the dressed stone is very similar to that of Sant Pere de Galligants. In a corner of this square is the **Casa dels Cornellà**, a rare example of Romanesque domestic architecture, solid and massy and cavernous in the lower regions with a more elegant first floor. Walking through the Plaça de la Llibertat, you will find the town hall and law court and an arcade still used as a market. The Carrer Major then leads up to Sant Viçens, a tenth-century church of fine proportions and extremely plain construction, though the capitals of the doorways are crowded with figures and display a pleasing sense of fantasy. From the apse of Sant Viçens a flight of steps leads up to the castle platform and the ruined church of Santa Maria.

On the lower side of the town the Carrer Pont Vell leads down from the Plaça de la Llibertat to a *mirador* with a fine view over the river Fluvià and a fortified bridge (which is almost as good an example of its kind as the bridge of Frías in Old Castile). There is

Mediaeval fortified bridge over the river Fluvià at Besalú.

also a little Jewish bath, said to be unique and requiring the municipal key. Besalú, like most cities of the time, had a Jewish quarter and this was still protected by the crown in the person of James I when the work on the bath was authorized in 1264. In all, a couple of hours can profitably be spent wandering about this unusually complete *conjunt*. A good cheap meal can be had in the bar facing Sant Viçens, where the locals go to play cards. This is preferable to the more pretentious Cúria Reial in the main square. The wine of the region is a rosé with a rather smoky taste.

On the return journey to Olot, a short detour can be made via Tortellà to **Montagut**, first home of the great retable by Pere Mates in the Girona museum. The Romanesque door with contemporary ironwork is still in place. Back on the main road you pass under the picturesque Castellfollit de la Roca on a spur at the confluence of the Turonell with the Fluvià. Descending once more towards Olot, your next major port of call will almost certainly be **Ripoll**, the most famous of the three important monasteries on the upper reaches of the Ter. But a word of warning here: once a great centre of learning and one of the leading lights of the early Middle Ages, Ripoll is now a rather rough, dour old place offering few blandishments to the traveller. This is perhaps appropriate in the Cradle of the Race, a title with primitive and sturdy connotations sometimes conferred on the town owing to the foundation of the monastery by Count Wilfred, first count of the house of Barcelona. But the fact remains that there is nowhere much to stay except the standard roadhouse, the Solana de Ter, two kilometres to the south of the town on the main road. There is therefore something to be said for sleeping in Olot and driving the thirty-odd kilometres to Ripoll in the morning.

The Benedictine monastery around which Ripoll developed is still the lion of the place. It was founded by Count Wilfred of Cerdanya-Urgell in about 880 and its first primitive church was consecrated in 888. In the following century the fame of its school began to spread abroad. In 967 it attracted the famous mathematician, Gerbert of Aurillac, who later became tutor to Emperor Otto III and then pope (Sylvester II) in 997. The monastery was then promoted energetically by the prodigious Oliba, abbot of both Ripoll and Cuixà (now on the French side of the border) and later bishop of Vic. Oliba was the brother of one of the counts of Cerdanya and a personal friend of Pope Benedict VIII, of Gaucelin, the great abbot of Fleury, and of Hugh of Semur, who was to become abbot of Cluny. In other words, he did not lack friends in high places or knowledge of the world. His reign at

Ripoll lasted from 1008 to 1046 and his great church, replacing earlier and humbler structures, was consecrated in 1032. By the year of his death the library had no less than 246 volumes and the school was known throughout Europe for its works of history, poetry, astronomy, music and especially mathematics – it is from this centre of learning that Arabic numerals appear to have spread across the Pyrenees.

After these glorious beginnings there followed a long decline. All sorts of vicissitudes befell the monastery in later centuries. It was badly shaken by the earthquake of 1428, it was sacked in 1463, a more fashionable Gothic vault was then imposed on it, neo-classical alterations played great havoc, it was sacked again in 1835 and by the mid-nineteenth century it was a ruin, as contemporary prints attest. Restoration began in 1886. Thus the church now standing is a faithful attempt to reproduce Oliba's original cruciform conception of a great barrel-vaulted nave with double aisles and long arms each containing three apsidal chapels on either side of the main apse. This is what you see today – patiently, efficiently and solidly rebuilt, but with none of the feeling that animated the original masons and craftsmen. In order to appreciate the exterior of Abbot Oliba's apsidal layout you must skirt the town hall and walk up Carrer del Doctor Reguier.

Inside the church there are a number of tombs, not only belonging to members of the house of Barcelona but also to the counts of Besalú and Urgell. Count Wilfred himself was exhumed during the abbey's reconstruction and now lies in a casket on the left-hand side of the crossing; this still awaits an appropriate monument. Count Ramon Berenguer III (1093–1131) is more grandly interred at the end of the right-hand transept.

However, the most famous item, which somehow survived, is the *pòrtic* (entrance) now enclosed by a glassed-in porch which, sadly, in the last resort will not protect it against the incurable cancer suffered by the soft stone. Michelin makes a gallant attempt to describe the carvings section by section. For even greater detail, buy the little guidebook on sale at the kiosk, in which you will find a transparent sheet of tracing paper entitled 'Iconography' with eighty-seven compartments; when placed over the photograph of the entrance this identifies every scene. Here are the Exodus, Moses and the Rock, Jonah and Daniel, David and Solomon, Cain and Abel, Peter and Paul, the other Evangelists and the twenty-four elders of the Apocalypse, to mention only some of the personages. Entrances of this kind were the grand texts of Christianity before Luther started distributing

Bibles. The columns too are decorated, some with a rope pattern, some in filigree, while others resemble the trunk of a palm. The design is firm and bold, so the effect is not fussy and you can contemplate this great work with pleasure that is not lessened by familiarity.

The richly iconographic portico of Abbot Oliba's great church at Ripoll.

The cloister with its double tier of arcades is grand as a whole but only the lower gallery abutting on the church is of the twelfth century; the rest of this level was completed in the fourteenth with deliberate archaism, though the later date of the capitals is quite clear. Parts of the upper gallery are of even later date but the general effect is harmonious. The museum, which you enter from the *plaça,* offers a pleasant (and mercifully small) hotchpotch that includes embroidered side-saddles, Catalan baroque painted bedsteads, ceramics, utensils, regional clothes, figurines and dolls. The collection also underlines the importance of Ripoll's 'metallurgical' industry: from the sixteenth to the eighteenth centuries the town was one of the most important centres of small arms' manufacture in Europe; there were also more than a hundred workshops making nails, tools, keys and locks. Because the forges were water-powered the centre's demise was brought about by the rise of the coal industry and the introduction of steam power in the Basque country and Asturias.

I had been on the lookout for sundials ever since my arrival in Catalonia because of the following passage in Ford's introduction to his section on Barcelona: 'The dial, emblem of the Catalan's knowledge of the value of time, is now placed on most of the stuccoed and painted houses. . .' So far my expectations had been disappointed, so my delight may be imagined when I found a handsome one on the wall of the building housing Ripoll's museum, complete with the unanswerable inscription *Volat irreparabile tempus.* I am glad to say that from this point on sundial-spotting became a more rewarding pastime.

From Ripoll it is only a few kilometres northwards to **Sant Joan de les Abadesses**, a smiling town compared with its more rugged neighbour. Access to the old centre is easy – so is parking. The abbey from which the township takes its name was founded in 885, again by Count Wilfred and in this case for his daughter Emma, who became the first abbess. The present church dates from the twelfth century and was consecrated in 1150. The layout of five apses and a short nave is unique in Catalonia. The main apse and the two flanking it are arranged radially; the other two are square on to the transepts. The carving of the capitals throughout shows mature Romanesque assurance and inventiveness. After the collapse of the cupola in the earthquake of 1428 simple barrel vaults were adopted throughout the building. The free-standing wooden figures of the Descent from the Cross behind the high altar date from about 1150. The scene is still formal and solemn but the new naturalism and with it the incipient tenderness of the next century are beginning to break through – the Roman soldier is particularly well observed. The few items of Gothic alabaster carving on display are of very high quality. You are handed a descriptive sheet in the language of your choice on entry, which you return on leaving. In addition to

Apse with blind arcades at Sant Joan de les Abadesses.

Sant Joan's graceful Gothic cloister.

the sheer interest and beauty of the place, the experience of contemplating it is made pleasant and easy through the free

115

availability of the relevant information. This is in rather marked contrast to the *conjunts històrics*, where you are liable to find yourself dependent on some cultural commissar. But Sant Joan is also a proper modern town with light industry and does not have all its eggs in its cultural basket. The late Gothic cloister is very elegant and peaceful – and perfect for noble nuns, though by the time it was built the abbey had passed into the hands of Augustinian canons.

The small (again, note small) museum contains pieces from various other churches in the town. The fourteenth-century wooden Virgin (20) is attractive; the arms of the choir stalls (23) are amusing; there is some very fine embroidery, especially 25; the expectant Virgin with the fully formed Christ child revealed in her belly (45) is unusual; everything is well chosen and can be seen in twenty minutes. The adjacent grandly styled *palau* of the abbots is actually a modest house with a Romanesque patio, which is used for exhibitions. (The Catalans love exhibitions: painting, sculpture, embroidery, photography, history, archaeology, anything that can be demonstrated visually – you name it and they will lay it on, not for foreigners but for themselves.) The rest of the old town is very pleasant, less enclosed and built of warmer stone than Ripoll. The ruined church of Sant Pol has an early tympanum of God the Father between Peter and Paul. The old bridge was thoroughly restored, not to say rebuilt, in 1972–6; at this point the river Ter runs between wooded slopes to the east and high Pyrenean moors rising above the tree line to the west.

The third of the trio of famous monasteries on the upper Ter is at **Camprodon**. If you are coming from France via Perpignan and Prats de Molló or going into France or just visiting the region, this is perhaps the best place of all to stay. It is within easy distance of both Sant Joan and Ripoll. The Hotel Güell is one of those old-fashioned good hotels which gets only one star because it has no lift. Another old bridge, restored in 1930, crosses the river here. The main street has something of the frontier-town look about it, with souvenirs and booze in the shops; it is in fact the last Spanish town of any substance before France, or the first coming the other way. At the far end of the Carrer Major is the parish church, which features a rustic belfry and a fine wide ribbed vault between rounded arches, very much a successful Catalan attempt to cover a large space without a tiresome forest of columns. Above this on the left is the Romanesque monastic church of Sant Pere de Camprodon with its octagonal belfry: it belongs to the mature Romanesque period of the mid-twelfth century but is simpler than Sant Pere de Galligants or Sant Joan de les Abadesses. All the same, it is a great building with a domical vault on squinches and two curious little passages leading from the nave into the transepts, which have semi-circular barrel vaults, while those

Square belfry of the Romanesque church of
Sant Pere de Camprodon.

over the nave are slightly pointed as the church caught up with the times during its construction. When I saw Sant Pere it was very effectively hung with pure white streamers and curtains and bunting in celebration of the one hundred and twenty-fifth anniversary of the composer Isaac Albéniz, a son of the town.

I strayed on a bit further and found, almost on the main road which bypasses the town, a grand Modernist villa in a state of near collapse. The terrace balustrade had Gaudiesque capitals, the tower a niche with a mock fifteenth-century Virgin; there was a profusion of tiles and – two scored in one day – there was a sundial. Its eclecticism might cause purists to pull a long face but

117

I hoped someone would soon take it in hand and restore its former self-confident disregard for the strict canon of good taste. Strolling back towards the centre, I noticed a handsome middle-aged woman knitting on the pavement outside her house. Quite unlike

Eclectic Modernist villa, Camprodon.

the Andalusian custom, whereby the women point their chairs inwards towards their doorways and present their backs to the world, this lady was facing boldly outwards as she plied her needles with great skill and speed. I suspect that Catalonia is a profoundly matriarchal society: the women run the hotels, the bars and most of the shops. More ephemeral pastimes like politics are left in the main to men, though women too have now learned to appreciate the joys of belonging to the municipal or higher bureaucracy. But whatever their role, they are self-confident, a bit loud, cigarette-smoking, often handsome – sometimes superbly so with classic Greek or Iberian features. In late September lorry loads of firewood were being deposited in the streets, impeding the traffic, and it was mainly women who were shifting the wood into baskets to carry it indoors. (And women, incidentally, were the backbone of the defences of Girona and Zaragoza in the Peninsular War.)

If you are not in a hurry, Camprodon is also a good centre for its own immediate valleys. **Llanars** has a pleasing little church with a pyramidal spire; it also retains doors with the original Roman-esque ironwork. **Setcases** higher up the valley has swollen from seven to at least a hundred houses, mostly modern in the rural pastiche style, and has two hotels and several restaurants to accommodate visitors in pursuit of winter sports.

Heading north from Camprodon on the road to France, a turning to the right after a few kilometres leads over the Coll de la Boixeda and steeply down into the valley of the river Beget with splendid views to the south. The hamlet of **Rocabruna** nestles in the flank of the hill and has a finely placed twelfth-century church. A single-track road leads on beneath the castle of Rocabruna to the village of **Beget**, where there is another ancient church containing a much venerated image of the Saviour which is credited with miraculous powers. Returning along the same route – for there is no other – and regaining the main road north, **Molló** next rises on the left with its handsome church and tower. Shortly afterwards you reach the frontier at **Coll d'Ares**. This is a very pleasant way either into or out of Catalonia and is certainly to be preferred to El Portùs on the main road from Perpignan to Girona, where considerable queues can build up at the customs. Up here you are waved through almost immediately. Whoever leaves Catalonia by this route has a very pretty run down to Perpignan through Arles (with its Benedictine abbey founded as early as 817, shortly after Charlemagne had pacified the area), Amélie-les-Bains and Céret. Whoever enters by this road has the pleasures of Camprodon, Sant Joan and Ripoll in store and then the choice of Girona via Olot or a straight run down through Vic to Barcelona.

Whether coming or going through French Roussillon, the traveller will naturally make some comparison between the two sides of the modern border. Winding roads, high pastures, alpine cattle and splendid views are common to both. In southern Roussillon Catalan is spoken, the names of towns and villages are signposted in both languages, the odd Catalan flag is draped over a balcony and words like *mas* (the traditional farmhouse with a shallow pitched roof and open loft – or arcaded gallery in the grander versions) are used as in Catalonia. Although French centralism will always prevail over fissiparous Spanish tendencies, and it is a long time since Count Wilfred and Abbot Oliba straddled the Pyrenees, all the same in Perpignan you sometimes hear: 'Catalonia? Bah! We are the true Catalans. They are just Spaniards.'

4

From the Pyrenees
to the Plain

Driving south into Catalonia from Perpignan there are four possible routes. (I discount the points of entry via Andorra and Viella, which would normally be approached from Foix and Tarbes respectively.) These include the coastal route via Cervera de la Marenda and Portbou (which can also be taken by train), the main road via El Portùs and La Jonquera, the less frequented Coll d'Ares described in the last chapter, and Bourg-Madame and Puigcerdà. The last of these has the advantage of an extremely good mountain road and the frontier is open all round the clock. It also enables you to call in at Sant Miquel de Cuixà and Sant Martí del Canigó.

Cuixà retains some of the grandeur of a great Benedictine abbey. Its cloister (demolished and plundered but partly rebuilt and featuring some original capitals) was enormous; there were two towers of which only one now stands. But it is also something of a medley: the nave puzzles experts still and is variously described as pre-Romanesque, Visigothic or Mozarabic. The church was remodelled between 1009 and 1040 by the ubiquitous Oliba. His seven apses have been partly destroyed but the remaining tower shows a strong affinity with those of Ripoll and Sant Pere de Rodes. Oliba has been credited with introducing the so-called Lombardic style to Catalonia and it is the case that these towers all share the common features of *ajimez* (or *coronella*) windows, set within recessed panels surmounted by the little

121

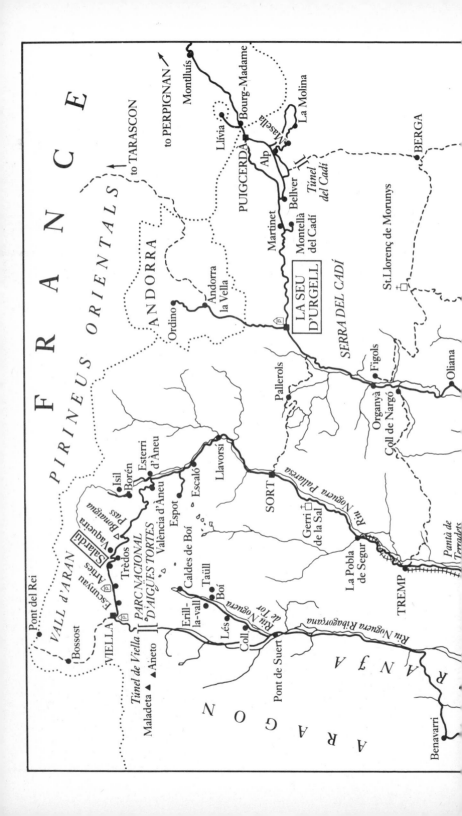

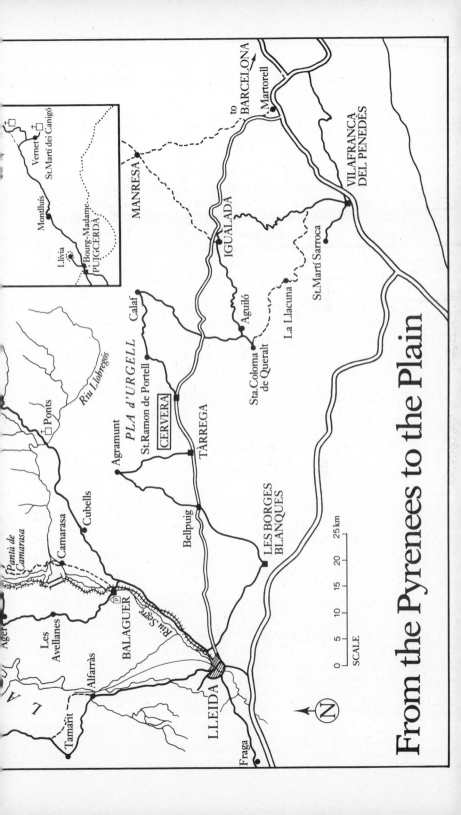

From the Pyrenees to the Plain

blind arcade which is characteristic of Lombard decoration.

You can continue from Cuixà to Vernet without rejoining the main road and from Vernet follow the river bed upwards to the village of Casteil, whence you proceed on foot to **Sant Martí del Canigó**. A note of warning here: it is a steep climb that will take twenty-five minutes if you are in good shape and longer if you are not. The first part of the trek in the glaring sun is the most trying. Then you enter a chestnut wood and the going becomes much easier in the shade. The monastery is tucked into the lower folds of King Canigó's leafy robe; there are no dramatic views of it, so you cannot cheat and photograph it from a distance – you just come upon it. This is yet another monastery with which Oliba was connected for it was founded in 1002 by his brother Guifré, count of Cerdanya, who retired here himself as a monk about fifteen years or so before his death in 1050. The church is built on two levels with a long crypt underpinning the tunnel-vaulted nave, which has only ten interior supports and is lit from the ends. So sturdy is this construction that it suffered little deterioration during a century's neglect after the abandonment of the site in 1785. The tower here is also very fine. The climb is well worth while. Though less venerable than Cuixà, Sant Martí is more isolated and has a less worldly air; it breathes contemplation and peace.

Rejoining the main road at Vilafranca de Conflent, you come upon a great fort with typical Vaubanesque features – the Pyrenees have never been as effective a barrier as is sometimes supposed. In the western or Basque sector the peaks are high, the passes narrow and the inhabitants fierce, as Roland discovered to his cost in 788 when the rearguard of Charlemagne's army was cut down not by Moors but by Basque mountaineers. But the more open upland pastures of the Cerdagne are another matter. Over the centuries they have provided an easy route for abbots and monks, kings and armies. It follows that control posts were required, becoming more than ever necessary, in French eyes, after the cession by Spain to France of Roussillon and what is now the French Cerdagne in 1659. The main trans-Pyrenean valley could not be left open as a high road for all and sundry as the Spaniards might feel minded to reoccupy their lost territories. Thus it was that Louis XIV commissioned from Vauban not only the fortress at Vilafranca but also one higher up at Montlluís.

And so to Bourg-Madame and back into Spanish Catalonia at **Puigcerdà**. Raised on a hump and forming a nexus of old streets with a fringe of apartment blocks, this town is a motorist's nightmare. If parking can be found, the Plaça de l'Ajuntament has an extensive view over the Catalan *comarca* of Cerdanya, which is watered by the river Segre. There are few remaining antiquities in the town: the principal monument is the octagonal tower of the demolished church of Santa Maria, dominating the lively *plaça* of that name. On the outskirts is a round pond which has been promoted by local pride to the rank of lake, where there is one hotel which looks reasonably quiet. The Hotel del Prado, down below, very near the customs post, is efficient and keeps a good table but the traffic is disturbing. On the whole, I am inclined to advise a night in Llívia rather than in Puigcerdà itself.

Llívia is a curious Spanish enclave across the French border. It is only five kilometres from Puigcerdà and can be reached by a 'neutral' road with a token customs post; there are no further formalities. Like so many ancient places, Segovia among them, it claims to have been founded by Hercules. What is more certain is that it was known as Julia Livia under the Romans and lay on the road from Ruscino (Perpignan) to Ilerda (Lleida). Both the Tet on the French side and the Segre on the Spanish side rise very near it, so it is almost exactly on the watershed and is a natural centre of communication between the two flanks of the mountain range. It thus became the original capital of the feudal county of Cerdagne before Puigcerdà was founded in 1177. It owes its present status to a bureaucratic error in the treaty of the Pyrenees of 1659, which only specified the cession of thirty villages to France: Llívia was a *vila* or town with a proper charter and thus was not included. It is a distinctly more attractive place than Puigcerdà. It has a partly fortified church with an ample Gothic vault. The small museum is mainly devoted to the utensils, containers and fittings of a pharmacy first mentioned in 1592 and later run by the same family for two centuries. The baroque dresser is charming, like a small retable with pots of unguents and powders instead of saints, though there are plenty of saints painted on the herbal containers, presumably just to be on the safe side. The dispensary has been reproduced with its reference books and retort. Medicine has been revolutionized since then, but not so upper Llívia. A hen-house window from which the usual cackles are emitted opens directly on to the Plaça Major. The lower town has become a ski resort with apartments and a number of hotels.

As you descend along the Segre from Puigcerdà, Ford's words do not seem out of place: 'This charming river and mountain ride seems made for the artist, angler and sportsman.' Alternatively, you can start off on the road to Ripoll and Barcelona and turn off to **Alp**, which provides access to the new Túnel del Cadí that pierces the mighty mountain spur and shaves an hour off the time to Barcelona via Berga. Alp is an old village, existing long before the coming of alpine sports to the area. Its neighbouring villages – Das, Urús – have similarly primitive names but all are now sprouting chalets on the flanks of the *serra*. From Alp you can continue up to **La Molina**, the oldest ski station in Spain. Nearby is Masella. Altogether they comprise a large complex and there are within the area thirteen stations offering a total of 271 kilometres of skiable slopes. (For further details consult the local tourist office or, preferably, the Spanish National Tourist Office in St James's Street before leaving.)

Taking care not to get sucked into the maw of the Túnel del Cadí, you can rejoin the course of the river Segre at **Bellver de Cerdanya** where a restored *casc antic* is finely sited above the river. **Martinet** is an agreeable little timber-trading village at the confluence of the Arànser with the Segre. It has a public swimming pool and riverside walks. Facing it on a bluff across the main river is Montellà del Cadí, which offers panoramic views both southwards over the Cadí's great hump and westwards along the course of the Segre, which becomes more serpentine as it enters a winding gorge before emerging in the vale of La Seu d'Urgell.

Without claiming Hercules as its founder and without known Roman antecedents, **La Seu d'Urgell** is nonetheless a very ancient place. It sent its first bishop, Sant Just, to the Visigothic councils of Toledo (527) and Lleida (546). It was taken by the Moors, reconquered in 785, acquired a bishop again in 799 and a count of Cerdanya-Urgell in about 820. By 839 it boasted a cathedral though this was replaced by another, consecrated in 1040 by Ermengol, another bishop and saint. His church survived a bare one hundred years, its poor state giving rise to the construction of the present building. All this building and rebuilding made the seat of the bishop the most important place in the town, which thus acquired its name Seu or Seo (episcopal seat). There are other *seos* in Spain, notably Zaragoza's, but they have not been similarly incorporated in the name of the city. This does not mean there was no civilian or commercial life in Urgell. On the contrary, it was the development of La Seu as a market town after the revival of commerce at the end of the Dark Ages which made possible – through taxes on traders – the building of this cathedral.

The exterior makes at first a rather stern impression, human-

*The modest but assured west front of the cathedral of
La Seu d'Urgell.*

ized by the odd little two-tier tower above the west-front pedi-
ment. The transepts end, unusually, in low massive towers, whose
military aspect is somewhat mitigated by large panels with
Lombard bands. Then as you move round to the east end you
begin to appreciate the real elegance and assurance of the design.
Upper transept windows on this side prepare the eye for the very
beautiful open gallery on twinned columns at the same height
which tops off the main apse. Above this rises a rose window and
the whole is crowned by the cimborium with its simple belfry.
Below this very successful and homogeneous east end of the
church there is a little public garden with a lovely view over the

vale of Urgell, lush with fruit trees, willows and poplars and ringed by wooded hills. The highest point of Cadí (2,567 m) rears up to the south-west. This is a very choice spot to which you may

The gracious galleried apse of La Seu.

wish to return; you can also continue happily to the left under the little eleventh-century church of Sant Miquel, into the square dominated by the bishop's palace and finally into the old shopping arcades of the Carrer Major.

But first the interior of the cathedral calls, as it still does to hundreds of citizens when evening mass is celebrated on Sundays and holidays. Not for nothing have the inhabitants contributed through their industry to this building from very early times. There is no exclusive box for the clergy in the middle of the nave – everything is open. It is still the people's church, where they can listen to the gospels and epistles in Catalan. If you raise your eyes, you will see that the barrel vault of the nave springs from piers decorated with a curious ball motif reminiscent of Avila. And in fact this church, not at all Gothic in any of its essentials, does invite comparison with early Gothic Avila, possibly because of its use of granite, its militaristic features and the appearance of gauche rusticities within a strong formal design. Four shallow apsidal chapels are scooped out of the thickness of the transept walls while the triforium windows shed welcome light on the transverse axis of the church. The crossing is covered by an elliptical vault with small embrasures which admit little or no light. The main apse with its semi-cupola has Lombard columns on the inside and, in its east wall, almost like a mihrab, is another apsidal recess in which the image of the Virgin of Urgell holds court.

To reach the cloister you have to buy a ticket to the museum, whose main trophy is one of a number of illuminated versions of *The Apocalypse of Saint John the Divine* by the Beatus of Liébana. This work, usually illustrated profusely, was extremely popular in the tenth to thirteenth centuries; the manuscript belonging to La Seu dates from the end of the tenth century and shows marked Mozarabic influence. You are introduced to the school of Lleida by an interesting fourteenth-century painted stone retable (87); there is a good painted wooden sarcophagus of the same century (103); the high Renaissance retable (111) of about 1550 is a good example of its kind; the best piece is the retable from La Conca (138), possibly by Pere Serra in the 1370s or thereabouts – the blues and golds seem to indicate provenance from his studio.

The cloister retains three sides of the thirteenth-century arcade on single columns. The massive granite capitals featuring humans and beasts in grotesque postures are of a more robust stamp than those of Ripoll or Sant Joan: they are said to have been carved by craftsmen from Roussillon; the same hands appear to have worked on the west front. The cloister affords a very satisfying view of the composition of the cathedral and also provides access to the smaller, slightly earlier church of Sant Miquel, whose nave is covered by a tentatively pointed barrel vault.

I hope I have managed to convey that La Seu is a fine piece of architecture, harmonious and assured but with some agreeably countrified touches. Its immediate surroundings are helpful to its appreciation and it is pleasant to wander under the wide old shopping arcades or *porxos* of the Carrer Major and neighbouring streets, which preserve some attractive shop fronts. Urgell also has a good broad *rambla* roofed by plane trees just on the edge of the *casc antic*. Here you will find most of the restaurants, hotels

Market scene, La Seu d'Urgell.

and banks. I am not a terrific fan of the National Paradors, whose growing network now smacks of Trusthouse Forte, but I think it is just worth staying at the Parador de la Seu, which is situated just a step from the cathedral. It is a modern building incorporating an old cloister which has been ingeniously turned into a combination of lounge and conservatory. Ask for a room facing out over the countryside. Those on the townward side are liable to suffer from the barking of chained guard dogs – country dogs bark too but in a more relaxed manner and they tend to shut up at night.

From La Seu it is only ten kilometres to the frontier with **Andorra**. A dispute between the count of Foix and the bishop of Urgell as to who owned these high narrow valleys and peaks was resolved in 1278 by giving the inhabitants independence under joint suzerainty. This arrangement applies to this day, the only difference being that the French state has inherited the count's role. 'Geographically considered', says Ford, 'the district ought to belong entirely to France, to which it is subject in civil matters, being in spirituals under the Bishop of Urgell, a sort of Prince Bishop in a phantom palatinate, and nominal republic.' In fact, today there is more evidence of Spanish administration and influence than French. The pillar boxes and hotel categories are Spanish; you hear more Castilian and Catalan spoken in the streets than French. The local government is administered by an elected council of twenty-four; their deliberations are held in Catalan, the official language of the little state.

It is tempting to sneer at contemporary Andorra for its commercialism, and indeed the lower valley, 'full of alpine charms' in Ford's day, is little more than a series of large drive-in supermarkets culminating in the capital **Andorra la Vella**, where the scarcity of building sites has given rise to a curious architectural style which might be called 'skyscraper-chalet'. However, despite (or perhaps because of) this development the town has been able to afford a rather splendid modern promenade and music centre immediately adjacent to the old church. And if you take the road up to Ordino you soon come into very delightful country where the river Valira bubbles down to join the Segre. But it is the shops and traffic that stick in the mind. And Andorra is not the best route into Catalonia unless you are coming from Toulouse and Foix. From Provence or Roussillon access is far better by Bourg-Madame/Puigcerdà. There are also likely to be queues at the Spanish customs on leaving Andorra, while they ferret around for all the duty-free booty you are supposed to have acquired in the principality, for they can conceive of no other purpose for going there. In a sense they are right – that is the typical Spanish view – but the delay can be tiresome.

From La Seu those who wish to continue into the Pyrenees can take the road via Pallerols and Vilamur to Sort, where I will join them in a couple of days. First, I want to follow the Segre further downstream and temporarily exchange alpine airs for a whiff of the heartlands, where Catalonia is untouched by foreign influences in the form of beachlife, supermarkets and winter sports.

The Segre continues attractively southwards through water meadows until it enters the gorge of Organyà. The town of **Organyà** is the home of the famous *Homilies,* considered to be the oldest known written document in Catalan and dating from the end of the twelfth century; they are in fact marginal notes to a collection of sermons in Latin and are written in a very plain and direct style. (Though there is no known earlier written text, it is generally held that spoken Catalan became current in the ninth century – see 'Catalan Language'.) Across the river from Organyà is **Figols,** a typical upper-Segre village complete with statutory Romanesque church. Below the gorge the river enters the Oliana reservoir, which consists of mudflats in high summer, but the stream threads its natural course through these regardless of

Towers great and small: the grand octagonal tower of Sant Pere de Ponts and the tapered tower of the primitive Visigothic or Mozarabic church of Coll de Nargó.

human attempts to swell it unnaturally. From the head of the reservoir a road branches off to Sant Llorenç de Morunys and Berga. Continuing south on the main road it is worth turning off at **Coll de Nargó** to see the primitive pre-Romanesque church a few hundred yards beyond the village. This is said to date from about 1000 but the tower appears to be earlier, featuring Visigothic or Mozarabic keyhole windows below the belfry. From here a rough road leads west to Tremp, which I shall approach by a less adventurous route. At the lower end of the reservoir, just above Oliana, the dam collects whatever water is left after a long dry summer. Downstream from here the Segre is allowed to revert to its natural size and runs on pleasantly down to Ponts, where it is joined by the Llobregós.

The towns are rougher in these parts and set no snares for tourists. There are fewer brightly informative signs and monuments are harder to find. Such is the case with **Sant Pere de Ponts**, which really deserves a visit. It is only two or three kilometres above the town of that name. The first sign to the left is clear enough; it is then best to ask at the first bar you reach. The track is not bad in fact and at the end is a very impressive octagonal tower (in the process of being restored) rising splendidly above a trefoil of apses; the church is a ruin and the site is deserted but what remains belongs to the very best period of the mid-twelfth century. No doubt it will all be put busily to rights in due course but at the time of writing the traveller has it all to him or herself.

The road now loses the river and you have a hot dusty run through grainlands with humpy hills crowned by the odd village, which may look splendid in silhouette but is often squalid on closer inspection. **Cubells** is one of these, an old semi-fortified, half-ruined place with a wide view of the Pla d'Urgell (Llano de Urgel), so called from the southerly extension of that county during the reconquest. On the horizon are towns such as Agramunt and Tàrrega. The landscape is somewhat reminiscent of the aching distances of New Castile. Down at this level you begin to regret the fresh airs and alpine views you have left behind, but it would be quite wrong to neglect these flatter, less dramatic lands if you want to understand Catalonia. It was here, between Aragon and the sea and between the Pyrenees and the Ebro, that the predecessors of the present inhabitants repopulated this most typical of Catalan regions, which has received less foreign influence than either the mountains or the coast. Here people are without airs and graces, straight in their approach but remarkably helpful, dropping any task just to show you the way.

I pushed on to **Balaguer**, capital of the *comarca* of La Noguera and a rather unusual place. This is Moorish territory, an important stronghold of the Islamic splinter kingdom of Lleida which existed independently after the break-up of the caliphate of Córdoba until its reconquest in 1148–9. The river Segre, of substantial girth here, divides the new town from the old, which slopes up under a stretch of wall remaining from the Moorish fort and culminates in the large Gothic church of Santa Maria with its splendid wide nave in the great Catalan tradition and an octagonal tower dated 1671 at the base. Immediately below the church is a warren of primitive alleys where gypsies make baskets on the steps; further down the hill is the old centre with the by now familiar *porxos*. It is all old and a bit seedy on this side, but when you cross the bridge to the modern side with its well-lit promenade, the dual effect is quite impressive. The east bank has recently been put down to lawn with willows and other shade trees, the modern blocks and hotel windows look straight across at the old quarter and its dimly lit river front, and the two banks seem to generate a sort of mutual satisfaction, each taking pride in the distinctive features of the other. But old Balaguer also has a foothold in the new quarter: just across the bridge is the church of Sant Dómenec, which features another successful wide vault and a particularly graceful semi-circular east end. Facing this church is the modern Parador Conde Jaime de Urgel, which is large and comfortable. You can do much worse than spend the night here.

The zig-zag pattern of this chapter is dictated largely by the lie of the land. The Segre and its two major tributaries, the Noguera Pallaresa and the Noguera Ribagorçana, flow from north to south down three deeply scoured valleys, making it difficult to follow a consistent east–west route along the Pyrenees, except by the link from La Seu to Sort, which cuts out considerable stretches of countryside and some interesting places. The western sector of the Catalan Pyrenees contains the highest peaks of all, and I decided at this point to describe a loop from Tremp via Sort up to Viella and back along the Aragonese border to Lleida with various detours on the way. Those wishing to proceed directly to Lleida will find it described later in this chapter.

From Balaguer there are two routes to Tremp and they meet at the north end of the Camarasa reservoir. The quicker of the two is via **Camarasa** itself, an old strongpoint on a hump with a small Roman bridge over the Segre. The Marquisate of Camarasa is one of the many titles of the dukes of Medinaceli, whose sway thus extends from Seville right up into the heart of Catalonia. The longer but more agreeable route is via Les Avellanes and Àger. This is almond country and it must be breathtaking in the early spring. The almond loves highish dry ground, preferably not too flat, so the terrain is ideal here. The plantations, some old, some new, extend along most of this route. You pass the largely modern monastery of Les Avellanes with its older Gothic church and vineyards and almond groves. Everything is very neat and well tended by the monks. **Les Avellanes** itself is capital of the nut: almonds occupy the core of the village. You climb now through holm oaks and oak scrub to the pass known as Port d'Àger, from where there is a tremendous view over the escarpment of the Serra de Mamet, under which lies yet another valley rife with almonds. You descend past the unexpected railway station of Àger – a line has been drilled through the mountains from Lleida to La Pobla de Segur – and shortly join the road from Camarasa.

Here you make your first acquaintance with the Noguera Pallaresa (so called because it flows through the *comarca* of Pallars Jussà), which feeds into the Segre just above Camarasa. Following it north, you are soon in the awesome defile of Collegats. The road twists under overhanging rock faces and through an ingenious tunnel, which is pierced both longitudinally and laterally in the wall overhanging the river with a sort of crude arcade that admits light. It emerges from this at the foot of another reservoir, that of Terradets, which unlike many of its kind is extraordinarily pretty with low hills and lush vegetation rather than oppressive crags. All in all, this is an extremely rewarding drive which offers a great variety of scenery. And so to Tremp.

Tremp is the capital of the *comarca* of Pallars Jussà. It is a pleasant, rather gentle town with several shady squares and walks. The apse of the main church and a tower surviving from the original fortifications act as dovecotes. Inside, the church features a typical wide Catalan vault, though on rounded arches with Gothic ribbed vaults in between. The Hotel Siglo XX is very adequate for a night. The next town upstream, **La Pobla de Segur**, is the terminus of the nature-defying railway line from Lleida. Its river, the Flamicell, is really a *rambla*, dry in summer, waiting for the melting snows to give it life. Here you have a choice of directions and the circuit of Viella can be taken either way. I chose the right-hand fork, following the main river, up to Sort in order to link up again with those readers I left in La Seu d'Urgell.

Not far upstream from this junction is the very old village of **Gerri de la Sal** with its saltpans down along the river, as its name implies. The foundation of the Benedictine monastery here dates back to 807, just after Charlemagne had established the Hispanic march as a buffer state of feudal counties to protect his southern flank against the Moors. It is thus one of the very first fruits of the Benedictine expansion following the pacification of the Pyrenees. The twelfth-century church (reached by a footbridge over the river) has a delightful three-tier rustic belfry with ogival decoration in the windows. On the south flank there is a window which appears to be Mozarabic – it is possible that a tiny Christian community maintained itself up here throughout the Moorish occupation until the monks arrived following the flag. The south front is host to the village cemetery; an open loft runs under the roof – you almost expect to see bales of straw tucked into it. It is hardly surprising that this delightful site on the bank of the Noguera Pallaresa, with the bonus of its salt deposits, should have attracted settlement or that the monks should have decided to

*The early Benedictine monastery of Gerri de la Sal,
delightfully situated on the bank of the Noguera Pallaresa.*

build here. The church enjoys one of the most magical settings in
Catalonia.

We come next fo **Sort**, capital of Pallars Sobirà, the higher (or
upper) of the two *comarques* of this name. It is built round the
junction with the road from La Seu d'Urgell, to which I have
already referred; the road is well surfaced and the link is perfectly
feasible. North of Sort you enter a world of slate-tiled pyramidal
church spires at **Llavorsi** and **Escalò**, the latter on the site of a
Visigothic monastery. A turning to the left shortly after Escaló
leads up to **Espot**, a pleasant little hill station that has grown up at
one of the entrances to the national park of Aigües Tortes, a
labyrinth of streams and lakes of which Sant Maurici and the
Estany Negre are among the largest. You can drive up as far as
Saint Maurice's lake, which is the point of departure for a whole
network of jeep trails and paths that enable you to walk right over
to the west side of the park and down via the Vall de Sant Nicolau
to emerge in the valley of the Noguera de Tor near Erill-la-vall and
Boi, or north and over into the Vall d'Aran coming down near
Tredòs and Salardú. There is a local walking, trekking and
climbing tradition which well precedes imported sports, so it is
not hard to obtain the necessary directions (the owner of the Hotel
Saurat at Espot is an expert); the reverse side of the Firestone

136

*Old bridge across the Noguera Pallaresa with the belfry of
Gerri de la Sal rising above the trees to the left.*

*Mountains above the Estany Negre (Black Lake) in the national
park of Aigües Tortes (Winding Waters).*

1:200,000 map T24 also provides a useful enlargement of the
whole park and its main trails. **Superespot** is a ski station above
the village, patronized mainly by Spaniards. It is not open every

137

year so anyone with designs on it should check in advance with the Spanish National Tourist Office.

From Espot the main road continues up the very pretty Vall d'Aneu, where you will find more churches with Nordic spires and a number of modest but very acceptable hotels, to **Esterri d'Aneu** (agood breakfast is served at the Hostal dels Pirineus). From here a branch road follows the upper waters of the Noguera Pallaresa.

The village of Borén reflected in the waters of the Noguera Pallaresa.

I added another sundial to my collection from the church tower of Isabarre. **Borén** is picturesquely situated at the head of the reservoir named after it. The river here is lined with walnuts and poplars. Just before **Isil** is the ruined Benedictine church of Sant Joan, an early foundation of the ninth century. It has a pointed apsidal recess but is otherwise fully Romanesque and is in the

Primitive capitals flanking the entrance to the ruined Benedictine church of Sant Joan, Isil.

process of being restored. The capitals of the entrance are curiously primitive. This valley is not much frequented by tourists as it offers no attractions but itself.

Returning to Esterri, one climbs to another pleasant village, **València d'Aneu**, with its two welcoming hostelries. Here begins the very grand drive up to the pass of Bonaigua, where the road crosses the main watershed of the Pyrenees. I felt that hitherto I had been pussyfooting around in the foothills. First, the great bald peaks on the French border come into view, then the road enters tight curves under pine-fringed crags from which the occasional cascade of water bounces down through the trees; untended cattle, ponies and sheep can be a hazard and should be looked out for on this road. From the top of the pass (2,072 m) looking west towards Aragon, you can identify the highest peaks of all, Maladeta (3,308 m) and Aneto (3,404 m): the white streak near Aneto's crown is a sixty-foot-deep glacier which superbly disregards the melting of the transient snows and glints evilly in the autumn sun.

After Bonaigua the road slides down swiftly into the Vall d'Aran, which is presumptuous enough to have its own dialect. You are immediately met by *benvengi* instead of the Catalan *benvinguts* (welcome) on the signs. I was told that *catalanoparlants* can understand seventy-five per cent but miss the refinements. The tongue is apparently a version of the old Gascon language, which seems plausible as the whole *comarca* was virtually cut off from the rest of Spain except by smugglers' tracks until the building of the roads and especially the Viella tunnel in the 1940s. In the circumstances the easier natural communications with France must have been a dominant influence.

Vaqueira is a modern ski resort (and a ghost town in summer) but you come shortly to **Salardú**. whose fine octagonal church tower has a sundial, which predisposed me in its favour. Inside, there are wooden galleries at the rear and along both sides of the nave. The entrance portico is still Romanesque despite an early Gothic interior. The village is extremely peaceful. On sale here are miniature models of '*joies romaniques del Pirineu de Lleida*' ('Romanesque jewels of the Leridan Pyrenees') – for this is the northern limit of the province of Lleida – so the collector can eagerly snap up a figurine of *Bossost s. CII* or *S. Climent de Taüll s. XII* for his or her mantelpiece. Nearby is **Tredòs**, some of whose parish church frescoes are in New York. A couple of hundred yards on foot above the bridge is a sanctuary with a charming old belfy in a leafy setting. You suddenly realize that the bright bubbling little river Garona is the French Garonne.

Cottages at Arties on the bubbling river Garona, which rises in the Vall d'Aran.

*Church towers at Salardú and Arties: the slate spire
is a feature of the Pyrenean valleys.*

From Salardú a single-track and mainly metalled road leads up to the reservoir of Santa Coloma and if you follow the stream that feeds this upwards and southwards you will eventually emerge again in the lake district of Aigües Tortes. **Arties** is another very charming village a little lower down the valley. In all these places the sawmills and carpentry shops are busy making shutters for chalets; there is no cause for alarm yet on this account, as the environment so far remains unthreatened and the building materials are all traditional, while the great impulse is provided to the local economy. The road continues downwards past other attractive villages – Casarill, Escunyau – to Viella, capital of this linguistically independent *comarca*, situated at the head of the valley where the Garona is joined by the Negre.

Viella has undergone considerable development since the piercing of the great tunnel to the south; it is slightly reminiscent of Andorra but the architects of its high-rise buildings have worked out a rather more successful modern vernacular and are in any case less cramped for space. The river Negre rushes down through the town centre. The church features an octagonal tower and early Gothic doorway, which bears witness to the French connection as thirteenth-century church entrances in the rest of Catalonia are still mainly Romanesque. On the front of the town hall there is an inscription, dated 1924, which reads: 'Don Alfonso XIII being King of Spain and a Military Directorate forming the Government, a Spanish Monarch trod the soil of Aran for the first time.' This gives some idea of the valley's remoteness from the centre, for the Bourbons always liked to get about, particularly on shooting trips. I also rather like the innuendo that when a king finally did put in an appearance he was only a puppet.

The Vall d'Aran is, to my mind, the most attractive of the Pyrenean valleys in Catalonia and I would prefer it for a walking holiday to Espot, which is more immediately enclosed by peaks and aspires to ski-station status without always being able to deliver the goods. In the Pyrenees it is important, I think, to distinguish between two types of valley: those with skiing facilities and those without. The former develop a distinct form of ski culture with more shops, bars and chalets – usually in a semi-traditional style using local materials – and more big hotels. Ski culture in the Vall d'Aran is confined mainly to the area round Vaqueira at the head of the valley. The next valley I propose to investigate, that of the Noguera de Tor, belongs to the latter group.

Before leaving Viella it is worth noting that there is an easy run to the French frontier at Pont del Rei via Bossost. This is a handy point of entry to Catalonia for anyone coming from Pau, Lourdes or Tarbes and a good way out for the whole of the south-west of France. From Viella, heading south again, the road climbs sharply above the town to the mouth of the great five-kilometre tunnel. Built in the 1940s, its surface is not particularly good – beware of wet patches. Emerging from it, the drive down the valley of the Noguera Ribagorçana seems uneventful after the grandeurs of the Bonaigua pass. Pont de Suert is a town of little interest at the junction of the Noguera de Tor with the larger river. The turning

*Sant Climent de Taüll, perhaps the most striking Romanesque
tower in Catalonia in an unmatched position overlooking
the Boí valley.*

143

into the tributary valley and up to the village of Boí is located two kilometres north of the town. This should not be missed.

Passing through Lés with its small reservoir, beneath Coll and its twelfth-century church (this involves a three-kilometre digression) and under Cardet's tiny sanctuary on a crag, you come after fifteen kilometres to **Boí,** which is the best base for the valley. It too has its Romanesque church, rather a good one (presently under reconstruction) with a neat two-storey tower. But the lion of the valley is **Sant Climent de Taüll** (often described on maps in the Castilian version as San Clemente de Tahull) three kilometres above Boí. This church has become something of a shrine for admirers of the Romanesque owing to the perfect articulation of its three apses in the shape of a trefoil and its exceedingly handsome six-storey tower (rivalled in Catalonia only by the cathedral tower of Vic which is, however, less dramatically situated). The windows here are interestingly arranged: a single slit at the lowest level gives way to a double arch (or *ajimez*) on a single column at the second stage and then to a triple arch on two columns at the third stage. Stages four, five and six revert to *ajimeces* which increase in size the higher they go, and every set of windows is set in an identical recessed panel within a Lombardic frame. Between the stages there is the additional local variant of a dentellated course of brick. I indulge so lovingly in these details to show that this is a very sophisticated piece of building; the simple rudeness of the interior with its circular columns rather disappoints. The frescoes of the pantocrator and other figures in the main apse are reproductions of the originals which have been removed to the Museu d'Art de Catalunya in Barcelona and serve as a reminder of the tremendous importance of murals to the interiors of these churches, which look somewhat impoverished without them.

Mr Kenneth Conant, author of the excellent Pelican volume *Carolingian and Romanesque Architecture (800–1200),* sees Sant Climent as being almost archaic for its date (1132). This may well be true of the nave but not so of the tower and apses, which continued to set the architectural tone well into the following century. Santa Maria, in the centre of the village, is very similar to Sant Climent in its interior construction, though it is slightly larger, but it loses points in its four-storey tower. Facing Boí and Taüll on the other slope of the valley is the village of **Erill-la-vall,** which outbids Santa Maria with a tower of five storeys; there may well have been an interesting rivalry at the time. All these churches use the same dentellated pattern between the different stages. Erill also has a rather uncharacteristic porch along one side, like one arm of a cloister.

The works of man in praise of God are very fine up here, but what God has done for man is equally noteworthy. Higher up the valley are the thermal springs of **Caldes de Boí**. There is a spa here and two substantial hotels complete with therapists and so forth. The spa in fact provides the main economic impulse to the life of the valley; it also helps to preserve it from the brasher developments of ski culture. On reflection, I think this valley shares the honours with the Vall d'Aran. Either from Boí, which offers the Hostal Fondevila (*simple mais convenable*) or from Erill and its several hostels, jeeps may be hired for trips into Aigües Tortes while the more active can plan excursions on foot. The latter, as Ford would say, should 'look to the provend' in case they are benighted.

From Pont de Suert it is possible to return to Tremp via Sarroca, but I decided to take the road to Lleida via Benavarri and pass out of Catalonia into Aragon. Hardly have you crossed the river than the Aragonese border is proclaimed and signs are firmly to Lérida. You seem to be back in the empire of the majority culture but be careful of appearances. At **Benavarri** (Benarrabe) I first learned about La Franja (the Fringe), which seems to stretch about twenty kilometres westwards from the Noguera Ribagorçana marking the border and includes such villages as Arena, Roda and Aler, as well as Benavarri itself. In this northern sector of La Franja they speak Ribagorçano, a dialect of Catalan. A little further south around Tamarit de Llitera and westwards the native tongue is nearer to standard Catalan. At Binéfar, however, twelve kilometres west of Tamarit, Castilian rules absolutely. 'We are all little republics in these parts,' said the Tamarit barman with a mixture of local pride and humour.

It is not purely for romantic or nostalgic reasons that the people of these parts cling to Catalan. In fact, it can be argued that economic reasons are more important. In Tamarit they boast openly that La Franja is the richest part of the Aragonese province of Huesca, and Lleida, not Zaragoza, is the great mart. The inhabitants of La Franja therefore tend to cleave both commercially and linguistically to Catalan prosperity. This is understandable enough because, even within this more favoured belt, initial impressions of Aragon are that it is distinctly poorer than Catalonia – as it always has been historically. Ruined farm buildings and forts are more common. The sheep are thinner. There are fewer signs proclaiming the public works being carried out by the autonomous government of Aragon. As a result of this little expedition I found myself reflecting that I had come across virtually no poverty in Catalonia to date: most of the buildings were well kept and there was much new construction, particularly of chalets in the Pyrenees. There was some begging in Barcelona but this seems to be the case in large cities in general. At Alfarràs the road re-enters Catalonia proper, and the signposts again read Lleida rather than Lérida.

Rather larger and more industrialized than Girona and with a less pronounced *casc antic*, **Lleida** is situated on the Segre, almost on the border of Catalonia with Aragon, and is thus an important centre of communications between the two halves of the old confederation. Its long and chequered history entitles it to a certain respect and it is still capital of one of the provinces of the old régime and of the revived *comarca* of Segrià under the new. But do not approach it in too solemn a spirit, as the semi-blue videos on show in many of the bars at night indicate its willingness to participate fully in contemporary life.

Having supported the Carthaginians in the Punic Wars, Lleida also supported Pompey against Caesar. Later it was a *municipium* under Augustus and in the Dark Ages it became a Visigothic bishopric. After the disintegration of the caliphate of Córdoba in 1031 it was the capital of one of the splinter kingdoms or *taifas* until it was recaptured by Ramon Berenguer IV and the count of Urgell in 1149 – shortly after the union of Catalonia and Aragon. It rose against the crown in the War of the Reapers (1640–52) and was eventually retaken by Philip IV. In the War of the Spanish Succession (1700–13) it sided against Philip V, the first Spanish Bourbon, who closed its ancient university after his confirmation on the throne by the treaty of Utrecht. In the Peninsular War (1808–14) it joined the popular resistance against the French and was a victim of the atrocities unleashed by Suchet. All in all, the city's passport is stamped with all the right visas but it is not a place that finds an easy way into the visitor's affections. Traffic is fierce and competitive; parking is difficult; the Parador is badly sited on the autoroute; and there is only one reasonable lodging in town, the Residencia Principal in the Plaça de la Paeria.

None of these is a sufficient reason for avoiding Lleida – as Ford inexplicably did when few of these modern problems existed. Oddly enough many of the street names are still in Castilian with Catalan protest stickers plastered over them. La Seu Vella is one of the most imposing monuments in Catalonia. Access from the lower town is rather circuitous: from the Carrer Major you take the steep Carrer Caballeros and then climb to the Plaça Wilfred I (*sic* – a curious variant of the usual Guifré) from which you gain the Plaça de la Sardana to emerge finally on the fortified platform with ramparts of various periods on which La Seu stands, one of the few Spanish cathedrals which remains a landmark and a beacon for many miles around.

This great church owes its battered appearance to its long service as fortress-cum-barracks-cum-prison from the early eighteenth century onwards, when Philip V had it Vaubanized with little domical sentry-boxes at the salient angles to serve as a command post from which to cow a population that had opposed his claim to the throne (just as he created La Ciutadella to control the rebellious Barcelonese). It ceased to be the seat of the bishop when a new cathedral was erected in the lower town in 1760–81. It now has no real function other than for exhibitions and musical events but without it Lleida would be just another sprawling pueblo of the plain.

La Seu is transition in action on a very grand scale. Founded in 1203 and consecrated in 1278, the plan of the church, with its

La Seu Vella, or old cathedral of Lleida, rising from a fortified platform above the town.

massive piers and engaged columns, is still thoroughly Romanesque. The tall capitals of the nave, the intricate foliage and figured scenes, belong to the mature Romanesque tradition, though foliage and interlacing patterns predominate here over

147

iconography. The roof is supported on hefty, slightly pointed arches of square section with bulky ribs securing the vault. The upper windows are firmly Romanesque, but the octagonal lantern raised on squinch arches at the corners óf the crossing is fully Gothic. The chapels are of various periods from flamboyant to plateresque, mostly very deteriorated and hacked about by the soldiery. But none of these later developments (or the vandalisms) very much affects the grand Romanesque plan.

The cloister is remarkable not only for its size – it is gigantic – but also for its situation attached to the west front of the church, to which it acts as a kind of vast forecourt or atrium. This is attributed to the earlier existence of a Moorish courtyard of ablutions on the same site in front of the mosque, which (as was usual) served as the first Christian cathedral after the reconquest in 1149. The decoration of the cloister is fascinating. The arcade abutting on the church, which includes the main west portico, has Romanesque columns with capitals of great intricacy, the work, some say, of Moorish craftsmen or Mudéjares. Certainly there are some reminiscences here of the honeycomb capitals of the caliphate of Córdoba. Above these rise Gothic flamboyant windows unusually framed within a chevron frieze. The Saracenic patterns continue round the four inner and outer piers of the southern wing of the cloister and a little way along the northern wing, but then Gothic scroll capitals take over and all the arches are filled in with decorated Gothic tracery. These discrepancies are apparently due to work having been suspended between 1286 and 1334. Regardless of this patchwork, the cloister of La Seu is without doubt one of the wonders of Catalonia: it triumphs in particular in its open *mirador* or belvedere of five bays along the southern wing, providing a wide-ranging view of the river and the plain with its grain silos, factories and acres of irrigated orchards. It comes as something of a relief, after twisting around in the mountains for a week, to be able to confirm the existence of a great swathe of flatlands including the plain of Urgell and ringed roughly by the towns of Balaguer, Agramunt, Cervera, Tàrrega and Les Borges Blanques.

A walk around the outside of the massive building confirms the Romanesque triapsidal plan, but the southern apse has been removed to make way for two Gothic chapels. The two south doors – those of the transept and the Porta dels Fillols, the latter recessed under a Gothic arch – feature Saracenic Romanesque decoration, which is probably a bit earlier than that in the cloister. Only the main exterior doorway to the atrium-cloister,

*The gigantic early Gothic cloister with belvedere of
La Seu Vella.*

the Porta dels Apòstols, is fully Gothic with the pantocrator in
the tympanum. The great pile is completed by the handsome
octagonal tower, the beacon of the plain, erected between 1364
and 1416. It is said to have been finished by Charles Gaulter of
Rouen, who designed the cathedral of Seville. There was almost
certainly a minaret here, or nearby.

The lower town need not detain you for long. The town hall
façade on the Plaça de la Paeria is a reconstruction of its
appearance in the thirteenth century. The traffic-free Carrer
Major leads to the new cathedral, erected during the enlightenment of Charles III; it is a frigid neo-classical building, extremely

dark, faintly reminiscent of the great Renaissance cathedrals of the south such as Granada or Guadix but without their ambition or thrust; it contains a good collection of tapestries. The old hospital facing the cathedral steps has a grand entrance with great radial voussoirs surmounted by a smiling Virgin and Child of the fourteenth century. Climbing behind the cathedral you come to the Plaça de Sant Llorenç. St Lawrence's church is the most venerable and interesting building in this quarter. Constructed mainly at the end of the thirteenth century, it features a wide barrel-vaulted nave and Gothicized aisles. The Gothic retables have traces of painting but are hard to see properly. There is a quintessentially Catalan painting of a bishop on an embossed gold background in the chapel next to the font. The chapel to the right of the high altar contains a striking fourteenth-century alabaster Virgin and Child. This is yet another transitional church. It has a good atmosphere and is a pleasant place to pause on the descent from La Seu.

El Segrià is Lleida's market garden. The northern half of the *comarca* is irrigated from the Canal d'Urgell and is intensively cultivated with fruit – apples, peaches and above all the pear. Every year during the last week of September Lleida is host to the largest fair of agricultural machinery in Catalonia. In the Camps Elisis (Elysian Fields), as the public park is rather presumptuously called, you pass stand upon stand of small tractors suitable for ploughing between fruit trees. There is no doubt the region is flexing its muscles for the Common Market – and not only in fruit, if the ministry of agriculture's monograph *The Organization of the Meat Market in the European Community* is anything to go by. Lleida is thus eagerly poised to contribute to the various mountains and lakes of the Community's common agricultural policy. The south of Segrià is not irrigated and does not pose this threat of glut. It is an area of old olives and almonds on carefully tended terraces. The inhabitants live in rather large plain villages with the odd grace note, a baroque doorway or a fountain. Across the Aragonese border the southerly extension of La Franja takes in Fraga and Mequinesa, where the people are bilingual.

Leaving Lleida, I decided to see the towns of the plain. This involved some more zig-zagging in order to take in those not situated on the main road to Barcelona. I started on the Tarragona road as far as **Les Borges Blanques**, which I thought a rather strange place. The large handsome parish church was closed at midday on a Sunday, while in a backstreet an extraordinary ranting sound drew me to a poor building from whose windows issued a virulent harangue in Catalan on the evils of the Church, princes, bishops and all such instances of vanity: as the preacher worked himself up to each climax, he would pause and the small congregation would chime in lustily with a loud *amén*. The meeting place was called the Església Evangèlica Filadèlfia (the Philadelphia Evangelical Church). The winds of religious tolerance have obviously blown freely and freshly in Spain since the 1960s when I was told there were only some thirty thousand Protestants in the whole country.

From here I turned north-east to **Bellpuig**, capital of the old barony of that name, situated on the main road to Barcelona, which I crossed before continuing on the same course to **Agramunt**, a small agricultural town with a particularly fine specimen of a transitional church. The east end is traditionally triapsidal in the Romanesque fashion but employs slightly pointed arches, which are continued westwards throughout the building. The transition is most eloquently expressed by the tall Romanesque acanthus capitals which top the engaged columns of the massive piers and act as launching pads for the pointed barrel vault of the nave. Despite the tentative Gothic of the interior (I have for a long time thought 'pointed Romanesque' a better term) the west front reverts to type with a gloriously intricate and thoroughly Romanesque portico incorporating a very fine sculptured group of the Adoration in the centre of the composition; the column capitals and imposts and the intrados of the arch are almost exhibitionist in their use of the Romanesque repertoire. This is a very interesting building imbued with the Romanesque spirit of the rural areas and dented only slightly by the new fashions from France. *Vaut le détour* if you are really interested in this sort of thing.

Next I headed south for **Tàrrega**. This is in the plain of Urgell, a *comarca* a hundred kilometres south of the capital of the old county of Urgell, La Seu, whose district is called Alt Urgell. The name of the county thrust southwards with the reconquest and its counts marched shoulder to shoulder with the more puissant counts of Barcelona, who nonetheless needed them until they were able to incorporate their allies' fief in their own domains. It is a plain in all senses with long plain but not drab town streets. The pride of these places is expressed in their churches, which are usually large like Tàrrega's domical Jesuitical temple with its grand baldachino over the high altar. (You are a long way from the tiny early churches tucked into the folds of hillsides; here a commanding position and the tall octagonal tower are the rule.)

Main entrance of the fine transitional church of Agramunt.

These are prosperous self-respecting communities. Tàrrega, a town of eleven thousand inhabitants, boasts a culture centre, a drama and dance school, a municipal school of music, an archive, a museum, a school of arts and crafts and a multi-sport stadium. The crops are maize, alfalfa and apples, apples and yet more apples, all irrigated by the Canal d'Urgell, which is fed by the Segre.

A few miles east along the main road stands another substantial town, **Cervera**. The Carrer Major is built on a long spine above the plain. Some way down it on the left is the house which held the *corts catalanes* or parliament that established the Generalitat de Catalunya in 1359 (see 'Political Life and Institutions'). Here too in 1469 the marriage contract was signed between Ferdinand of Aragon and Isabel, heiress to the throne of Castile, a union pregnant with far-reaching consequences. At the far end of the

Details of capitals and archivolts at Agramunt.

street is a town hall of 1786 which features curious local figures supporting the balconies; these eighteenth-century gargoyles (though they do not spout water) are most unusual in a period when strict neo-classicism reigned. Behind this building is the main church of Santa Maria with its fine octagonal tower, vying with its fellows in the rest of the region. From the Plaça Major a semi-subterranean passage runs parallel to the Carrer Major at a lower level. The local corporation has attached to it, no doubt with an eye on the tourists, the cumbersome title of Alley of the Thirteenth-century Witches (the last execution for witchcraft in Catalonia took place in Terrassa just outside Barcelona in 1619, when four were accused, all tortured and two burned alive).

At the opposite end of the Carrer Major to Santa Maria and close to the present town centre rise the large university buildings erected by order of Philip V after he suppressed all the other universities in Catalonia for their part in the War of the Spanish Succession. Once you have passed the porter's lodge with its scrolls and frills, the buildings are severely institutional. There is a long forecourt with two clocks and a sundial (a precaution against mechanical breakdown) to ensure that the students of the *Cervariensis Academia* were not late for their Bourbonic lessons. Beyond this are two further quadrangles. The first-floor chapel is now used to satisfy the Catalan appetite for exhibitions. Its pretty baroque altar is the only relief mitigating the interior severity of this barrack-like, custom-built, short-lived university whose status as such was terminated in 1841, when its faculties were moved to Barcelona. It is now the backdrop for the annual fair when swings and roundabouts are set up under its walls for four days in late September.

From Cervera I decided to turn north-east again to Calaf, which had tempted me from both Manresa and Solsona, but not quite enough. The road passes through **Sant Ramon de Portell**, whose monastic church is proclaimed on signs as the Escorial of the Segarra, a piece of local hyperbole that can safely be disregarded. **Calaf** itself is a typical town of the region featuring a good tower of

Capitals and columns at Santa Coloma de Queralt.

the by now familiar shape. This detour is not obligatory except for fans of Catalan church towers; I would counsel others to proceed south-east from Cervera directly to **Santa Coloma de Queralt**, which along with closely neighbouring Aguiló was one of the forward outposts of the reconquest in the tenth century. Here you are almost at the foot of the wooded hills where Islamic tribesmen were able to prolong their resistance. Santa Coloma has a good sturdy parish church of Catalan Gothic stamp and a pleasant porticoed square. A little way outside the village towards the hills is the thirteenth-century church of Santa Maria de Bell.lloc on a platform overlooking the Serra de Queralt. It has a fine doorway with some Saracenic motifs; carved on one capital is a bird of prey swallowing a human, head first. There is also an eroded Adoration in the tympanum.

From here you may continue, if you so please and without remonstrance from me, south-east again via La Llacuna to

Vilafranca del Penedès, where I will shortly rejoin you. I felt it my duty to inspect Igualada first. To the right of the road **Aguiló** perches finely on its mound and then you climb on to the ridge running towards Igualada. Up here the southern face of the Serra de Montserrat comes suddenly into view. It took me somewhat by surprise because the Virgin's beams had lost some of their power as lesser goddesses made their bid for supremacy in other sanctuaries in the regions to the north. But the re-emergence of the jagged massif at once reminded me that the great Diana of the Mountain is no mere local Barcelona cult but exercises a far wider attraction over the towns and villages of the plain.

Igualada is a large busy town. It has a leather and textile museum, a Modernist slaughterhouse and a church by Gaudí's assistant Joan Rubió. These attractions are not really sufficient to make struggling with the traffic worth while. As I was not quite ready to re-enter the atmosphere of Barcelona, I took the road over the Serra de Queralt and down through the wine-growing district of the Penedès to its capital **Vilafranca del Penedès**. This is another prosperous, well-kept place. Its centre has the air of refinement often associated with wine-producing districts. The old quarter is well lit but not over-lit by night. The town hall is spotless. The parish church was built on a truly impressive scale: a wide Catalan vault has been achieved on very slightly pointed arches; there are no aisles and the sharply pointed side chapels, each surmounted by a rose window, are accommodated in the thickness of the wall. These chapels are all closed off by iron grilles, much less usual in Catalonia than in the south and bearing witness – as do some of the shop signs – to the existence of a local wrought-iron industry.

Facing the west front is an old mansion, in which Peter III (the Ceremonious) died in 1387. This now contains various collections, the most interesting of which is the Museu del Vi with its extensive display of presses, viticultural tools, barrels, bottles, glasses and leather containers. The Plaza de Jaime I (still in Castilian here) on to which these buildings face is very handsome with other Gothic mansions, one or two buildings showing Modernist influence and a curious carved monolith in the centre inscribed *Als Castellers*. This is a monument to the contests held during the August fair when all the villages of the district compete to build the tallest human tower or 'castle' with one man supporting another on his shoulders and so on, the whole edifice being buttressed by a sort of scrum of supporters at ground level. The champion *castellers* achieve pyramids with three figures forming the lower tiers, which reduce to two and then to one, and rise as high as eight or nine tiers in all. There is usually a child on his father's shoulders on top. The practice is also widespread in the adjacent *comarques* and particularly in the town of Valls, capital of Alt Camp. In Vilafranca the Hotel Pedro III el Grande is very comfortable and can be recommended for the night.

Whilst at Vilafranca it is well worth driving ten kilometres to **Sant Martí Sarroca**, where on the castle hill above the village there is a thirteenth-century Romanesque church with a grand Lombardic apse. This affords excellent views of the vineyards of the district, whose rusty green grape produces agreeable light fresh wines in rather welcome contrast to the heavy vintages of Aragon, La Rioja and (nearer home) El Priorat down in New Catalonia.

The return to Barcelona from Vilafranca can be accomplished in an hour or so. I paused first to try to give some coherence to my impressions of the cities and towns of the plain, whose core is the Pla d'Urgell, known also to the Catalans of the coast as *les terres de ponent* (the lands over to the west). It is not an area that will appeal to the tourist eager for instant thrills but the discerning traveller will find much to savour in it and will come closer here to the unadorned spirit of Catalonia than on the coast where foreign influences are more pronounced. Here the people have had to draw on their own resources, patiently building their own institutions – schools, churches, co-operatives, businesses, clubs – which they guard with determination and pride. There is a sense of space and distance and dry clear air which is sometimes reminiscent of New Castile, but the views are less wearisome, for the wooded foothills are seldom far off and indeed the landscape changes with surprising rapidity. The old towns feature sober but substantial churches and confident well-kept public buildings; there is none of the sense of ennui that permeates Castile, so well conveyed in Antonio Machado's 'Poema de un día' (1914). From the northern fringe Solsona is an extremely pleasant base for exploring southwards as far as the main road. To the west Balaguer may be a more convenient centre than Lleida and is close to Agramunt. The belt of towns across the centre – Bellpuig, Tàrrega, Cervera and Santa Coloma – merits a visit and Cervera itself is a good base camp from which to explore them all. On the southern fringe Vilafranca del Penedès serves as a jumping-off point for the Costa Daurada and the Cistercian route – both of which are explored in the next chapter.

5

New Catalonia

New Catalonia is the southernmost part of the present-day autonomous region. It was largely brought within the fold of the house of Barcelona by Counts Ramon Berenguer III (1093–1131) and Ramon Berenguer IV (1131–62). The former repopulated Tarragona and restored its old archbishopric; the latter pushed the frontier right down to the Ebro. Conventional wisdom holds that below the Llobregat French influence wanes and Moorish airs are wafted up from the south. I was by now ready to explore the truth of this, especially as the metropolis tends to become oppressive and airless in the autumn as it waits for the first rains – so I was not averse to a change of air and was almost tempted to make one great stride to Tarragona along the autoroute. But it would have been a pity to miss Sitges, still by far the most agreeable resort on the Costa Daurada. The coast road via Castelldefels with its dark sand, followed by a number of inlets occupied by cement factories, is not particularly attractive, so it is on balance worth taking the autoroute as far as the exit marked to Sitges and Vilanova i la Geltrú.

The great virtue of **Sitges** is that it has the proper marine parade with palm trees of a well-established seaside town that was not thrown up overnight. The church is nicely situated right above the water and the pleasant old buildings behind house various bequests from distinguished Catalans which make it clear that this was a place dear to local people before the tourists came. It is

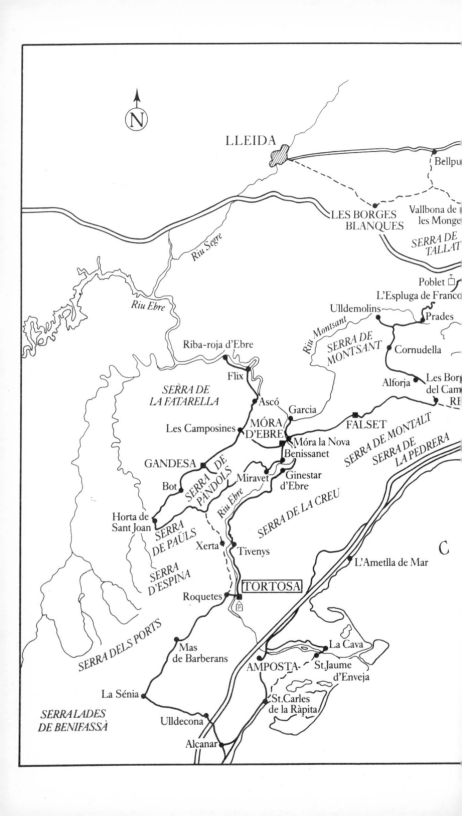

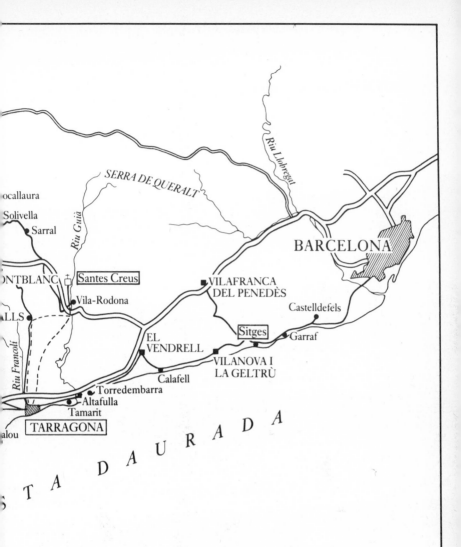

ocallaura

Solivella
● Sarral

SERRA DE QUERALT

Riu Guià

Riu Llobregat

BARCELONA

ONTBLANC   † Santes Creus

● Vila-Rodona

■ VILAFRANCA
DEL PENEDÈS

Castelldefels

LLS ●

Riu Francolí

EL
VENDRELL

Sitges

Garraf

VILANOVA I
LA GELTRÙ

● Calafell

● Torredembarra
● Altafulla
Tamarit

TARRAGONA

alou

S T A   D A U R A D A

New Catalonia

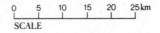

0   5   10   15   20   25 km
SCALE

worth while looking in on the Museu Cau Ferrat, which is the house or assemblage of old houses put together by Santiago Rusiñol, the Modernist painter and writer (see 'Modern Art') and left to the town by his widow. The ground floor of this shrine of *fin de siècle* nostalgia is almost excessively quaint but there are some good pieces of mediaeval alabaster and, upstairs, a collection of ironwork – how Spain loves threatening iron spikes! This is one respect in which Catalonia is no different from Castile. There are also two El Grecos bought by the painter in Paris. His own and other contemporary work is mainly of interest to Hispanists and Catalanophiles. The adjacent Museu Maricel offers somewhat second-rank Catalan Gothic paintings. The Casa Llopis in the upper town, built in 1793, was the home of a family of diplomats. Now dignified with the title Museu Romàntic, it displays *in situ* the fixtures and fittings of a cultured nineteenth-century bourgeois household. (The romantic period in Spain runs from 1820 to the 1860s strictly speaking, but it tends to get stretched to include most of the century.) None of these museums is obligatory

Parish church rising above the yacht basin of Sitges,
the most civilized of the Catalan seaside resorts.

but an agreeable few hours can be whiled away in them if you are staying in Sitges.

Next comes **Calafell** and its long strip of not very prepossessing seaside development under the old village and castle. The road then turns slightly inland to El Vendrell, where it joins N 340 and shortly curves down to the coast again. On the next strip there are two Roman monuments, foretastes of Tarragona. The plain

On the approach to Tarragona: the Torre dels Escipions,
a monument to the brothers Scipio, who resisted the
Carthaginians in the second Punic War.

Roman arch of Berà is actually on an island in the middle of the road. Not long after the Torre dels Escipions appears on the right, surrounded by a good deal of picnic filth and litter (unusual in

Catalonia). It consists of a large plinth with two mutilated figures of later date than the Scipios; there is no evidence that they were buried here. However, the monument does serve to remind us of Tarragona's foundation by Publius Cornelius Scipio in 218 BC during his advance from Empúries to the Ebro at the outset of the second Punic War, when he required a more southerly base from which to subjugate the tribes of the interior who supported the Carthaginians. Also, Tarraco had the makings of a better port than either Empúries or Barcelona. It was later elevated by Augustus to the rank of *colonia* and became the capital of the province of Hispania Citerior or Tarraconensis – throughout the Roman period it was a much more important place than Barcelona.

The road passes through Torredembarra and Altafulla, both of which possess castles and standard beach developments. The ramparts and cathedral tower of **Tarragona** rise into view some distance before the town. Aim for La Rambla Nova. No sooner have you parked and begun to circulate on foot than it is clear that this town is very different from Barcelona. Of course, it has in modern times been overtaken in size by the capital, but the more significant difference lies in its relationship with the sea. La Rambla, a very wide grand promenade, culminates in a *mirador* overlooking the sea, whose influence really permeates and freshens the whole town, whereas in Barcelona the sea seems to be an alien element and is largely ignored. The only time the Barcelonese seem to make contact with the sea is when they go to eat in the fish restaurants of Barceloneta, where they observe it from glassed-in verandahs. Columbus may be looking dramatically seawards from the foot of Las Ramblas but there is no sensation or smell of a great seaport. Here, by way of contrast, Roger de Llúria, the great corsair and national hero of the late thirteenth century, faces inland but the sea breezes blow around him and the youth of Tarragona flock to the base of his statue and along the parapet of the *mirador*. On the strip between the beach and the bluff on which Tarragona stands run the coast road and the railway, and you can see the modern port with its great mole and cranes. Usually there are several tankers or other vessels lying offshore. The whole feeling here is infinitely more maritime than in the capital; it is a great relief, quite literally a breather, to come here after the febrile late September festivities of the *Mercè* in Barcelona, when there does not seem to be enough air to go round (see 'Popular Culture'). The Hotel Residencia Lauria near the seaward end of La Rambla Nova is very agreeable and can be recommended.

Another noticeable difference is that the Tarragonese do not seem quite so earnestly Catalan; there is a good deal of Castilian spoken in the shops and streets, probably because Tarragona was a provincial capital under Franco and as such became home to functionaries speaking Castilian and expecting the same of local shopkeepers and traders. All the same, if you speak Castilian but only rudimentary Catalan it is quite a welcome experience to feel that you are not speaking a forbidden tongue. (However, in neighbouring Reus, a large bustling industrial town with a long textile tradition, the population is rabidly Catalan.)

I think chronological niceties should be preserved in Tarragona. There is such a Roman flavour here that you should resist being sucked immediately into the cathedral. In fact, the Roman pull exerts itself quite naturally. Immediately below the Passeig de les Palmeres at the end of La Rambla Nova are the remains of the amphitheatre. This was superbly sited to take advantage of the natural fall of the land down to the beach and its shape has been roughly reproduced with modern masonry. It is hard to understand, at any rate at first glance, exactly what purpose was served by the ruins still standing on the floor of the arena – were they cages for beasts, exits for gladiators, tanks for water battles? Then you suddenly realize that you are looking at the remnants of a quite large twelfth-century church, which replaced – so you learn – an earlier Visigothic one commemorating Sant Fructuós and his deacons Auguri and Eulogi, who were martyred here in AD 259. It is a rather curious experience, sitting here on the eastern rim of this ancient place of entertainment and laughter, blood and sacrifice, with the railway and coast road immediately below, the port cranes to the south and the tankers lying at anchor in the bay. The main hotel, the Imperial Tarraco, rises on the town side, its hemicycle cunningly following the contour of the amphitheatre, though its functionalist style leaves something to be desired. But altogether this is an unusual and suggestive urbscape which sums up Tarragona, past and present.

The next port of call is the archaeological museum (for archaeological read Roman) in a modern, purpose-built structure adjoining the Roman *praesidium*. On its outer walls it bears the large legend *Tarraco Scipionum Opus* on one side and *Colonia Julia Urbs Triumphalis Tarraco* on the other. The museum contains an important collection, as you might expect. There are mosaics from villas, often made by itinerant craftsmen (the craft of pebble mosaics, which are found in many of the resurfaced streets, thrives to this day). There are the usual vitrines with terra

Second-century bust of the Emperor Marcus Aurelius.

sigillata ware, oil lamps and so forth, but of special interest are the lead coffins and lead plumbing pipes and in particular the examples of refined bronzework: keys, nails, doorknobs and even needles. There is an impressive display of portrait and official sculpture, the latter much stimulated by the foundation of the monarchy in 26 BC and the demand for busts of the reigning god-emperor in every nook and cranny of his empire. There is also a section on Roman villas which reminds the visitor that these were not merely retreats for recreational purposes but important economic units producing crops, cattle and even industrial goods and including the cellars, stables, warehouses and other buildings necessary for these purposes; in some ways they foreshadow the economic activity of the monasteries (see 'Monasticism').

Next I would be inclined to cross the old town to the Passeig Arqueològic, which keeps museum hours. This means skirting the cathedral to the south. All the hotels and the local tourist office provide an excellent town plan. The streets in the old quarter follow those of the Roman town and most of the houses have very ancient foundations. As Ford remarks, 'The Roman inscriptions embedded here and elsewhere are so numerous that the walls are said to speak Latin.' The archaeological promenade provides a pleasant walk between the later outer defences and the walls of the citadel, whose dressed blocks of Roman sandstone are raised on enormous granite boulders said to be remnants of an earlier Iberian settlement. There are two or three openings in this primitive base of the wall bearing the legend *Puerta Ciclòpea*; these have hefty slabs as lintels and are attributed to the third century BC. The most prominent tower, the Torre de l'Arquebisbe, dates in its upper portions from the fourteenth century. There is an eighteenth-century salient with cannon and a Vaubanesque lookout point. Below the outer wall is the public garden, the Camp de Mart, with its modern statuary, including an extraordinary bronze of Wagner in the nude with a robe thrown over his knees like a bath-towel (Wagner was and still is extremely popular with the Barcelona bourgeoisie – see Palau de la Música, Barcelona, pp.66–7). The exit from the promenade is located at the north angle of the great wall, whence you can re-enter the old town by an arch in the Passeig de Sant Antoni or continue round the rest of the wall, coming back full circle to the archaeological museum.

The other principal Roman remains are the aqueduct and the forum. The Pont del Diable (the Devil's Bridge), as the aqueduct came to be called in popular parlance, is five kilometres out on the road to Lleida and should certainly be seen whether you are proceeding in that direction or not; it comprises two tiers 26 metres high and 217 metres long and was built in the second century. The main forum was located in the lower town; it has been excavated and, though there is little left standing, the descriptive signs give a good idea of the layout and the various activities which took place in it. You are still, I am afraid, not quite let off the Roman hook, because there is an important intermediate step to the flowering of Christianity, which is quite excellently portrayed in the Museu i Necròpolis Paleocristiana in the middle of later industrial developments on the bank of the river Francolí. It was the building of the tobacco factory that brought this site to light. Here, in the third century, were buried Fructuós, Auguri and Eulogi, the martyrs of the amphitheatre, and in all more than two thousand tombs were unearthed, ranging from *tegulae* (flimsy little constructions of brick and tile) through common ditches, wooden coffins and clay urns to lead, stone and marble sarcophagi imported from Italy. The humbler tombs can be seen *in situ*, preserved under corrugated canopies by courtesy of the tobacco company (an early instance of cultural sponsorship by a commercial firm). The museum contains the grander sarcophagi and some very interesting mosaic coffin lids. The point of this visit is to gain a privileged insight into the continuity between late Christianized Roman culture and the fragile flame that continued to flicker through the Dark Ages in such places as Terrassa (see pp.62–4). Later it was fanned into new achievements and new ambitions by the empire of Charlemagne, from which sprang both pre-Romanesque and fully Romanesque architecture. It was all part of the same chain and this museum reveals an important link.

With this in mind it is now appropriate to visit the cathedral. The Visigoths made Tarragona the seat of a bishopric and here Saint Hermengild was martyred by his father King Leovigild for espousing the Roman rather than the Arian faith, which was then the official Visigothic cult. Not long afterwards King Reccared was converted to Rome. The Moors sacked Tarragona and then abandoned it; it became a no man's land between Christianity and Islam until the end of the eleventh century. In 1118 it was granted by Ramon Berenguer III to the Norman adventurer Robert Burdet, but it was not until 1171 that a new cathedral was begun. It is now hemmed in by both earlier and later buildings. The best approach is from the oblong Plaça de la Font (with the decently imposing, but not ostentatious town hall) up the Carrer Major, which affords a narrow gunsight view of the west front. The steps are steep but not operatic as at Girona. Above the portico is a superb decorated rose window. The central column of the divided doorway is graced by a very beautiful Virgin and Child surrounded by a good flanking cast of saints and worthies. The pity is that the pinnacles of this façade were never completed, while the broken gable looks positively dangerous (this neglect is surprising in view of the number of good architects in the restoration trade in Spain).

As I have indicated, the church is rather difficult to see and appreciate fully from the outside. On the north it has been encircled by the perfectly respectable early nineteenth-century bishop's palace. The clearest available view of the tower and lantern is from the cloister. It is therefore best to enter through the cloister (tickets are available at the gate), as you are obliged to do unless you happen to coincide with a service. Once inside, it is immediately apparent that despite the Gothic west front this is essentially a Romanesque – or pointed Romanesque – building. I am not an uncritical devotee of the grand Norman/Romanesque style, which had to be superseded, if only to pave the way for the

Cloister, apse, lantern and belfry of Tarragona cathedral.

glories of mature Gothic; I only wish to emphasize that it was a long, slow, painful process for the thoroughly Romanized Iberian peninsula to escape from its Roman heritage. (See also 'Romanesque' and 'Gothic Art and Architecture'.)

This is, then, yet another grand example of the transitional style, whose ground plan is in every respect Romanesque. There is no ambulatory and the main apse is severe within and fortified without. All the main structural arches – crossing, nave and aisle arcade – are pointed but of heavy square section, deriving from the barrel vault. The capitals have Romanesque decoration, though this becomes more perfunctory as you move west and there are some structural advances, notably in the octagonal ribbed lantern over the crossing. The massive piers also have the welcome addition of a stone bench running round their bases.

There are some good interior fittings. The choir, of fine late Gothic workmanship, has the virtue of not being closed off at the west end. There is a single row of stalls on either side of the nave with two tiers in the *capella major*. The main apse is partitioned by a splendid retable of 1426–34 with an elaborate predella of scenes from the life of Saint Tecla in painted and gilded alabaster: you are shown graphically how fire failed to consume her or lions to devour her. The tremendous pinnacles crowning the main figures of the retable rise almost to the vault. The alabaster altar frontal beneath dates from the late Romanesque period. The side chapels are of various periods, ranging from the fourteenth century to high baroque. They contain, among other things, three painted Gothic retables whose quality is hard to judge through the protective grilles. The *tresor* (treasure) consists of large monstrances, vestment chests and some tapestries. The museum off the cloister contains nothing of vast interest, though there are three painted woodcarvings of the Virgin which aptly illustrate the progression of Romanesque polychrome sculpture through three phases: in the first the Child is standing hieratically, in the second he is seated on his mother's knee and in the third he is finally humanized to the extent of stretching up to suckle at her breast. This is the prelude to the tender fourteenth century.

The large cloister communicates with the church by a particularly fine mature Romanesque doorway with God the Father and the symbols of the four Evangelists in the tympanum. The cloister itself employs a rather successful design of triplets of rounded arches contained within slightly recessed pointed panels; each panel has two round windows above the arches and – eager for evidence of Moorish influence in these more southerly climes – I was delighted to find the little polylobulated blind arcade immediately under the eaves. The southern arm of the cloister is really the best point from which to appreciate the pleasing relationship of tower, lantern and apse, which is obscured from most other viewpoints. Skirting the church on the outside, I was struck by the warlike aspect of the main apse, by two smaller Romanesque apse protuberances indicating an original five-apse plan and by the old doorway under the bell tower. Outside the west front children use the portico as a football goal, but the Virgin and Child who are right in the line of fire on the centre column seem quite unperturbed.

In the immediate vicinity of Tarragona are the impressive castle and church of **Tamarit** on a promontory over the sea. The beach has been taken over by ultra-efficient German and Dutch campers with powerful cars and caravans, whose tented extensions have all the commodities of a living room. But their settlement is discreet and this is not a bad place to bathe. There is a (non-shanty) restaurant right on the beach. The locals seem to prefer **Salou**, further south, despite the proximity of industrial and chemical plants and the tanker jetty. The tourist end of the bay has an extremely long and hot esplanade of young palms which made me yearn for the mature trees and more domestic scale of the seafront at Sitges. But Salou is an old port with some claim to fame, as it was from here in 1229 that the conquerors of Majorca set out.

Signs on the way out of Tarragona signal the monasteries of Poblet and Santes Creus. Certainly the latter is reached very quickly and easily from Tarragona and Poblet is not far distant. But the great Cistercian trio is incomplete without Vallbona de les Monges and I think a base further inland and nearer all three is desirable. Montblanc or Valls will serve but both are rather raucous towns with poor lodgings. My preference is for Santes Creus itself, which can be used as a delightfully quiet base for the other two. For the moment, however, I was determined to push on to the southernmost rim of Catalonia to see whether *catalanisme* was as pronounced where the culture had been exposed for much longer than in the north to corrupting Moorish influences. Also, it seemed fitting to postpone the pantheon of the monarchs of the Aragonese–Catalan confederation at Poblet to the very end of my tour.

From Tarragona southwards for a long stretch the carob is king, shouldering out even the ancient olive on the hillside terraces. To the west runs the not very high but nonetheless forbidding chain formed by the Serres de la Creu, de Montalt and de la Pedrera. The coastal plain is rough and stony and the coastline is mainly rocky with small pools and coves. The first appealing town is **Amposta**, a pleasant old place on the south bank of the Ebro and capital of the *comarca* of Montsià. Here you meet the great green river, some three hundred yards wide at this point, for the first time. If you want to get a smell of the delta, which is quite a little world of its own, a pleasant circuit can be made by recrossing the river over the modern castellated bridge at Amposta and taking the first right for Deltebre and La Cava.

Rice is the great crop of the delta, which is one of the main ricebowls of Spain. The road runs through paddy fields criss-crossed by irrigation channels; round the villages are market gardens specializing in artichokes. At **La Cava** there is a *transbordador*, as the signs indicate; this is an expertly manoeuvred steel raft which will bring you back to the south bank and thus to

Sant Jaume d'Enveja. From here, instead of following the river back to Amposta, the more adventurous may care to zig-zag their way across the delta to Sant Carles de la Ràpita. Ask for directions in Sant Jaume. Castilian serves as a lingua franca but the delta folk are *catalanoparlants* to a man– with a Valencian accent. I am reliably informed that the difference is no greater than, say, Yorkshire is from southern English, though each sub-region tends to stress the differences out of local patriotism. Madrid too has tended to play up minor linguistic differences in order to weaken the movement for a Greater Catalonia (see also 'Catalan Language'). There is no doubt, however, as to how deeply rooted the language is here: Catalan is the language of the schools; Castilian is not taught except as literature.

Weaving across the paddy fields (and steering by the sun when in doubt), I saw great piles of brown rice being cleaned and sifted in the open air. With a bit of luck and a few more friendly directions I emerged at **Sant Carles de la Ràpita**, as it is called these days. It was founded as San Carlos de la Rábida by that zealous improver, Charles III, who envisaged a great seaport within the protective arm of the sandbank running south from the delta. This never developed as anticipated but Sant Carles, attractively situated under the Serra de Montsià, is a serious Mediterranean fishing port, with boats of all sizes, from trawlers tied up along the mole to smaller craft on the mud flats; there is also a small yacht basin and marina. Sant Carles will leave you in no doubt of the aggressiveness of the Spanish fishing industry. A good fish lunch in an authentic setting may be had at any of the several restaurants down on the port. *Catalanitat* is evidenced by such delightful street names as Carrer Xicago, which makes Chicago sound positively Mexican.

If you want to stay within modern Catalonia, you must leave the main Valencia road some ten kilometres south of Sant Carles and head for Alcanar, which is only two kilometres inside the so-called border (there were in fact customs between Castile and Aragon-Catalonia in the eighteenth century to protect the Castilian markets from being plundered by adroit Catalan salesmen). From Alcanar the road climbs a little to descend on **Ulldecona**, which has a church that exemplifies to perfection, if not on a grand scale, the main achievement of Catalan Gothic, the covering of a considerable space with a single vault, dispensing with aisles and rounding the interior off with a graceful semi-circular east end where tall windows are separated by finny ribs. In all these buildings there is evidence of the democratic Catalan urge to suppress the recesses and shadows and mysteries associated with earlier church architecture by creating a type of hall church without barriers between the priesthood and the people (see 'Gothic Art and Architecture').

La Sénia, right on the border of Catalonia with the likewise autonomous community of Valencia, has a church very similar to Ulldecona's in inspiration, though it is probably somewhat older and has subsequently been reconstructed on the inside. This is a strange sprawling place under the grey escarpment of the Serralades de Benifassà, which seems to have experienced a short-lived burst of Catalan industrial development. Catalan is again spoken here with a Valencian accent.

Leaving for Tortosa, it is well worth taking the higher road via Mas de Barberans, which passes through a great expanse of ancient olives, some of which must be centuries old with their split trunks, gnarled stems and open crowns; many of them are as large as holm oaks. A fine crop was hanging from the branches in September. **Mas de Barberans** is a plain village under a mini-Montserrat range of mountains, the Serra dels Ports. It affords a terrific view over the olive groves and orchards which stretch as far as the eye can see into the old kingdom of Valencia.

Tortosa on the Ebro was a strongpoint in Roman, Visigothic and Moorish times. It was the seat of a splinter kingdom or *taifa* from the collapse of the caliphate of Córdoba until its recapture by Ramon Berenguer IV in 1148. The southern fringe of Catalonia thus missed the two or three centuries of relatively peaceful Christian development enjoyed by the north. On the castle hill there are the remnants of fortifications of various periods, but the building of greatest interest is the cathedral, immediately beneath the citadel on a site formerly occupied by a mosque.

The present cathedral was begun in 1347. Behind the incongruous baroque front lies a fully mature Gothic church with no transitional traces at all. The piers are slender and delicately modulated at the base; the capitals are vestigial; the engaged columns and vaulting ribs fly upwards without let or hindrance; and the main arches supporting the vault are no longer of heavy square section as at Tarragona but are slimly moulded. Although the aisles have not been suppressed as at Girona, they are high and well lit and still allow for clerestory windows over the nave. The double ambulatory is particularly beautiful: there are altars against the inner wall of the lower outer arcade but this has not been subdivided into box-like chapels and you can circulate freely both on the inner and outer circles. The decorated tracery behind

*Roof and buttresses of Tortosa cathedral;
in the background the Ebro nears its estuary.*

*Tortosa cathedral's baroque façade, one of
the few examples of the style in Catalonia.*

the high altar is very fine. Though farthest from France, this is, curiously, the most French of the cathedrals of Catalonia.

The interior fittings are rather sparse, no doubt as a result of the ravages of both the Peninsular War and the Civil War, when the Ebro divided the two sides for a year. There are no choir stalls. But the two fifteenth-century stone pulpits, which have largely escaped mutilation, are worthy of note: the one on the left has bas-reliefs of the four Evangelists, each busily writing his gospel, with his symbol at his shoulder or knee (see p.46) – Saint Mark's lion seems to be disagreeing with his master's text. On the right-hand pulpit are the four Doctors of the Church: Saints Gregory, Jerome, Ambrose and Augustine. The large baroque chapel of the Mare de Déu de la Cinta contains an object of great veneration, a belt popularly believed to have belonged to the Virgin Mary. In the adjacent bay is a carved font or basin which apparently belonged to the schismatic Pope Benedict XIII, otherwise Pedro Martínez de Luna (1328–1422), whose extraordinary life and enforced retirement to Peñíscola are so well described by Blasco Ibáñez in *El Papa del Mar*. Between the westernmost pair of nave piers is a fine High Renaissance iron screen or *reja*, which effectively turns the first bay of the church into a sort of narthex.

The small cloister with its very pointed arches seems rather plain after the great Romanesque cloisters and their elaborate capitals crowded with grotesque figures and biblical scenes, though it scores a point from me for its two sundials, now rather overshadowed by cypresses. Ironically the cathedral's west front (1705–57), one of the most ambitious attempts in Spain at a grand baroque façade, is completely wasted on the eye owing to the continued existence of a block of older buildings between itself and the river. Only a broad flight of steps to the river front could have given it the space it requires. Do not be deterred, incidentally, by its forbiddingly shut doors: access except on high days and holidays is through the cloister.

The bishop's palace, which is partly responsible for cramping the west front, has a fine fourteenth-century doorway with radial slabs and a good staircase. There is not much else to see in the lower town, though there are other façades of a similar stamp; the church of Sant Dómenec and the college of Sants Jaume i Mateu, founded during the reign of Charles V, both have plateresque entrances, a style not much in evidence in Catalonia, presumably because the Catalans found it too fussy, inclined as they are towards the plain and grand. Rising from a pier in the middle of the river is a monument redolent of General Franco's era – eagle, fasces, cross, angel, star – and dedicated 'to the combatants who found glory in the battle of the Ebro'. That could of course be interpreted to include both sides, but the style and symbolism leave little doubt, as Michelin remarks, that it 'commemorates the Nationalist victory'. Unusually for Catalonia, Tortosa is a rather dirty run-down town with beggars and gypsies; there is nowhere really to stay except the Parador Nacional installed in the castle. This is, however, splendidly sited with a superb view up the Ebro valley and across to the mountain system comprising the Serres dels Ports, d'Espina, de Paüls and de Pàndols, which mark the south-westernmost limit of the region ruled by the Generalitat. Although the drive up requires a detour, the Parador is located directly above the cathedral, which can easily be reached on foot by an alley called Carrer del Castell. If you are reluctant to pay the price of a Parador dinner, there is a good fish restaurant, the San Carlos, almost on the junction of the ascent to the castle with the riverside road.

If you intend to follow the Ebro upstream, you can take either the east (in local terms left) or west (right) bank. If you have the time and inclination, a complete circuit can be made from Tortosa to Móra d'Ebre on one side and then back via Gandesa and Xerta on the other; otherwise I think the left bank is the more rewarding. The other road does indeed follow the river as far as Xerta but then it enters a series of *barrancos* (ravines) through the *serres* towards Gandesa and the river is lost.

The left-bank route makes a very pleasant drive through lemon groves and peach orchards to **Tivenys**, a modest and friendly little village which, rightly confident of fine weather until the end of September, celebrates its *feria* (fair) on the last Sunday of the month. The road then veers up into the Serra de Cardó, with more magnificent views over the Ebro basin. There really is no need for mapmakers to mark panoramic vistas or scenic routes in these parts: they are the rule rather than the exception. And do not be misled by the usually reliable Roger Lascelles 1:300,000 regarding a bridge over the river to Miravet – there is none. There is indeed a ferry but it is not very active and I failed to locate the ferryman. You have to continue to Ginestar d'Ebre and thence to Móra la Nova before coming across the next bridge. But nothing is lost for everything is pleasing to look at and it suddenly occurred to me that the Ebro valley is the Andalusia of Catalonia. The analogy should not be pushed too far, but there are all sorts of reminiscences here of the deep south of the peninsula. The olive and the vine are the most obvious ones – indeed, there are more and better vines up here than in Andalusia (excepting Jerez, San Lúcar and Montilla) and I was particularly struck by the marvellous pruning of the olives, which open their crowns to the sun and direct their loaded branches downwards for easier harvesting. Here I think the Catalans have tended to persevere with the cultivation of this crop because the land is too rugged for any other, whereas those Andalusians with less than top-grade trees have tended to convert quickly, with government inducements, to other types of monoculture, in particular to sunflowers and cereals. The similarities between the two regions also include the pomegranate and even the prickly pear, and there are geraniums in painted tins. The biggish villages – of two or three thousand souls – with their baroque churches likewise recall the labourers' villages on the rim of the Guadalquivir plain. There are, however, significant differences. There is little or no whitewash in these parts; the villages are brown, ochre, grey, orange – the natural colours of brick and stone. And the great green serpentine river, swollen like a python by lakes and dams, is a mightier stream than the Guadalquivir.

I turned south via Benissanet and Miravet towards Gandesa. **Miravet** has a large ruined Templar fortress-monastery, erected shortly after the town's recapture by Ramon Berenguer IV in 1153; it became an important strongpoint of the new frontier. Today the crumbling village is again very Andalusian: somnolent dogs and lizard-eyed men at the café tables watch the world go by. **Gandesa**, at the junction of several roads, features a church with a geometrical Romanesque doorway, though most of the interior has received the baroque treatment. It also has a wine co-operative in the Modernist style (see 'Modernisme'). There is a good roadhouse on the road to Móra, the Piqué, which offers an excellent cuisine and is patronized by local gourmets. Try the partridges in season but beware the local white wine, which has an alcoholic content of fourteen per cent.

From Gandesa I went via Bot to **Horta de Sant Joan**, an old fortified village in the hills with an arcaded *plaça* and warren-like streets; the corners of the buildings make angles impossible for the motorist. A Templar outpost was established here in 1197 as part of the order's line of fortress-monasteries along the Ebro. More recently, Picasso came here with his friend Pallarès in 1898 and stayed for eight months, living for some of the time in a cave. It is said that the artist's paintings and drawings were thought by the locals to be the works of the devil, but the small rural scenes on board of this period, now housed in the Museu Picasso in

Barcelona, are unlikely to have excited this reaction. Now Horta claims proudly that the arcaded *plaça* inspired Picasso's first Cubist painting, disregarding the fact that he did not return until the summer of 1909 and his Cubist period is generally held to have started with *Les Demoiselles d'Avignon* in 1907. At all events, they have dedicated a street to his memory and the whole place is very picturesque in the conventional sense of the word. Other artists followed Picasso, notably Miró, who painted here in 1917. Impressively sited under a great fang of rock facing the town is the monastery of Sant Salvador d'Horta. The drive back to Gandesa via Prats de Comte is memorable for its dramatic crags and fragrant pines.

Between Gandesa and the Serra de la Fatarella to the north-west stretches an undulating expanse of vineyards which produce some of the region's potent wine. But Gandesa has a more serious claim to fame: two kilometres outside the town on the road that winds into the wine district stood General Franco's command post during the battle of the Ebro in 1938. The Republic had advanced across the river in the hope of drawing off the main Nationalist thrust towards Valencia. The offensive failed owing to lack of supplies and air cover, and the Republican army was pinned down in its trenches for four months; sixty thousand men died. The locals take a macabre relish in telling visitors that ironically Franco's headquarters was located on the site of an Iberian necropolis. The village of **Corbera**, four kilometres along the road to Móra, is still largely a ruin and the church a mere shell, as it received much of the brunt of the Nationalist shelling from Gandesa and the Republican response from Móra d'Ebre. Here in Gandesa veterans congregate every year to commemorate the battle, among them Americans from the Abraham Lincoln Brigade.

After Gandesa I wanted to get back to the river, so I took the left fork at Les Camposines leading up to Ascó and Flix. The former is not of great interest but **Flix** has unexpectedly large chemical and hydroelectric plants and both towns have railway stations, for they are on the main line from Barcelona to Madrid – so you may see the Talgo, Spain's superexpress, whizzing through the rocky terrain. Above Flix is **Riba-roja d'Ebre**, a quiet old town whose church has a good provincial baroque portico of 1772 (well after the arbiters of taste had decreed the dawn of neo-classicism). Ask in the *plaça* for La Penya, a *mirador* overlooking the railway and river. Here the Ebro emerges from one of its python bulges where it has been joined, a little further upstream, by the Segre, which I followed from La Seu d'Urgell to Balaguer. From this vantage point I had the satisfying sensation of having encompassed most of Catalonia, for the Catalan nation is cradled on the west by an arc of rivers, starting with the Noguera Ribagorçana rising high in the Pyrenees and feeding into the Segre, which then descends through Lleida and in its turn feeds into the mighty river along whose course so much Spanish history has been made and so much Spanish blood spilt.

Returning to Ascó, you can cross the river and take a good road that hugs the east bank via Garcia to Móra la Nova, whence the main road to Reus and Tarragona runs through a further large expanse of vines, some terraced up on to the hillsides. **Falset** is another old porticoed town, capital of the vinous *comarca* of the Priorat. The deep reds are rightly called black; the whites have a not unpleasant smoky or earthy flavour but like those of Gandesa they are high in alcoholic content and should be treated with respect. The towns and villages hereabouts – Falset, Pradell, Les Borges del Camp, Mont-roig – are rust and ochre in colour, rising out of the landscape almost like natural outcrops, distinguished and defined mainly by their octagonal church towers. It was to **Mont-roig** that Miró was drawn back from Paris almost every summer between 1920 and 1932 (see 'Modern Art').

At Les Borges del Camp I turned up into the Serra de Montsant with the object of approaching the monastery of Poblet by this route. **Alforja**, as its name implies in both Castilian and Catalan, was an ancient centre of the saddlebag trade. Cornudella and Ulldemolins follow the general style of villages in these parts. **Prades** has a particularly pleasing square and fountain (the latter reproduced in the Poble Espanyol in Barcelona – see p.53) and an old gateway and church of rose-coloured stone. The mountain system formed by the Serres de Montsant and Roquerola is a maze of spines and spurs which are tree-clad almost to the summits. Here you will find pine, chestnut, carob, ash, oak scrub and wild olive. If you think of Spain in general terms as barren, you should remember how densely wooded is much of Catalonia. And so down to **Poblet**. If evening is closing in, there are a number of hostelries within a mile or so of the monastery; and also in the town of **L'Espluga de Francolí**, where the Hostal del Senglar is the best.

The royal monastery of Poblet, rising below the tortuous *serres* and overlooking the Conca de Barberà, another *comarca* rich in vines, has all the amplitude of a grand, rich foundation. From the days of Alfons the Chaste (1162–96) onwards it was favoured by most of the count-kings of Aragon-Catalonia as their final resting place and it was designated definitively by Peter the Ceremonious (1336–87) as pantheon of the royal family. Through the first gatehouse lie several dependencies. The chapel of Sant Jordi stands just outside the next gateway, where tickets are now sold; the thirteenth-century church of Santa Caterina is just within the main forecourt on the left. Then the whole long multiple façade comes into view: the Renaissance church entrance under an old rose window, two fourteenth-century machicolated towers further to the left marking the entrance to the palace, two watch-towers and the two lanterns of the church itself. This has all the

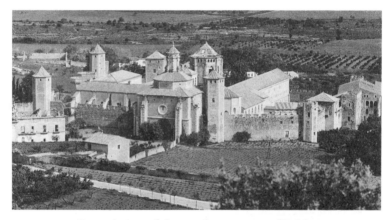

General view of the royal monastery of Poblet.

stamp of that special mix of fortress-palace-monastery beloved of Spanish monarchs, whether Castilian or Catalan (the Escorial and Guadalupe, though of very different periods, immediately spring to mind). Ford's romantic attribution of the word 'Poblet' to the name of a hermit imprisoned by a Moorish emir but set free on three occasions by angels is no longer taken seriously; Father Agustí, the present archivist, opts more sensibly for the derivation from *populetum* (poplar grove).

The foundation dates from 1151; the church was begun in the following decade. Immediately inside the west door is a narthex, which is followed by seven bays of slightly pointed arches of square section as far as the crossing. The arcades between the aisles and the nave are likewise slightly pointed but framed in larger round-headed panels containing the clerestory windows. The capitals, of Romanesque profile, are completely plain. The aisles are more pointed than the nave and have rounded vaulting ribs. They connect across the transepts with the ambulatory but a great plateresque alabaster retable now partly obscures this. Considerably hacked about in its lower sections, this is otherwise fairly intact and extremely impressive in its way with a delightful Virgin and Child as centrepiece, but like other 'improvements' undertaken under Charles V, who knocked down part of the Alhambra to make way for his Renaissance palace, it is completely inappropriate for its setting and ruins the effect the steeply pointed ambulatory arcade would otherwise have made. If you arrive in the evening, there is a good chance of hearing the Cistercian community of some thirty monks singing vespers in the great church, to which they returned in 1940 after more than a century in the wilderness.

To see the rest of the monastery you must join a guided tour, which starts from the palace entrance. The cloister is beautiful.

Poblet's fourteenth-century cloister and pavilion.

Off it open the old kitchen, the refectory, the library and the fine chapter house, on all of which the multilingual guide will dilate informatively. But it is the cloister itself that should detain you. What is remarkable is the successful combination of Romanesque capitals with Gothic tracery filling the arcades (rivalled only by the grand cloister of La Seu Vella at Lleida – see pp.148–9); there is also a charming octagonal pavilion with a basin and fountain on the north side of the quadrangle. There is a good deal of new carving owing to depredations but the overall effect is magnificent. When Ford saw the monastery it had recently been abandoned. 'The mitred abbot, purple as his wines, reigned in Palatinate pomp', he tells us, but 'in the recent reforms, July 24, 1835, he and his monks fled; then the axe felled his fruit trees and the torch fired his cells; ruin and robbery have since been the order of the day and the glories of Poblet are past. . .' (Eighteen thirty-five marked the beginning of the famous *desamortización* – disentailment – of the monasteries by Mendizábal to pay the national debt and provide the government with some ready cash from the sale of the monastic lands, a reformation three centuries behind our own.)

The royal tombs, as seen today, are the result of a superb job of restoration. As Ford informs us, 'The ashes of the lines of kings cast to the wind were in part collected by a local curate named Sorret and removed to the cloister of the cathedral at Tarragona.' In 1952 they were returned with such fragments of the tombs as had been preserved, which were ingeniously reconstructed by the sculptor Frederic Marès to form the impressive gabled sepulchres raised on shallow arches on either side of the crossing of the church. This arrangement faithfully reproduces the plan of Peter the Ceremonious, so superior in my view to the claustrophobic subterranean mausoleum later built for the royal house of Spain at the Escorial.

A curious feature picked up by Ford is that some of the royal personages appear twice, that is to say with effigies on both sides of the gabled lid of their sepulchre. This is the case, on the north side, with James I (the Conqueror), who is carved on one face as a soldier and on the other as a monk, having taken the habit a few days before he died after a reign of sixty-three years. Ferdinand of Antequera, the first Castilian-born king of Aragon (d. 1416) also has two effigies. His wife Leonor of Albuquerque is included only because Ferdinand the Catholic believed her remains to be here, whereas they are actually in Medina del Campo. On the south side, John II (d. 1479), father of Ferdinand the Catholic, is again shown twice; so is Alfons the Chaste (d. 1196), as both soldier and monk. As Ford acutely observes:

This is truly characteristic of the mediaeval Spaniard, half-soldier, half-monk, a crusading knight of Santiago; his manhood spent in combating for the cross, his declining years dedicated to religion. No country has ever produced more instances of kings retiring to the cloister nor of soldiers resigning the sword for the crucifix, and washing off the blood from their hands, making their peace with God after a life of battle for his cause.

Whatever else may divide Castile and Catalonia, there is at least a common trait here. The guidebooks on sale at the bookstall identify each monarch and queen on a useful plan. What might cause some surprise is the homogeneity of the carved images of rulers who spanned more than three centuries; apparently Peter the Ceremonious had new likenesses made of his predecessors and those who succeeded him in the next century followed the same style. Senyor Marès did the rest.

Curious though these details may be, it seems in some way inadequate to treat the royal tombs merely as objects of antiquarian or archaeological interest, when their occupants had such a tremendous effect on the fortunes of Aragon-Catalonia. The dynastic intricacies and rivalries which put an end to the trans-Pyrenean ambitions of the house of Barcelona, the agreement that Murcia would fall within the Castilian zone of the reconquest, thus terminating Catalan expansion on the mainland, and Catalonia's consequent yearning for a Mediterranean empire based on communications by sea – these developments moulded the whole thrust of Catalan and Aragonese political objectives for several centuries and, when the Mediterranean dream fell apart, Castile was left very much the master in the peninsula. (For a fuller discussion of this topic see the Introduction.)

Among the other things to see at Poblet is an enormous dormitory which accommodated some two hundred monks in the monastery's heyday; this connects by a flight of steps directly with the main crossing of the church; the same arrangement is also found at Santes Creus. The upper level of the cloister no longer exists but you pass by way of the roof of the lower arcade into the palace built by Martin the Humane (1396–1410) for his retirement. This is underpinned by a huge cellar and now contains on the upper floor a museum detailing the process of restoration. Poblet requires a whole morning or afternoon.

Just down the road from L'Espluga de Francolí, going towards Valls, is, to use Ford's words, 'the decayed town of Montblanch, pop 4,000, with its old walls, towers and four gates'. Though its population has only increased to 5,200 or so, **Montblanc** – which has dropped the Castilian *h* along with other towns like Vic – is now a bustling place, where I found tractor drivers queueing to weigh in their share of the grape harvest on the scales of the wine co-operative before tipping their loads into great communal vats. Montblanc is also busily rebuilding those stretches of its wall which have fallen down since Ford's time, apparently in an attempt to rival Avila. The main church boasts a splendid example of an aisle-free Catalan vault with a radial east end, which is attributed to the Englishman Reinard Fonoll (or Raynard Fonoyll), who worked on the cloister at Santes Creus and appears to have imported the English decorated style into Catalonia.

From Montblanc I headed for Vallbona de les Monges, which I could have visited from further north but had preferred to reserve for inclusion in the Cistercian Triangle, where it belongs historically. There is no need to group the Cistercian foundations together in this way; you may find it more convenient to make the shorter detour from either Les Borges Blanques or Bellpuig d'Urgell. The route from Montblanc passes over the Lleida–Tarragona autoroute to La Guàrdia dels Prats and thence via Solivella and Rocallaura to the monastery.

Vallbona de les Monges has been continuously occupied by Cistercian nuns since its foundation in 1157 – an astonishing record. It is much smaller than its two great male contemporaries and, being rather more off the beaten track and less visited, it is a place of great tranquillity whose main business in life is prayer. The cloister is curious in that all four arms are different: the one

The church lantern and the irregularly designed cloister at Vallbona de les Monges.

farthest from the church where the entrance is situated is very simple twelfth-century Romanesque; the eastern arm is later Romanesque featuring triplets of arches under wheel-shaped windows and capitals that sprout pine cones; along the flank of the church the arcade is decorated Gothic; while the most recent, fifteenth-century addition is the archaic western arm, presumably designed to tone in with the Romanesque work facing it. The chapter house with its splendid Gothic double doors contains tombs of the abbesses let into the floor; they are shown on the lids complete with mitre and staff, just like the mitred abbots in the male monasteries. They were no doubt as formidable.

The church has an aisleless nave which contains the nuns' choir. The vaulting arches and ribs are sharply pointed, rising from brackets rather than columns or pilasters. The arches of the crossing, which is earlier than the nave, are slightly pointed and crowned by a later lantern raised on squinches. The nuns are very proud of the octagonal lantern which lights the church and makes a grand effect outside in conjunction with the lower and likewise octagonal belfry; they claim that neither Poblet nor Santes Creus produced anything as impressive. On one side of the chancel is the tomb of Violante of Hungary, second wife of James the Conqueror, and on the other that of their daughter Sancha. There are more abbesses' tombs in the floor of the nave. The entrance for local churchgoers is by the fine Romanesque portico in the north transept; the Virgin of the Rose of Jericho – a manifestation previously unknown to me – is supported in the tympanum by an angel on either side. Although Vallbona is less grand than its masculine counterparts, it has a potent air of continuity. It never succumbed to the French; it should not be missed.

From Vallbona I drove back to Solivella, where I turned left and then right to Sarral. This land between the Serres de Tallat and de Roquerola is the Conca de Barberà, which gives its name to the *comarca*; it is indeed a corrugated conch whose little spines and cols are topped with pine copses and whose declivities are filled with a profusion of vines. From Sarral you continue south via Pla de Santa Maria (passing twice under the motorway) to the crossing just outside Vila-rodona, where the final leg to **Santes Creus** is clearly marked.

This monastery enjoys, I think, the most charming setting of the three. The single-street village is flanked by a leafy walk and vineyards; little market gardens fringe the monastic walls. The immediate approach, through a large baroque gateway leading into an oblong *plaça* dedicated to Saint Bernard and surrounded by ex-monastic dependencies (now ordinary dwellings), is also delightful. The latter are all decorated with *esgrafiado* or stencilled white patterns, some geometrical, others floral, in pleasing contrast to the severe castellated west front of the church. On the right at No. 1 was the abbot's lodge with its tiny Gothic cloister.

You enter through the main cloister. It is evident that from early times there was rivalry between Poblet and Santes Creus, whose founder and patrons carried slightly less clout. Certainly the two foundations strove mightily in their cloisters to outshine

Gothic cloister at Santes Creus –
the pavilion is a forerunner of Poblet's

each other. The Englishman Fonoll was brought in to build the south arm here (1331–41) and in a sense this early fourteenth-century cloister is 'purer' than Poblet's: the slender columns are fully Gothic with small scrolled or floral capitals while some of the capitals of the larger piers, particularly at the entrance to the octagonal pavilion, exhibit a new exuberance, a taste for popular scenes such as the vintage, which is normally absent from the more geometrical or iconographic Romanesque decoration. Here there is no lack of humorous or grotesque figures and the atmosphere conveys more of an urge to celebrate than to instruct. You are in the more cheerful world which immediately preceded the dreadful scourge of the Black Death.

The octagonal pavilion or *templete* with basin and fountain is a feature of the grander mediaeval cloisters and was probably inspired, if unconsciously, by the fountains in the courts of ablution of the mosques, which they very often replaced. Here the pavilion is earlier than the rest of the cloister; it may have served as a model for Poblet's – which is more elegant, however. Opening off this cloister is the rebuilt chapter house with tombs of the mitred abbots let into the floor like those of their brethren at Poblet and their sisters at Vallbona. There is a second, older cloister called the Posterior owing to its location towards the rear of the church. This gives access to the cellar, kitchen, refectory and, in the far corner, the royal apartments. The latter are on a much more modest scale than at Poblet but conserve a delicate Gothic staircase and first-floor gallery.

And so into the church. The interior is markedly different from Poblet's. The slightly pointed nave vault is carried on arches of very wide square section, projected by pilasters on rolled supports about ten feet above the floor – rather than from columns as at Poblet or from brackets as at Vallbona. The huge piers are thus plain and rectangular without clusters of columns, relieved only by the pilasters and their own indented corners. The rounded arches opening from the nave into the aisles are also of square section; the ribs of the nave and aisles are likewise square, in contrast with the slightly shaky ribs of circular profile at Poblet, which do not always join at quite the right places. There is no ambulatory. The rectangular east end is extended on each side by transepts, so that the church of Santes Creus, or Holy Crosses, is appropriately shaped like a Latin cross. The fine rose window is partly obscured by the retable. Each transept has two chapels along the east wall. As at Poblet a flight of steps leads up from the body of the church to the great dormitory. The general effect, which is very grand, is of greater austerity and solemnity.

In terms of royal sepulchres Santes Creus scores fewer points than Poblet, largely because Peter the Ceremonious arrogantly decreed that all his successors must be buried with him at Poblet on pain of their vassals' refusal to swear allegiance. Prior to the union of the two states, the kings of Aragon were buried at San Juan de la Peña, high in the Pyrenees, and the counts of Barcelona at Ripoll. It was Alfons the Chaste, the first count-king of the federation, who chose Poblet for himself, possibly to avoid wounding the susceptibilities of either half of his domains. But it was not until the decision of Peter the Ceremonious that Poblet became the Escorial of the royal line. In the meantime, two monarchs had preferred Santes Creus. On the north side of the

*The church and lantern from the arcaded cloister walk
at Santes Creus.*

crossing, in a carved and painted stone casket, raised on a strange
sort of porphyry urn or bath, which rests in its turn on a pair of
antique Mesopotamian lions, lies Peter the Great (1276–85). The
tomb is enclosed in a pavilion of Gothic tracery and let into the
floor; immediately beside it is the resting place of the corsair
Roger de Llúria, whose statue faces down La Rambla Nova at
Tarragona and who is said to have brought back the urn and the
lions from one of his expeditions to the east. In the equivalent
position on the south side are the effigies of James the Just (1291–
1327) and his wife Blanche of Anjou, also enclosed by a pinnacled
pavilion.

Impressive though these royal sepulchres are, Santes Creus
lingers in the memory for the simple grand proportions of the

church, the beauty of the cloister and not least its pleasant surroundings. There is a bit less of an industry attached to this monastery than at Poblet. There is also an excellent lodging, the Hostal Grau, just outside the first gatehouse. It is reached easily from Tarragona and could serve as the jumping-off point for the rest of the triangle. Equally, I can think of no better place in which to review your impressions of New Catalonia.

The alleged difference of this region from its northerly counterpart attributed to more prolonged contact with Moorish culture has some foundation in historical fact, though this should not be given undue weight. After the battle of Poitiers in 732 the Moors fell back fairly rapidly from their overextended position, allowing the very early establishment of Benedictine monasteries on both faces of the Pyrenees (see 'Monasticism'). In 801 Louis the Pious took Barcelona. Charlemagne then struck a short-lived pact with the Saracens which resulted in the establishment of a frontier running through the present wine-growing district of Penedès and the *comarques* of Alt Camp, Conca de Barberà and Garrigues in the direction of Lleida; on the Christian side this gave rise to strongholds and fortified villages such as Santa Coloma de Queralt and Aguiló. The relative stability of this line of defence during the ninth and tenth centuries allowed a flourishing trade (especially in slaves) to develop between Christian Barcelona and Valencia and the Balearic islands, both still in Moorish hands. These close economic relations naturally had some effect on the Catalans, who took from Islam such instruments as the astrolabe and adopted Arabic numerals.

This period was not all harmonious interchange, however. In 985 Al-Mansur sacked Barcelona and in his last famous raid in 1002–3 he ravaged the county of Urgell, destroying Manresa on the way. In 1010, by way of reprisal, nine thousand Catalans carried out a successful expedition as far south as Córdoba. In the years 1010–31, which saw the collapse of the caliphate, Islamic Spain was divided into a mosaic of independent kingdoms or *taifas*, among them Dénia, Majorca, Valencia, Tortosa and Lleida, which gave rise to the large Moorish forts whose remains can be seen in the latter two cities and at Balaguer. These kingdoms lasted a little more than a century, Tortosa and Lleida paying tribute to the counts of Barcelona as the price of their survival. El Cid, as all the world knows thanks to Charlton Heston, took Valencia in 1094 but this wide-screen epic was of short duration: the city was retaken by the Almorávides in 1102 and it was not until 1238, nine years after Majorca, that James the Conqueror finally incorporated the great Levantine trading mart into his empire.

All these connections, whether pacific and commercial or antagonistic and warlike, were clearly bound to influence Catalan culture in one way or another: Saracenic decorative motifs were adopted by Romanesque sculptors at Lleida and Tarragona; Islamic cloths, textiles and ceramics were imported and copied by Catalans; philosophical and scientific texts were translated from Arabic, notably at Ripoll. But these influences would be of much greater account if this book were to cover the whole of the empire of James I, including Valencia and Majorca, where Islamic power persisted for much longer and where, after the reconquest, the Morisco (Moorish) population remained in very considerable numbers as artisans, craftsmen and farmers until their final expulsion by Philip III in 1609. This is the *Gran Catalunya* whose restoration is still a gleam in the eye of some contemporary Catalan nationalists, though the constitution of 1978 prohibits the political union of two or more of the seventeen autonomous regions by voluntary agreement among themselves.

If we confine ourselves to the territory covered by the 1979 autonomous statute of Catalonia (the same area as that governed by the Mancomunitat of 1914–25 and defined by the statute of 1932), which is the subject matter of this book, Moorish characteristics are much less pronounced for a number of reasons. On recapturing Toledo in 1085 Alfonso VI of Castile proclaimed himself king of the Christians, Jews and Moors and there was at any rate a period when these groups lived in relative harmony within the same city walls in many parts of Spain. The Moorish element in this racial and linguistic tripod was lacking north of the Ebro. In 1179, under the treaty of Cazorla, Aragon-Catalonia renounced any further southerly interest in the reconquest, abandoned Murcia to Castile and turned its attention to Mediterranean expansion: thus land-based contact with Islam diminished rapidly, despite important Catalan contingents at the capture of Cuenca in 1177 and the battle of Las Navas de Tolosa in 1212. Then the Cistercian influence took firm root in southern Catalonia from about 1150 with the almost simultaneous foundation of Poblet, Vallbona and Santes Creus. These became outstanding social and economic forces in a region no longer in military dispute, whereas further south and west Castilian aristocrats and military orders of warrior-monks were to wage intermittent war with Islam, on an almost sporting basis, for another three centuries or more; all of the Trastamara kings delighted in

Moorish architecture and some wore Moorish dress. Most of these cultural interchanges were absent from Catalonia north of the Ebro – the relatively low level of Moorish influence is, I think, summed up by the lack of any real penetration of the Catalan tongue by Arabic words, which is such a distinctive feature of Castilian Spanish and constitutes one of the crucial differences in the development of the two languages (see 'Catalan Language').

The conclusion, in my view, must be that Catalonia as presently constituted under the Generalitat is – whether north or south of the Llobregat – remarkably homogeneous in its culture and aspirations, and that the 'Moorish' south, though not without some foundation in history, is a bit of a red herring these days. There are of course very considerable scenic, climatic and stylistic differences within Catalonia, and Islamic decorative influences are in evidence, but the sense of nationhood and political ambitions do not alter very much whether you are in the Pyrenees, in the sober old towns of the central plain, in the industrial heartland round Barcelona, in busy textile towns like Reus, in Gandesa and Móra with their memories of the battle of the Ebro, down on the delta of the great river or in Tortosa, once the seat of a Moorish kingdom. All are attracted by the powerful magnet of Barcelona's industrial tradition and cosmopolitan connections. This is what makes Catalonia so solid, self-conscious and determined a nationality and differentiates it so markedly from the militaristic, landowning and lackadaisical culture of Castile with its much more pronounced Moorish influences. Africa certainly does not begin at the Pyrenees or even at the Llobregat; the Ebro may be nearer the mark but you must push on further south into Valencia or west into Aragon to begin to sense the real impact of Islam on Spain. Catalonia – Old and New – belongs essentially to Europe and the western Mediterranean.

If this alignment makes Catalonia seem more prosaic than romantic Andalusia or Castile, the traveller who has followed the itinerary I have described (or almost any variant of it) will by now have realized, I am sure, that such distinctions are too simple to be of much help in defining a complex culture. Busy productivity and eager marketing notwithstanding, Catalonia is amply endowed with retreats for the renewal of the spirit, such as here at Santes Creus, where the austere grandeur of the church, rising out of painstakingly terraced vineyards and carefully tended market gardens, is expressive of precisely those qualities that have enabled Catalonia to endure so remarkably through all the vicissitudes of its history.

PART
TWO

6

Romanesque Art and Architecture

The Romanesque style, in all its variations, has attracted passionate enthusiasts in recent decades. Although these loyalists do not necessarily reject the Gothic revolution – they may well have a soft spot for Chartres or Burgos – they see the Romanesque flowing in the channel of a great tradition from Rome through the Dark Ages and the architecturally timid Carolingian renaissance into the period of 1000–1200, during which some of the greatest churches of all time were built: Durham, Ely, Dijon, Cluny, Tournus, Vézelay, Arles, Conques, Caen, Salamanca, Zamora, Trier, Worms, Pisa, Verona, Palermo. In their view 'barbaric' Gothic should be seen as a mere interlude of three or four centuries in the great classical tradition, which was resumed with the Renaissance and continued through the baroque period into neo-classicism and right into the nineteenth century, when it began to be questioned again by the Gothic revival. And this is, I believe, one good reason for devoting a short essay to the Romanesque in this book.

Moreover, the Romanesque style in Catalonia differs considerably from that on the pilgrim route to Compostela or on the Castilian meseta. Much of it is earlier and therefore more primitive. What the Catalans call pre-Romanesque and others call Carolingian began to make its way southwards over the Pyrenees shortly after 800. Much of the impulse behind this progress was monastic and predominantly Benedictine (see

'Monasticism'). It is usual to date Romanesque proper from about 1000; a 'mature' Romanesque style appeared in about 1150. Having established a firm base in the hearts and expectations of the people, it then clung on well into the Gothic period to such an extent that most transitional churches are entirely Romanesque in spirit and layout, a slightly pointed arch being the only innovation. This is the style I sometimes refer to as pointed Romanesque and it is associated with deliberately archaic cloisters and capital carvings which survived well into the fourteenth century.

There were, of course, early churches along the pilgrim route to Santiago de Compostela in Galicia, but there was no major church there until 950; the present cathedral of Santiago was begun in 1078. One of the great little churches of the pilgrim route, Frómista, was founded in 1066. By contrast Pyrenean and Catalan dates encompass Arles (817), Cuixà (879), Ripoll (880) and Sant Joan de les Abadesses (885). In short, Catalan Romanesque got off the ground much earlier.

Another major difference between Catalan and Castilian Romanesque concerns material. In Catalonia churches tended to be built of a roughcast stone and rubble mixture; only the grander ones attained dressed ashlar masonry. There is very little use of brick in this period in Catalonia, though along the pilgrim route there developed an astonishing flexibility in brickwork owing largely to the efforts of Morisco craftsmen, who introduced Mudéjar motifs and produced a hybrid style known as Romanesque-Mudéjar, which features blind arcades of horseshoe shape to decorate apses and entrances. The tower of San Lorenzo at Sahagún is a fine example. No such influences existed in Catalonia, where the predominant form of exterior decoration was and remained the Lombard band, which entered the region from North Italy via Provence and Perpignan. This is simply a form of blind arcade in which each recessed panel is capped by two or sometimes three semi-circular arcs that in the grander versions (La Seu d'Urgell and Sant Pere de Galligants in Girona) rest on slender engaged columns. It is a form of decoration also employed on towers in the panel surrounding the *ajimez* (or *coronella*) windows. Fundamentally, however, Catalan Romanesque is less elaborate than other versions of the style and this restraint had its effect on later Gothic architecture.

Further differences between the Catalan and the Cantabrian or Castilian versions of Romanesque lie in a difference of purpose. Along the pilgrim route there was a tendency to emulate the

*Apse of the Romanesque church at Olius, decorated with
Lombard bands.*

Cluniac layout, which comprised a semi-circular east end that
opened on to a number of radial apsidal chapels where relics
could be housed and venerated; these were directed at the
growing pilgrim industry. In Catalonia radial ground plans do
not appear until the Gothic period. Montserrat did not become
a centre of pilgrimage until the mid-twelfth century and was of
more regional appeal; also relics seem to have held less of a
fascination for the Catalans than the Castilians. The nearest
approach to multi-apsidal treatment is in Abbot Oliba's reconstructed Ripoll, but here the five apses are merely protuberances
from the square end of the church. A triapsidal or trefoil east end,

195

or a single apse in humbler churches, is more common. Yet
another difference marks off Catalan Romanesque from that of
Segovia and Avila, where very substantial parish churches are
supplemented on one or more sides by elaborately carved porch-
arcades, in which meetings of local worthies, early municipal
councils and local parliaments were held; these are hardly found
at all in Catalonia (there is one at Erill-la-vall), where the earlier
advent of the Romanesque style coupled with more serious
considerations of defence presumably made exterior porticoes
less desirable meeting places. (There were swingeing raids by Al-
Mansur right up into Catalonia in the early eleventh century when
church building was well advanced; by the time the Avilan and
Segovian churches were under construction the Moors had been
thrust permanently south of the Tagus.)

Thus, whether large or small, grand or modest, Catalan Romanesque buildings are basically simple in purpose and design,

*The plain early Romanesque church of Sant Viçens, Besalú,
branches into fantasy in its capitals.*

though some of these are most impressively sited, such as at Cardona (early eleventh century) and Sant Pere de Rodes (consecrated in 1022). The apogee is usually held to have been reached in the mid-twelfth century. Sant Pere de Galligants, finished in 1131 (the cloister was completed slightly later), is a good example of a fully mature Romanesque church as are the later cathedral of La Seu d'Urgell (1131–82) and Sant Joan de les Abadesses (consecrated in 1150). Severity of design is relieved only by the carving of capitals and doorways but the reasons for this detail were doctrinal and iconographic rather than decorative: this is certainly the case with the celebrated mid-twelfth century portal of Ripoll, whose many compartments containing more than a hundred human figures and beasts narrate a number of biblical tales that would easily have been interpreted by the contemporary illiterate though even the most cultivated modern traveller requires a key to decipher them (see p.112). Cloisters, usually built later than the churches they served, often preserve fully Romanesque characteristics well into the Gothic period: the stumpy double columns with large twinned capitals provide ample opportunity for carving of iconographic scenes, formalized birds and beasts or geometrical patterns (some of the latter have been attributed to Moorish influence, though Celtic strapwork also comes to mind). But whatever decorative or didactic motifs are used, the overwhelming impression conveyed by the principal Catalan Romanesque churches is one of simplicity, gravity and restraint. These characteristics mesh well with the Catalan character itself, which perhaps explains the continuing popularity of the style well after it had been superseded elsewhere.

In Spain as elsewhere the church tower is important as a landmark, a beacon, a symbol of local pride and perhaps even of rivalry with neighbours. Although Gothic architecture is generally considered to be a more aspiring style than Romanesque, in Catalonia, curiously enough, the best towers belong to the Romanesque period. My own tentative explanation is that Romanesque builders, constrained by the essentially massive and solid structural requirements of their interiors, sought their upward thrust when they came to the towers; Catalan Gothic architects, on the other hand, solved their aspirations in the interior and were less concerned with external gestures. Be that as it may, there are several impressive Romanesque tower-belfries with *ajimez* windows framed by Lombard bands and I suspect there may well be some influence from the minarets of mosques here. Among the most prominent are the six-stage El Cloquer of

Vic cathedral; the six-stage tower of Sant Climent de Taüll; the five-stage tower of Erill-la-vall; the hollow but erect tower of Sant Pere de Rodes – all square so far; and the octagonal towers of Sant Pere de Galligants and Sant Pere de Ponts. None of the main Gothic towers, with the exception of the old cathedral at Lleida, achieves comparable effect. But a lighter and less emphatic octagon later caught on as the prescribed form for almost every parish church in Catalonia.

Consideration must not, however, be given only to the most important churches. There are about two thousand standing Romanesque churches catalogued in Catalonia, only a handful of which can be mentioned in this book. Some are tiny like Sant Quirze de Pedret (outside Berga) or Obiols or Tredòs. Many were or are still in serious disrepair and have not celebrated services for years. A long and painstaking rescue operation, initiated in the late nineteenth century by Puig i Cadafalch, the Modernist architect, has seen the removal of many of the remaining frescoes and other paintings and carved images to museums, principally the Museu d'Art de Catalunya, which contains the finest collection of Romanesque art in the world.

This brings me to Romanesque painting. It is generally assumed that the gravity of the Romanesque style found expression mainly in stone, and sometimes in wood or iron, but seldom in colour. This assumption leaves out of account two major art forms: frescoes, sometimes covering the interior of an entire church, and painting on wooden panels, usually to form the frontispiece of an altar. The style of both forms is linear, graphic in its formalized folds and primitive modelling, but boldly coloured. Again the purpose is didactic. The altar fronts in particular have been influenced by illustrated manuscripts and indeed there is a resemblance between the exquisite scenes on parchment and those transposed into coarser materials. Both art forms, fresco and on panel, can be seen to marvellous advantage in the great Barcelona museum, where frescoes from Sant Quirze de Pedret and Sant Climent de Taüll and works from many another abandoned or frankly ruinous church have found a safe and permanent haven. The period also gave rise to some quite remarkable wood carving, which is not restricted to the familiar innocent-faced seated Virgins with a stiff, hieratic Child seated on the knee, but includes such splendid works as the unpainted, gaunt, anatomical seven-piece Descent from the Cross from Erill-la-vall, which is to be found in the diocesan museum at Vic.

I come finally to the transitional style. This may appear to

Eleventh-century Virgin and Child from Vallbona de les Monges:
note the hieratic position of the Child with the dexter hand
raised in benediction.

belong more to the dawn of Gothic architecture than to the
evening of Romanesque, but this transition was a lingering affair
and the Catalans peeled off the comforting Romanesque plaster
with great reluctance. Thirteenth-century churches like the old
cathedral of Lleida and Agramunt with their tentatively pointed
arches remain fully within the Romanesque tradition as far as
the ground plans are concerned and tend to rush back to mother
for the doorways, archivolts and tympana, etc. (this roughly a
century after the Cistercians introduced their architectural reform). It may be that the hinterland was more conservative and
less susceptible to new influences than the more cosmopolitan
coastal strip, but there is no doubt that the Romanesque grew out
of the Catalan heartlands almost like natural outcrops from the
soil and that when the Gothic style finally penetrated the interior
it adopted a very sober countenance with no frills.

7

Gothic Art and Architecture

There are numerous theories concerning the Gothic style. It is often described as transcendental and aspiring with a tendency to create vertical rather than horizontal buildings, in contrast with the broad recumbent form of the classical basilica in which the Romanesque style has its origins. Though Celts and Latins played an important role in the development of Gothic architecture, a Germanic strain is sometimes suggested as a vital ingredient. According to Wilhelm Worringer in his celebrated *Form in Gothic* (1927), the Gothic 'will to form' dominates European architecture from very early Christian times and is latent in the Romanesque development and diversification of the very simple undifferentiated Roman basilica. In 'Romanesque Art and Architecture' I have touched on the alternative view, according to which Gothic is merely a hiccough in mainstream classicism, which was very properly revived by the Renaissance and has flourished ever since. Whichever interpretation you prefer, there can be no doubt that the Gothic style was only very painfully and tardily able to break out of the horizontal accentuation of Catalan Romanesque.

Gothic architecture did not arrive in any recognizable form in Catalonia until the Cistercians, taking advantage of the reconquest of the Ebro valley, established themselves almost simultaneously at Poblet, Vallbona de les Monges and Santes Creus in the mid-twelfth century. The new monasteries were situated fairly near Tarragona and well back from the new frontier with the Moors, which was protected by Templar castles. Building at Poblet began shortly after 1166 and was followed closely by Vallbona and Santes Creus. But each adopts a rather different system of construction. Poblet probably comes closest to a French Cistercian abbey: the slightly pointed vault of the nave still rests on ribs of square section but the aisles are more pointed with rounded vaulting ribs, and there is an ambulatory. Santes Creus, on the other hand, is rather less innovative, the only concession to the new style being the slightly pointed nave vault; instead of an ambulatory there is a square east end with a rose window – the overwhelming impression is of a grand building rooted in the old style. Vallbona is smaller and somewhat more Gothic in feeling than either of its neighbours: the aisleless body of the church has steeply pointed arches rising from brackets and there is also a successful lantern over the crossing, a feature absent from both male monasteries.

So it began. The real Gothic breakthrough, however, occurred not in the churches themselves but in the great cloisters that followed them – at Poblet, Santes Creus and Lleida (Vallbona's is a charming hotchpotch – see pp.182–3) where in the last years of the thirteenth and the first third of the fourteenth centuries the Gothic world finally breached the solid old ramparts of the Romanesque tradition. This breakthrough was neither complete nor consistent. At Lleida – whose cloister, the grandest in Catalonia, was begun before 1286 – Romanesque columns with exceedingly intricate capitals showing Saracenic influence launch flamboyant Gothic tracery; at Poblet too essentially Romanesque capitals are combined with a Gothic arcade; only at Santes Creus does a fully Gothic cloister with slender columns and purely decorative floral capitals replace the heavier, bulkier, iconographic carvings that have so far prevailed. The south walk at Santes Creus (1331–41) was designed by the English master mason Reinard Fonoll (who was also responsible for the church at Montblanc) and seems to clinch the Catalan acceptance of the by now international style.

While work proceeded on these cloisters the construction of the first great Catalan Gothic churches began: the cathedral of Barcelona in 1298, that of Girona in 1312 and Santa Maria del Mar (Barcelona) in 1329. Two main styles can be distinguished. The first aims to create a great church with an ambulatory, as in both Barcelona churches. This is what might be called the French tendency, which culminated in the cathedral of Tortosa (the most

French of all Catalan cathedrals), begun in 1347, whose double ambulatory is one of the supreme achievements of Catalan Gothic.

The second approach forgoes avenues of columns with narrow pointed vaults and strives to span the widest possible space under a much flatter vault: an outstanding example is Girona cathedral, whose vault is the widest in the Gothic world, outreaching Albi's by eleven feet. This system has a number of consequences: it dispenses with aisles altogether but thus also eliminates the possibility of an ambulatory; it requires solid buttresses running up to the roof so that the side chapels are reduced to little more than recesses between these buttresses. The design of these hall churches is not wholly unrelated to the developing mediaeval commercial exchanges; the aim seems to have been to promote openness and communication rather than mystification. At the cathedrals of Naples and Palma de Majorca (close structural cousins of Girona's) the affinity between very active trading communities and this method of church construction is particularly apparent.

In any event, the wide vault and the columnless space seem to have satisfied a desire rooted in the Catalan character for a great open uncluttered space in which the congregation and the priest could communicate without unnecessary barriers. There are fine examples of this design in Barcelona at Santa Maria del Pi and Sants Just i Pastor; at Vilafranca del Penedès; at Montblanc; at Sant Domènec de Balaguer near Lleida, and at Ulldecona right down on the southern border of Catalonia. Some of these churches, notably the latter three, achieve a particularly graceful solution to the east end, which is semi-circular and features tall windows separated by slender, finny, vaulting ribs. Other import-ant and successful churches such as Castelló d'Empúries do not manage to achieve this single span but their design is similarly inspired and their aisles are not low and crabbed, but tall and airy. The quest for width and openness, and the abhorrence of nooks and crannies, emerge as the outstanding characteristics of the Catalan Gothic style.

The fixtures, fittings and paintings – some of very high quality – commissioned for these buildings now demand consideration. Some can still be found *in situ*, others in the Museu d'Art de Catalunya and in local museums. Between the Romanesque and Gothic periods the predominant art forms changed: frescoes, large iconographic and didactic wall paintings, disappeared while the relatively small, painted wooden altar frontispiece gave way to the larger *retaule* (retable), which became an important feature behind the high altar. This house of many mansions, still on wooden panels but enclosed by Gothic tracery, became the essential framework of Gothic painting – here in Catalonia as in Castile.

Spanish painting as a whole lagged much behind the Italian and the French: Catalans and Castilians alike were too preoccupied with their struggle against the Moors to develop the arts of peace at an early date. In troubled times art tends to be portable: kings carried their favourite images at the saddle-bow; creative ingenuity found its outlets in tiny ivory triptychs, jewellery, church plate, clasps, bindings, caskets, processional crosses and the like. Although Catalonia, as it is defined today, became pretty well secure from the Moorish threat in about 1150, by this time the Romanesque had become so deeply rooted that, as in architecture, the Gothic style was slow to flower in religious art, and Gothic painting and sculpture did not really make their appearance before the fourteenth century.

Saint George and the Princess, central panel of a triptych by Jaume Huguet: the gilded estofado *halo, like a great golden platter, is still obligatory for saints in the late Gothic period.*

The Girona and Vic diocesan museums are essential to the understanding of Gothic artistic development, whose most persistent feature, as I stress throughout, is the continuing use of embossed gold *esgrafiado* backgrounds and the raised gold *estofado* treatment of haloes, garment hems and so forth long after these hieratic and iconographic devices had been discarded north of the Pyrenees. There are some remarkable painters, notably Pere Serra (1357–1409), Ferrer Bassa (active 1324–48), Ramon de Mur (1402–35), Lluís Borrassà (1380–1424), Jaume Ferrer II (active 1434–57), Bernat Martorell (active 1427–52) and the great Jaume Huguet (c.1415–92). Given this array of talent, the question arises

The celebrated retable of the Virgin of the Councillors by Lluís Dalmau, who was strongly influenced by the Flemings, especially Van Eyck.

why these artists allowed themselves to be confined by craft techniques which had been superseded elsewhere. The answer, I suggest, lies in the conservative nature of local taste and the power of the craft unions or guilds. It must be remembered that the painter started off as the poor relation of the carver, the glazier, the gilder, the carpenter and other associated skills; these guilds were particularly dominant in Barcelona throughout the Middle Ages and in many cases commissioned works for their own churches and chapels, not unnaturally according to their own tastes. Thus major painters continued to work within the confines of iconographic restrictions discredited by the Italian Renaissance. Castilian art was to some extent liberated by Fernando Gallego and Pedro Berruguete in the second half of the fifteenth century, but Catalonia had to wait until Pere Mates (d. 1558) for its release from mediaeval formulae (see pp.103–4) by which time Italianate mannerism had arrived on the doorstep.

Catalan humanism emerged earlier in sculpture perhaps because the restless search for movement, narrative and form on a flat surface which agitated painters such as Ferrer Bassa met no

La Mare de Déu de Boixadors from the diocesan museum at Vic is a supreme example of the tender humanism of the fourteenth century.

such technical impediments in wood or stone. The early four-teenth-century metamorphosis of the stolid Romanesque Virgins with the child resembling a miniature adult, into marvellously tender mothers with smiling faces, robed in naturalistic folds and carrying a playful babe in the crook of the arm is fascinating. There are three outstanding examples of this development in the Girona diocesan museum, while Vic possesses the superb *Mare de Déu de Boixadors* (*c*.1330–60). Other fine carvings of the Virgin and Child of this period can be found on the central column of the west front of Tarragona cathedral; in Sant Joan de les Abadesses; and in the church of Sant Llorenç in Lleida.

To sum up, the Gothic style was slow to establish itself in Catalonia, where the preference for the hall church and wide vault may be seen as the manifestation of a certain Catalan reluctance to surrender to the full verticality of mature Gothic; towers are adjuncts rather than the crowning glory of the whole. It is in the painted panels of the retables that the Gothic world finds its most vivid expression in this corner of the Mediterranean. The celebration of motherhood is the pervasive theme in sculpture and fourteenth-century naturalism provides the perfect vehicle for a return to the idealization of the human form, which is the foundation of classical art.

8

Monasticism

Because the Catalans are thought of primarily as traders and manufacturers, it is all the more important to give due weight to the spiritual side of their national life, which antedates their commercial activities and is by no means irrelevant or superseded today.

There were monastic communities in Catalonia as early as 385. Rules were devised for them at the councils of Tarragona (516) and Lleida (546); the council of Osa (598) gave bishops the power to decide which set of precepts would be followed by monasteries in their respective dioceses. The seventh century saw a further proliferation of Visigothic monastic rules, of which the most important were those of the brothers Saints Isidore and Leander and that of Saint Fructuós. This pluralism yielded in the ninth century to the rule of Saint Benedict, which was promoted by Charlemagne and Louis the Pious with the objective of spreading the special Benedictine mixture of the practical and the spiritual throughout the Carolingian empire.

As a result the ninth and tenth centuries saw the arrival of the Black Friars (an allusion to the Benedictine habit) on the northern and southern flanks of the Pyrenees. In the pre-Romanesque (800–1000) and fully Romanesque (1000–1200) periods approximately two thousand churches were built within the modern limits of Catalonia alone. (See also 'Romanesque Art and Architecture'.) Not all were monasteries or monastic dependencies and not all were Benedictine, but the main thrust came from that order, whose foundations include Gerri de la Sal (807), Banyoles (817), Cuixà (879), Sant Cugat (878), Ripoll (880), Sant Joan de les Abadesses (885), Sant Llorenç de Morunys (910), Sant Pere de Rodes (934) and Canigó (1002).

Most of these foundations, unable as they were to survive without protection, had strong feudal connections – Ripoll and Sant Joan were both founded by Count Wilfred for his children Rudolph and Emma respectively. Other great monasteries were built or extended by noblemen who wished to retreat after a life of action, a very Spanish tendency both inside and outside Catalonia. One way or another these noble connections were vital to the survival of the monasteries in a period when raids from Moorish territory were still not infrequent (the Cordoban warrior Al-Mansur swept right through Catalonia in 1002–3, destroying Manresa). The winds of reform, however, were already beginning to blow, with the name of Cluny in Burgundy to the fore. In order to free itself and other monasteries from overdependence on a corrupt nobility, in 949 Cluny placed itself fully under the protection of the pope; other monasteries followed suit. The motivation behind this was political as well as religious and the movement had the backing of the counts of the region, who saw the papal connection as a means of further loosening their links with the waning Frankish empire.

The Cluniac example was followed by other monastic groupings of the same kind. In the eleventh century Oliba, abbot of Ripoll and Cuixà and bishop of Vic, was not only a leading light of his age in terms of culture and scholarship but also had the energy and drive to found a number of other monasteries and abbeys, among them La Portella, Santa Maria de Montserrat and Fluvià. That Oliba was also well connected does not seem to have undermined his work; indeed his connections were probably essential to it. But other cases of empire-building by ambitious abbots were less successful. There were constant jurisdictional squabbles, and then a further complication: the counts of Barcelona, who at the turn of the eleventh century had acquired feudal dominion over several of the great counties of the French Midi, such as Toulouse and Provence, felt obliged to sweeten their new vassals, both civil and ecclesiastical, by granting them suzerainty over important Catalan monasteries. Thus Grasse and Moissac extended their sway south of the Pyrenees.

This political misuse of the monastic tradition for secular ends led to various reformist movements, among them that of the

Cistercians, who became known as the White Friars (to distinguish them from the black-habited Benedictines). Ramon Berenguer IV's reconquest of the Ebro valley opened up a larger and more secure world, of which Cîteaux was not slow to take advantage. Almost simultaneously, in about 1150, the monasteries of Poblet, Santes Creus and Vallbona de les Monges were founded, ushering in a new phase in which religious foundations were no longer mere mountain refuges or political pawns but large, active and efficient socio-economic organizations under royal patronage, the county of Barcelona having acquired the crown of Aragon by marriage in 1137. The Cistercian monasteries are substantially different from their Benedictine predecessors, not merely in the transitional Gothic style of the churches or the fully Gothic cloisters (see 'Gothic Art and Architecture'). They are also much larger: Poblet in its heyday had some two hundred monks, whereas Cuixà, though imposing enough, had only fifty. Then again, the buildings also served as a royal palace (Poblet) and as royal quarters (Santes Creus). This foreshadows that peculiar complex of fortress-palace-monastery which was to fascinate later Spanish monarchs and give rise to Guadalupe and eventually to the Escorial. Within these buildings Cistercian life was highly and hierarchically organized and included inspections and triennial general chapters. As the monks elected the abbot, this position was no longer the exclusive province of younger sons of the nobility.

While the principal aim of the Cistercians, who followed the rule of Saint Bernard (the most outstanding and erudite of the first abbots of Cîteaux), was to eliminate corruption and restore the purity of monastic life, it should not be forgotten how important an economic role was played by the monasteries in the Carolingian period and the early Middle Ages. The first foundations were in effect a form of repopulation in what had previously been Moorish territory. At Cuixà the community owned 500 sheep, 50 mares, 40 pigs, 2 horses, 5 donkeys, 20 oxen and 100 other 'large horned animals'; they also employed 20 servants. The monks were thus able to teach new settlers how to plough and rotate their crops, breed and care for farm animals and manufacture domestic utensils and agricultural tools. With greater political stability and the southward movement of the frontier, cultural dissemination assumed greater importance: Ripoll, Cuixà and Sant Cugat became renowned centres for the illumination of manuscripts and the translation of philosophical and scientific texts.

The military orders of monk-knights who played so prominent a part in the Castilian reconquest were less in evidence in Catalonia. The Templars were the leading order of this kind in the region and the greatest concentration of their foundations is to be found down along the course of the Ebro, where the frontier was established by Ramon Berenguer IV in the mid-twelfth century. Templar fortress-monasteries were immediately built at Tortosa and Miravet (1153) and a little later at Ascó and Horta (1197). Protected by these spiritual and temporal outposts, the Cistercian monasteries clustered round Tarragona were able to enjoy a stable and secure existence.

The mendicant orders made their first appearance on the Christian map under the papacy of Innocent III (1198–1216). Franciscans, Dominicans and later Carmelites provided the stimulus to monastic reform. The Dominicans, formed in response to the Albigensian heresy, which questioned much orthodox doctrine, were prominent in Castile but much less so in Catalonia, where many of the persecuted Albigenses had fled, bringing their wealth and trading skills with them. It was not until Ferdinand the Catholic imported the Castilian Inquisition to replace the much milder Catalan branch in the 1480s that the much feared Dominican inquisitors obtained a firm hold over the religious life of the principality.

To write about Catalan monasticism without referring to Montserrat would be like *Hamlet* without the Prince. Founded in the eleventh century by Abbot Oliba as an independent house, it later became a priory of Ripoll. The monastic community was reinforced by a dozen or so hermitages on the hillsides, whose occupants bound themselves to obey the prior of the order. By the twelfth century Montserrat was already an important centre of pilgrimage; it is from this time that the image of the famous black Virgin dates (see pp.69, 72). As I discovered on my journeys, Montserrat's influence is not confined to Barcelona alone: its spiritual beacon sweeps powerfully over the coastal strip, the central plain, up to Vic, down to Vilafranca and indeed over all Catalonia; the extraordinary massif is actually visible from a number of major towns such as Manresa and Igualada. In the Middle Ages Montserrat eventually outshone Ripoll in scholarship and its independence was conceded by the Spanish anti-pope, Pedro Martínez de Luna (Benedict XIII) at the beginning of the fifteenth century. But the centralizing zeal of the Catholic monarchs subjected it from 1493 to the Castilian Congregation of Valladolid, under whose tutelage it remained until the sequestration of the monasteries in the nineteenth century. In 1874 the monks returned and restoration began on the monastery, which had been sacked by the French in the Peninsular War. Throughout the Franco régime Montserrat was a casket in which the spirit and pride of the Catalans were zealously preserved. If Catalan culture is ever again subjected to the ferocious persecution of those years, it will be to the abbot of Montserrat rather than to the politicians that the nation will turn.

Whatever their backslidings and their involvement in political intrigue, there can be no doubt that it was the monasteries that kept the lamp of civilization burnished and burning from the collapse of the Roman Empire through the Dark Ages into the fragile Carolingian renaissance and beyond. This is particularly true in Catalonia, where invasion and repression have often prevailed, calling forth from the Catalans the virtues, nurtured in the monastic tradition, of endurance, work and prayer.

9

Catalan Jewry

It is difficult to pinpoint precisely when the Jews arrived on Catalan soil after the diaspora, but there is some evidence of their presence in the peninsula in Roman and Visigothic times and they are first documented in Girona in 889, when the city was still in Moorish hands. In Muslim territory they did not experience much adverse discrimination – their numbers were far too small to constitute a threat to Islam – and though they were confined for dwelling purposes to the *aljama* or *judería* they otherwise mixed freely with the rest of the population. Intellectually the Jewish contribution was valued, and their skills in the secular sciences were not thought to conflict with Islamic teaching; the philosophical debates which took place in Córdoba between the Aristotelian Maimonides (1135–1204) and the great Islamic thinker Averroes (1126–98) are well documented.

In Christian territory liberal coexistence did not survive much beyond the eleventh century; it was not acceptable to an increasingly powerful Church. As the reconquest advanced, the Jews were thrust into a subordinate position within the political and social order, which was later to take the form of a fundamentally servile role in the Christian feudal régime. They were confined to enclosed precincts within the Christian cities where their conditions were worse than in the Muslim equivalents. In Catalonia the Jewish *call*, especially in the thirteenth and fourteenth centuries, was an insalubrious warren of dwellings with a single

212

authorized entrance, where the inhabitants were confined between dawn and dusk. It was rare for the king or the bishops to
allow the extension of *calls* – and these were usually located on the
wrong side of the city drains. In Barcelona the *call* ran from the
Plaça de Sant Jaume down to Las Ramblas and bordered on the
prostitutes' area. The Barcelonese had the habit of depositing
their refuse at the gate of the *call* and then inveighing against the
Jews for any infections or pestilences that broke out. This was an
immediate cause of not a few popular risings against the Jewish
communities.

Despite these unfavourable conditions, however, the Jews had a
powerful defender in the person of the king. The crown punished
anti-Jewish demonstrations and the intervention of successive
monarchs in disputes between the Gentiles and the Jews had
some effect in cooling racial tensions. The doctrinal basis for the
crown's role as protector of the Jews was largely established by
Saint Augustine, who settled the judicial status of the Jews by
proclaiming them 'serfs of the king'. In 1176 the statute of Teruel
regulated the fines that might be imposed by the crown on its
Jewish subjects, the justification being that 'the Jews are the serfs
of the king and belong in perpetuity to the royal treasury'. Thus, in
addition to revenues from woods, mines, saltpans, markets and
fairs, the king was provided with a further source of income. It
should be added that the Jews belonged to the king alone; no other
person or institution, such as the Church, could possess them.

The crown thus had a vested interest in maintaining the Jewish
population, favouring their immigration and intervening to
prevent the invasion and destruction of the *calls*. When in 1391 the
Valencian *judería* was threatened with destruction the king wrote
to the governor reminding him of the monarch's obligation to
'defend the Jews and hold them under our special guard and
protection, because they are our coffer and our treasure'. But the
royal policy was not limited to intervening in violent incidents; it
went further along the lines of extending privileges and pardons
to all the Jews in the territory. Not gratis, of course: any excuse
(coronation, marriage, war, admission of new Jewish immigrants) was a pretext for levying a subsidy on the *calls*. The Jewish
fiscal contribution was significant not so much for its volume – it
was not, after all, the only or even the major source of the crown's
revenue – but for its coercive nature. The so-called serfs lacked
citizens' rights and any role in the political process; nor was it
necessary to call parliament to tax them. This had obvious
advantages, and it has been suggested that the conquests of James

I (1213–76) would not have been possible without the Jewish purse.

James the Conqueror was in fact one of the most liberal monarchs in his approach towards the Jews. His was an expansive period in Catalan history and in return for Jewish contributions he granted them a number of favours – for example, permission for a new Jewish bath in Besalú in 1264. Even so, some not very attractive duties fell to them. They had the dubious privilege of exercising the king's lions, these being the most usual form of present offered to Catalan rulers by ambassadors from North Africa. The lions were caged in the patio of the royal palace (today the Plaça del Rei) and were in effect the beginnings of Barcelona's zoo.

Apart from exercising lions, Jewish occupations and professions were essentially those they had practised for centuries and which allowed them to begin a new life almost anywhere if they were expelled. These occupations fell into four categories: craftsmanship (especially the craft of jewellery), financial services (including small loans), knowledge of and translation from Arabic and the practice of medicine. The Jewish contribution to Catalan life flourished in all these fields, but most outstandingly of all in medicine (which was of great importance in Lleida, where it was practised by both men and women). Jewish doctors often became royal physicians despite papal and conciliar disapproval. This was particularly the case in Catalonia. For example, in 1386 Sullam Deusloger of Cervera obtained royal permission to travel outside his *call* to attend to his many patients; on occasions such as this Jewish doctors were exempted from wearing the distinctive clothing the Jews were normally required to wear, so as to avoid insult or assault. Once a doctor had been examined and approved by two medical assessors, one Christian and one Jewish, he was given a licence to practise throughout the kingdom of Aragon. As late as 1468 Cresques Abnarrabí successfully operated on John II for cataracts.

In the religious field the special contribution of the Catalan Jews to their own faith was made by the cabalistic circle of Girona in the twelfth and thirteenth centuries. The *càbala* was a mystical and theosophical movement which originated in the Jewish communities of Languedoc and then spread through Catalonia and the rest of Spain. (Mysticism was also in the air in the Christian camp, witness the Franciscans and the works of Ramon Llull – see 'Catalan Literature'.) The great master of the Catalan *càbala* was Isaac el Cec, or the Blind (1165–1235) of Girona, author of the most obscure mystical speculations and possessor of thaumaturgical powers. He was the originator of an oral esoteric tradition; also, the talmudic work of one of his followers, Moises ben Nahman or Nahamònides (1194–1270) is claimed as the jewel of the literature of sephardic Judaism. As a result of this movement cabalistic doctrines became almost orthodox in Catalonia, and in the disputes provoked by *The Guide of the Perplexed* of Maimonides, who endeavoured to protect not only the Mosaic law but also the interests of Aristotelian philosophy – Catalan Jewry was firmly against the Cordoban.

All this intellectual ferment, however, was still confined to the cramped and squalid *call*. Synagogues were unable to comply with the law which required that they be built on a high place and feature twelve windows – and mediaeval documents suggest that there were not more than a hundred places in Catalonia where the Jewish rite was celebrated (cf. more than two thousand Romanesque churches). And if 'synagogue' is taken to mean a public place providing formal instruction, these probably did not exceed thirty. In Barcelona there were at most six synagogues, three in Girona and probably not more than one each in other cities with well-established Jewish communities such as Lleida, Tortosa, Tàrrega, Cervera, Tarragona, Balaguer, Agramunt, La Seu d'Urgell and Solsona. There are certainly no outstanding synagogues in Catalonia like those now bearing the Christian names Santa María la Blanca and El Tránsito (which houses the Museo Sefardí) in Toledo, both erected when Jewish treasurers were providing money for Christian wars. In general Catalan Jews were squeezed between their status as serfs of the crown and, ironically, the resentment of that special relationship by the Church and the Inquisition. In these circumstances there could be no beautiful synagogues on commanding heights.

Towards the end of the thirteenth century, there began a series of attacks throughout Spain on the Jewish *aljamas* and *calls*; outbreaks of anti-Judaism occurred in Girona in 1276, 1278, 1285, 1331, 1348, 1391, 1405 and 1418. Some sources suggest that these were inspired by the zeal of Dominican preachers, especially during Holy Week when they were able to rouse the Christians against the 'assassins of Christ', rather than by genuine social conflict. Gerald Brenan, on the other hand, holds that there is evidence of real economic resentment encompassing an implicit criticism of the nobility who frequently married into Jewish stock.

Be that as it may, the position of the Catalan Jews seems to have been somewhat preferable to that of their brethren in Castile and Valencia (where there was a particularly horrible massacre in 1391). The commercial and financial links the Jews had established with the rising Catalan bourgeoisie were important. Also, the Aragonese and Catalan Inquisitions were not as yet in the hands of hardline Dominicans and the most spectacular act of populist demagoguery carried out by Saint Vincent Ferrer, himself a Catalan, was to evict the Jews not from their holy places in Barcelona or Girona but from the Toledo synagogue now called Santa María la Blanca.

But the atmosphere undoubtedly worsened towards the end of the Middle Ages and conversions to Christianity were frequent, whether sincere or not. Even today Catalan surnames of Jewish origin are not uncommon, e.g. Benejam or Salomó, while others spring from the alternative course adopted by converts of assuming as patronymic the name of a saint as in Sanvicens, Sants, Santaulària, etc. This absorption of increasingly persecuted Jewry by Catalan society has had, I believe, important effects on the development of the Catalan nation. It should be remembered that in mediaeval times Jews were not bound by Catholic laws against usury and were thus able to make loans against interest and develop financial services in a way that was forbidden to Christians. With the commercial expansion begun under James I and extended under other mediaeval monarchs, these services became of great utility and the special skills and aptitudes they required were not lost when conversions took place. Several centuries later, when the Catalan industrial revolution got under way, banking and trading instincts were still alive. Savings also play an enormously important part in Catalan life, as is witnessed by the development of the powerful *caixes* or savings banks. These were and are essential to capitalist development, while reflecting the Jewish moral commitment to community projects and services.

After the expulsion of the Jews in 1492, it was not possible to profess Judaism publicly until the nineteenth century when there was a trickle back. In 1877 there were only 406 notified Jews in Spain, of whom 21 lived in Barcelona. In about 1930 there were 400 Jewish families with a total of 3,000 persons in Barcelona alone, which rose to some 5,000 in 1935. After Franco's victory Jewish numbers diminished again – the régime continued to inveigh against the 'Jewish, masonic, Marxist conspiracy' until its demise. Today the Jews of Catalonia probably number some 5,000 again, many of them of South American origin who have fled from anti-democratic régimes in that subcontinent. A very high percentage of the younger generation is marrying into Gentile families, so the process of absorption seems likely to repeat itself. Whether this trend continues or not, there can be no doubt of the significant and perhaps even seminal role played by the Jews in Catalan life. This is popularly recognized in the designation of the Catalans by the rest of the peninsula as the 'Jews of Spain' – and the same sort of jokes are made about them as are made about the Scots by the English. As much of this seems to be motivated by a certain envy of their commercial competence, the Catalans receive these pleasantries with equanimity.

10

Political Life and Institutions

This subject may seem out of place in a book mainly devoted to the attractions of Catalonia and its cultural heritage. But it is of tremendous significance to the Catalan people, is intimately linked with their culture and customs and lies behind the many outward and visible signs of Catalan nationalism – flags, street names, passionate attachment to the language – by which the traveller can hardly fail to be struck. In addition, the political life of Barcelona in the late nineteenth and early twentieth centuries became notorious for its outbreaks of violence, and it must be emphasized that not only the politicians and industrialists but also some of the leading cultural figures – architects, poets and painters – became deeply involved in proposing solutions. Therefore any account of Catalonia which sidesteps these aspects of the Catalan story would be inexcusably incomplete.

Catalonia is at present governed under the statute of autonomy of 1979, derived from the Spanish constitution of 1978. The supreme organ of government in the region is the Generalitat, a body of ancient origin headed by a president, who is elected by the Catalan parliament of 135 deputies for a period of four years: this implies approval of his programme of government and of his executive council or cabinet of twelve ministers responsible for the various areas of government devolved under the statute – they need not be members of the parliament. These bald facts give no hint of the strength of local feeling, suffering, endurance and sheer tenacity which were required over the years to obtain the modest degree of independence Catalonia enjoys today. So before looking at the present functioning of the statute it is worth going back to discover how and why this limited autonomy was secured from the central state.

The first point to grasp is that Catalonia has for centuries been justifiably proud of its early democratic institutions, which differed from those of the rest of Spain and have on the whole proved more durable. There were early parliaments or *cortes* in Castile and León, to be sure, but virtually their only function was to raise taxes for the monarch. The Catalan *corts* functioned as tax-raising bodies too, but they also developed a much stronger role in relation to the crown. Various explanations have been advanced for this, amongst them the absence of huge feudal estates and the early development of an urban bourgeoisie. Whatever its origin, the democratic spirit of the Catalans is abundantly evident today; it is particularly striking that the style of address *don*, to which every Castilian and Andalusian lays claim, is never accorded even to the most distinguished citizens: everyone is plain *senyor*.

As far back as 1025 Count Berenguer Ramon exempted the inhabitants of his domains from any jurisdiction outside his own. The *Usatges de Barcelona*, a feudal system of civil law, were drawn up in 1064–8. During the twelfth and thirteenth centuries, the repopulation of New Catalonia, which had been recaptured from the Moors, was accompanied by relatively generous charters of rights for the new towns in order to attract inhabitants. In 1193 an 'assembly of peace and truce' was held which followed earlier precedents, although on this occasion representatives of the commons participated for the first time; this was another step in the evolution of the parliamentary process. At about this time the municipal government was also developing and statutes of self-government were granted to Lleida and Perpignan (1197), Fraga (1201) and Cervera (1202). In the period 1249–58 Barcelona acquired the basis of its present municipal government. The celebrated *Consolat de Mar* was elaborated between 1258 and 1272; this was a code of practice regulating the trading relations of virtually all the Mediterranean countries and laying the foundation of maritime commercial law for the whole of Europe. In 1283 a parliament was held in Barcelona at which the powers of the merchant class were consolidated and the jurisdiction of the city's newly established Consell de Cent (Council of One Hundred) was confirmed. The forerunner of the Generalitat, in effect a permanent commission of the *corts* whose job was to collect taxes when the assembly was not in session, was created in 1289. During the reign of Peter III (1336–87) the Generalitat was given further functions and responsibilities, reaching the peak of its power in the early fifteenth century.

This steady growth and consolidation of independent civil and commercial institutions continued until the death of Martin the Humane without offspring in 1410. He was succeeded by a Castilian prince, Ferdinand of Antequera, who had pronounced authoritarian views. This tendency was further enhanced by the marriage in 1469 of Ferdinand of Aragon to Isabel of Castile, though even after the union of the two crowns Catalan institutions remained at least formally separate from those of the rest of the peninsula. It was not until the War of the Spanish Succession, and the Catalan espousal of the Austrian against the Bourbon cause, that the complete abolition of Catalonia's ancient liberties was brought about in 1716 by the first Spanish Bourbon Philip V (see pp.10–11). Military defeat and political emasculation did not, however, have a totally disastrous effect.

One of the by-products of the *Nova Planta*, as Philip's punitive measures were called, was that it concentrated Catalan minds on commerce, for which they had always shown an aptitude. The Barcelona chamber of commerce was founded in 1758. Other economic and learned societies sprang up, giving birth to an enlightenment not unlike that of Scotland in the same period, which suffered political repression after the Jacobite rebellion of 1745. In 1760 a claim was presented to Charles III, supposedly an enlightened despot, for the restoration of the rights abolished by Philip V. Charles refused to budge on this point but in 1778 he did lift the embargo on Catalan trade with the American colonies, which gave a boost to exports. Also, demographic growth led to an extension of cultivated land and more intensive agriculture, whose surpluses were invested in wool and cotton manufacture. Commercial success in its turn generated capital for the modernization of industry: the spinning jenny was functioning in Catalonia only ten years or so after its first appearance in England. At the same time the guilds decayed and the germs of a new industrial proletariat were sown; fuelled by the surplus population of the countryside, the proletariat grew in parallel with the expanding bourgeoisie. Despite these developments, it is hard to say exactly when the Catalan economy took off. In my view, it was a step-by-step process rather than a dramatic upward curve. But the important fact from the institutional point of view is that it happened without any sort of official intervention: local Catalan energies and private enterprise brought about a steady industrialization totally lacking in the rest of Spain.

Industrial progress was interrupted by the war of 1793–5 against the French revolutionaries and then by the Peninsular War of 1808–14. When industrialization was resumed, it changed gear, entering a more politicized phase, as the Catalan upper bourgeoisie became increasingly disenchanted with Madrid. It might be thought that nineteenth-century Spanish liberalism would have been sympathetic to regionalist aspirations but this was not so. The first attempt at a liberal constitution, that devised by the *cortes* of Cádiz in 1812, still envisaged a unitary state, but this was torn up immediately by Ferdinand VII on the restoration of the Bourbon monarchy by the treaty of Versailles. The liberal revolution of 1835 was no more sympathetic to the idea of a revived confederation of Catalonia, Aragon and Valencia mooted at the time; the liberal government of Baldomero Espartero also promoted free trade, which was anathema to the Catalan bourgeoisie, who saw their hemp industry amongst others ruined by imports of foreign jute. The progressive Madrid governments of 1840–3 and 1854–6 were thus not at all to the taste of Catalan business interests, particularly as workers' movements of a mutualist and co-operative nature gathered strength during these periods, culminating in a general strike in 1855. But it was the period 1868–74 which most shook the bourgeois entrepreneurs. The palace revolution of September 1868 sent Queen Isabel II into exile and introduced universal suffrage, the right of association, liberty of the press and religious freedom. The Catalan industrial workers increasingly saw their future within the framework of an international workers' movement rather than as a purely local issue – and they were more attracted to the anarchist than the socialist model. The bourgeoisie, alarmed by the popular and revolutionary trend of events, aligned themselves with the army and the monarchists and lent their support to the restoration of the Bourbon monarchy in the person of Alfonso XII; this was effected by the coup d'état of General Martínez Campos in 1874. But disenchantment was not far behind.

It is necessary here to refer to the phenomenon known as the *Renaixença* or Catalan renaissance. It must be remembered that the smouldering fires of Catalan nationalism, though damped down, had not been extinguished by the *Nova Planta* nor by the centralization and decatalanization favoured by the Madrid governments of both parties in the nineteenth century. The language, banned officially, continued in use in the farms, villages and country churches, in the popular (as opposed to the romantic) theatre and even in such formal acts as wills drawn up by notaries. There was thus no shortage of sparks to ignite *catalanisme* in all its guises. The *Renaixença* was fed from a number of sources: on the one hand it was populist, progressive and republican and linked to workers' associations; on the other it was literary, élitist and conservative, springing from a rediscovery of the language by the bourgeoisie and leading to the revival of the mediaeval *Jocs Florals* – a contest of troubadors – in 1859. This many-faceted phenomenon was not initially political but it undoubtedly created the climate for an upsurge of political *catalanisme* when the time was ripe.

From about 1875 the political scene in Barcelona becomes extraordinarily complex. At first the new conservative government in Madrid satisfied Catalan business aspirations by reimposing protective tariffs; there was a great burst of economic expansion known as *febre d'or* (gold fever). But in 1881 the liberals returned to power in Madrid and there was a renewed semi-tolerance of the workers' movements. In 1881 an anarchist congress was held in Barcelona. There were now three main tendencies in the political field: the business-dominated conservative right demanding protectionism; the progressive federalists, led by Valentí Almirall, demanding regional autonomy; and the fast-growing anarcho-syndicalism of the workers, increasingly uninterested in *catalanisme* of whatever stamp and drawn towards international solidarity. In 1885 the bourgeoisie presented a *Memorial de Greuges* (Memorial of Grievances) to Alfonso XII but without concrete results and from this time onwards they took up the banner of *catalanisme* no longer as a cultural and literary plaything but as an instrument to advance their own interests against a central state that was totally out of touch with the modern industrial world.

Before going any further it is instructive to appraise the Catalan haute bourgeoisie in their curious role as progressive reactionaries. This is best illustrated by the development of the *colonies industrials* along the rivers, where water power was available for the textile factories. These industrial compounds were isolated from the towns and villages and organized almost on feudal lines, complete with owner's mansion, workers' housing estate, school and church. There was an early morning bell to wake the employees in good time for a spot of procreation before clocking in: the future workforce had to be assured. In most cases cultural and educational provision was made by the proprietor with the genuine aim of counteracting the brutalization of labour through the factory system. In some cases the buildings were designed by eminent architects such as Antoni Gaudí (for the Conde Güell) or Puig i Cadafalch. Nonetheless, as a combination of paternalism and intrusiveness the industrial colonies were unparalleled – and a far cry from the aspirations of the workers' movements. Nor was there any disposition on the part of the Catalan industrialists to promote political legislation along the lines of the British reform bills or social legislation along the lines of the factory acts. Though the Catalan bourgeoisie were contemptuous of Madrid for its lack of understanding of the modern world, they can hardly be congratulated as progressive employers.

The period of approximately 1890–1910 is marked by a number of mainly right-wing Catalanist groupings and regroupings whose objective was to demand either protectionist legislation or regional autonomy (or both) from the central government. The Lliga de Catalunya of 1889 evolved into the Unió Catalanista of 1891, in which the architects Domènech i Montaner and Puig i Cadafalch and the conservative politician Prat de la Riba played an important part. In 1892 the Unió Catalanista approved the *Bases de Manresa*, a project for regional autonomy which again did not prosper. In 1895 rebellion broke out in Cuba and in 1898 the last straw came for the Catalan bourgeoisie when Cuba, the Philippines and Puerto Rico – all important trade outlets – were lost for good through, as they saw it, the incompetence and indolence of the Madrid government.

From this point on all the energies of the conservative industrialists were directed at disassociating Catalonia from the disastrous performance of Madrid. Any idea of national regeneration in which Catalonia would play a leading part was dropped: Catalan employers wanted to go it alone. Dr Bartomeu Robert, a leading conservative Catalanist and mayor of Barcelona, was quite unable to gain acceptance for additional taxes to pay for the loss of the Cuban revenues with the result that businesses simply shut up shop – and he was obliged to resign. The foremost Catalan businessmen broke away from their lifelong adherence to the national conservative party and founded the Unió Regionalista, which in 1901 evolved into the first exclusively Catalan political party, the Lliga Regionalista, founded with the objective of fighting the national elections on a regionalist ticket. There was then an attempt at an all-party Catalanist movement under the banner of *Solidaritat Catalana*, to which the Lliga subscribed. It was not supported by Alejandro Lerroux's republicans but it won the municipal elections of 1907 and did well in the next general election to the *corts*, to which Cambó the industrialist and Puig the architect were returned.

While the right was proceeding along the regionalist road, the left was going in the opposite direction towards internationalism. It was during this period that Barcelona acquired its lurid reputation as Bomb City. In 1888 the Partido Socialista Obrero Español, still the main Spanish socialist party today, and the Unión General de Trabajadores, still the largest Spanish trade union, were both founded in Barcelona, but their Marxist-based ideology was not congenial to Catalonia and in 1899 both removed to Madrid, leaving the field to Bakuninist anarchism. In 1893 Pauli Pallàs had attempted to kill General Martínez Campos and was executed: two bombs were dropped by way of reprisal in the Liceu theatre, killing twenty and wounding many more. Bomb City was in business. It has to be said that some of the bombings were carried out by government agents in order to discredit the anarchists. The Montjuïc trials of 1906 led to an international outcry and the fall of the government. The most violent incident of all was the *Setmana Tràgica* (Tragic Week) of 1909, when the workers' organizations rose against the government's call-up of reserve troops to fight in Morocco in defence of Spanish mining interests there, which were threatened by the tribesmen of the Rif. This was a classic and bloody instance of the deep desire of the Catalans to have nothing to do with the incompetent militarism of Madrid: 116 people died and some 300 were injured before the uprising was suppressed.

In 1911 a shaft of light broke through the storm clouds. Inspired by the intelligent conservative Prat de la Riba, author of *La nacionalitat catalana* and president of the Diputació (provincial assembly) of Barcelona, a proposal was elaborated for a voluntary confederation of the four Catalan provinces – Barcelona, Girona, Lleida and Tarragona – known as the Mancomunitat. The proposal was finally approved by the Madrid parliament at the very end of 1912 and came into being in 1914 with Prat as president. This was the first regional institution of a political nature to exist in Catalonia since 1714. It had no taxing power but could issue bonds. Assisted by the boom generated by Spain's neutrality in the First World War, it accomplished a great deal in the spheres of transport, infrastructure, communications, culture, education, forestry, health, social services and finance. Prat died young in 1917 and was succeeded by Puig i Cadafalch, who remained president until General Primo de Rivera's military coup. Puig made the mistake of supporting Primo in the belief that the Mancomunitat would be allowed to continue, but he was speedily disabused: it was effectively dissolved in January 1924 and formally abolished in 1925. Ironically it was Primo who gave the go-ahead and provided central government funds for the Universal Exhibition of 1929, which had been on the drawing board for twenty years. At the same time the Catalan language was again proscribed.

In 1930 Primo de Rivera fell and the municipal elections of April 1931 turned into a referendum on the monarchy. The republican parties won overwhelmingly and King Alfonso XIII was forced into exile. Such was the euphoria in Catalonia that Francesc Macià, leader of the Esquerra Republicana de Catalunya (Republican Left of Catalonia), proclaimed Catalonia an independent republic within an Iberian federation. He was quickly forced by Madrid to withdraw this bid for a separate status that would be quite unacceptable to the rest of the country; what the Catalans got in 1932 was a statute of autonomy with certain devolved powers to be exercised by the revived Generalitat. In the 1933 general elections the parties of the right were victorious. There was a general strike in 1934 and the Generalitat rebelled against the new government, but Macià's successor, Lluís Companys, refused to issue arms to the people and the revolt failed. It was followed by suspension of the statute and the imprisonment of the president and members of the Generalitat. In 1936 the popular front of marxists, anarchists and bourgeois republicans won the national elections and Companys and his fellow prisoners returned to power. But the respite was short. On 17–18 July much, though not all, of the army rose against the republic. The majority of the Barcelona garrison joined the rising but were overpowered by Security and Civil Guards, supported by militant workers and some soldiers. Thirty thousand rifles were captured from the Barcelona armoury. Companys encouraged anarchist leaders to set up a central committee of anti-fascist militias, one of which, the Partido Obrero de Unificación Marxista (Workers' Marxist Unification Party), was joined by George Orwell in December of that year (see pp.17–18).

The course of the Civil War is too well known to require repetition, despite the spell its heroisms, atrocities and complex political infighting on the left continues to cast over all Hispanophiles and many who still deplore the farce of noninterventionism which allowed the Germans and the Italians to intervene with impunity. When it was finished, Companys was captured by the Gestapo in France and handed over to General Franco's government. He was executed in 1940 in the fortress of Montjuïc. There followed the most brutal of all the repressions suffered by the Catalans. Philip V had decreed the death of institutions, not of people; Franco's revenge demanded both. The administration of the principality was returned to the four provinces, each with its civil and military governor and departmental delegates from the central ministries: all these posts were filled by Castilian placemen. The executions and the dead hand of central bureaucracy were accompanied by the most sweeping attempt ever made to stamp out the Catalan language; clandestine Catalan literature did of course circulate. In 1954 Josep Tarradellas succeeded Josep Irla as president of the Generalitat in exile in a solemn ceremony at the Spanish Republican Embassy in Mexico.

After General Franco's death in 1975 the Spanish constitution-makers recognized that they had to take account of the *semifracaso* (semi-failure) of the unitary state, which had still not gelled satisfactorily after five hundred years. But they were determined not to go down the federalist road. Devolution within the nation-state was as far as the king and the Madrid politicians would go or the army permit. Against assurances that the statute of autonomy would be restored, Tarradellas returned to Barcelona in triumph on 23 October 1977 as provisional head of the Generalitat. It has been claimed that a million people filled the streets to welcome him home. In political terms the statute that emerged in 1979 is fairly modest. On paper its main devolved areas of competence are: home office matters; economy and finance; education; culture and the media; health and social security; territorial policies and public works; agriculture, stockbreeding and fisheries; industry and energy; trade and tourism. However, these are very much circumscribed by the following factors. The two national police forces, the Policía Nacional and the Guardia Civil, are still in place and very much in evidence. The Generalitat has virtually no resources of its own and does not even collect taxes for the central government as in the Basque provinces and Navarre; it is therefore almost totally dependent on Madrid for funds, which are supposed to be paid automatically under a statutory formula. This gives rise to an annual wrangle generating not a little heat. But there is a compensating factor: Catalan culture has been given a completely free rein. This may not seem very substantial, but in view of the many assaults in the past on the spoken and written word, and on education in particular, it is of great importance to Catalonia, which has always sustained itself through thick and thin on its deep and ineradicable cultural roots.

A million people filled the streets to welcome Josep Tarradellas back to Barcelona on 23 October 1977.

As far as territorial organization goes, the traveller may understandably find this confusing. The Generalitat is the ultimate regional authority and there are plenty of large signs announcing improvements to roads, buildings, irrigation, etc. displayed under its auspices. At the same time there are other signs announcing rather similar projects and bearing the imprint of the Diputació of the province concerned. The explanation is that the provincial structure introduced in 1833 and used by successive governments (not only Franco's) as an instrument of central control has not yet been dismantled. There are still civil and military governors and provincial assemblies; the latter have lost some of their functions but they still exist – though superfluously, as the elected Parlament de Catalunya is empowered to pass laws in all the devolved areas of competence and to delegate their implementation to the Generalitat. In general, the provinces continue to provide a means whereby Madrid can keep a finger in the local pie.

Next come the *comarques*, of which there are thirty-eight in Catalonia. These smaller, more organic units are much older than the provinces and evolved from the system of communications established in Roman times. They were adopted as the lower tier of administration under the statute of 1932 and have thus acquired a hallowed status – they are the preferred unit of most Catalans. Within the *comarques* are the *municipis* (each governed by a council called the Ajuntament); some are tiny, some large and one – Barcelona – is very large. But the struggle is essentially between the *província* and the *comarca*. There are few signs that any Madrid government of whatever colour will lightly abandon a provincial structure that is such a well-tried instrument of centralism. Nor are the Catalans likely to abandon their cherished *comarques*. But sooner or later rationalization there must be if only for economic reasons: it is absurdly expensive to maintain four levels of local government.

This is the sort of issue which is discussed endlessly in parliament and the press. The parliament of Catalonia aids its deliberations by allowing members to smoke in the chamber: this extends even to the dignified figures on the presidential table above the podium from which speakers address the hemicycle. There is something almost Modernist about the beards and pipes and cigars: Ramon Casas, the deft turn-of-the-century portraitist, should be there to record them worthily. For there can be no doubt that these men and women take their responsibilities with the utmost seriousness. They do not see themselves merely as a regional body; they are the representatives of a nation which may not have the status of a nation-state but does have all the other attributes of nationhood: language, literature, historical boundaries and a viable economy. Catalonia, incidentally, is the only non-nation-state to have its flag on the moon along with those of the United Nations. The curious reason for this, I gather, is that the nuclear physicist Werner von Braun was born in Catalonia and insisted on it.

Sometimes the idea of a Greater Catalonia, which would include Aragon, Valencia and the Balearics – the whole *catalano-parlant* world of some ten million people – is advanced. But this can only be a gleam in the eye because the federation of two or more autonomous regions without the consent of the national parliament is expressly ruled out by the constitution, no doubt precisely with this wealthy and potentially powerful combination in mind. There are visionaries who are prepared to accept the chill winds of European competition within the Common Market because they see the European Community as the framework within which the nation-state as it is presently known will eventually wither away to be replaced by a federal Europe in which Catalonia will enjoy equal status and full statehood with Belgium, Holland, Denmark, Scotland, Bavaria and other historical entities of similar size. But the Catalans are also a highly practical people and until that day dawns they will make the best of their statute and keep Madrid up to the mark by insisting on the fulfilment of all its conditions down to the last letter, which probably means a busy life for the constitutional tribunal.

11

Catalan Language

The Catalan language is a potent force, perhaps the most potent in Catalonia. It is more than a means of communication, more than a literature; it is the badge of a determined minority culture and an important weapon of nationalist politics. It is by far and away the most frequently used language you will hear spoken around you. Basically you can adopt one of two attitudes to it. You can disregard it completely as, for example, the average English visitor to Wales disregards Welsh. You can get about perfectly well using Castilian Spanish, which is the joint official language and understood by all Catalans, even though they do not use it among themselves – and you will find that English and French are widely spoken in Barcelona and on the coast. It is interesting that Catalans who speak either of these languages actually prefer them to Castilian, so the earnest student of standard Spanish should not seek to practise it on Catalans if another means of communication is available.

The alternative – or perhaps really complementary – approach is to acquire some understanding of Catalan, which will in my view increase enjoyment of the trip with the bonus of a certain sense of achievement. The daily paper *Avui* (*Today*) is not difficult to read for anyone with some knowledge of Spanish and average school French. You can ask for leaflets in Catalan when they are on offer in several languages; restaurant menus, theatre programmes and so forth all help to fill in gaps. However, spoken

Catalan does present difficulties of the same sort of magnitude as, for example, Portuguese – which is also very easy to read and hard to understand. So before encouraging you any further along this road, I think I should attempt to convince you that it is worth while.

I had heard of Catalan as a distinct language and even of some Catalan writers long before I ever went to Catalonia, but this was largely in connection with the Catalan literary revival or *Renaixença*, which began in about 1833. Loosely I had assumed that a few literary gentlemen had got together in their salons and decided that it would be a good idea to revive the old tongue and award literary prizes at a revamped version of the mediaeval *Jocs Florals*, and that they had then gone on to decide that it should be taught as a second language in schools, and in this way a moribund tongue gradually began to breathe new life and gain widening acceptance. This was so ill-informed that I feel I must give a brief account of the truth before going on to make some practical suggestions.

First the current facts, as far as they can be pinned down. According to a reliable source in Barcelona, of the six million inhabitants of modern Catalonia, some three and a half million use Catalan as their habitual tongue in family and business life; another million or so are bilingual without using it among themselves; and the balance have varying degrees of understanding of Catalan but speak only Castilian – the latter category belonging almost entirely to the immigrant population from other regions of Spain. If you add those who speak Valencian and Majorcan, which are almost identical with Catalan, and those on the Aragonese border and in French Roussillon who also speak Catalan, the grand total of natural *catalanoparlants* approximately doubles. From this it is clear that Catalan is in business in a way that Welsh and Gaelic and other minority languages are not.

Catalan is derived from vulgar Latin and belongs to the same group of western romance languages as Occitan, French, Castilian, Portuguese and Galician. It has some grammatical forms common to the Iberian branch of this group but it is phonetically and lexically nearer to the Gallic branch and in particular to Occitan (called the *langue d'oc* in the Middle Ages and more recently Provençal). Initially it was the spoken tongue of a mainly illiterate population. The evolution from low Latin to Catalan was slow and to the participants imperceptible. The most basic changes from the Latin root probably took place in the seventh and eighth centuries but this is difficult to pinpoint because such documents as existed were written in Church Latin with little relationship to the current vernacular. Then the vernacular began to break through into written texts. By the ninth and even more in the tenth and eleventh centuries there is an increasing appearance of distinctively Catalan words and even whole phrases in Latin texts, which suggests that the spoken language then was essentially what it is now. The first known Catalan written text is the twelfth-century *Homilies d'Organyà*, a marginal commentary on a collection of sermons in Latin.

The language spread as territory was recovered from the Moors: first into New Catalonia, then into Valencia and the Balearic Islands and finally overseas (it is still spoken by twelve thousand people in the town of Alghero in Sardinia). Thus Catalan became the national language of the mediaeval Catalan-Aragonese confederation, though it did not become the native tongue of Aragon, which retained separate political institutions and laws. Nonetheless, there is even today a fringe of Catalan speakers penetrating about twenty kilometres into Aragon (see p.145). As to Valencian and Majorcan, which are only distinguished from Catalan by local accents, successive Madrid governments – on the principle of divide and rule – have constantly sought to emphasize the minimal differences that exist in order to enlist local pride against any idea of merger. This ploy is designed to diminish the linguistic (and economic) community of interests which spurs on the advocates of Greater Catalonia, who would restore the federation as it was in the thirteenth and fourteenth centuries.

From the end of the fifteenth century to the early eighteenth century, despite the subordination of Catalonia to the Spanish crown, Catalan continued as the official language of the Aragonese and Catalan territories. It is perhaps surprising that this degree of cultural independence should have been accepted after the centralizing efforts of the Catholic sovereigns and the first Habsburgs, but it obviously reflected a reality that could not be overcome. So, despite the War of the Reapers (1640–52) and other serious clashes with the government of Madrid, the language continued in general use. Under both Philip III and Philip IV the minor nobility was bilingual and spoke Catalan for preference; only the grandees who lived at court repudiated their linguistic heritage.

The first major campaign to undermine the language came with the arrival of the Bourbons. The suppression by Philip V from 1716 onwards of all local political institutions was accompanied for the first time by a prohibition of the official use of Catalan. Obviously it could not be suppressed in ordinary parlance – and this was important at a time of very high illiteracy – but it was ruled out of all public business. Of course it survived in other spheres: there was no other way of teaching children who knew no Castilian, or of making wills for simple people, or of taking popular theatre to the fairgrounds – though smart drama and private correspondence among the upper classes both made increasing use of Castilian. Curiously enough, however, it was not until the reign of that enlightened despot Charles III that a law was passed requiring that secondary education, in the hands of compliant religious orders, should be taught in Spanish. But the universities still used Latin and primary schools still taught perforce in Catalan. The law thus proved unworkable and was revoked in 1771. The next attempt was made under the liberals in 1857 – Spanish liberalism, curiously enough, has always shown pronounced centralist tendencies – but by this time the renaissance was well under way.

The Catalan *Renaixença* is a phenomenon that is hard to define. Its first literary text was *L'oda a la pàtria* by Bonaventura Carles Aribau, published in 1833. Various literary and satirical magazines sprang to life. The *Jocs Florals* of Barcelona were revived in 1859 in imitation of the mediaeval contests of the troubadours. Jacint Verdaguer and Joan Maragall became popular romantic poets. Valentí Almirall founded the first Catalan daily newspaper *Diari Català* in 1881 and summed up the whole autonomist movement in his book *Lo catalanisme* in 1886. The most important point to grasp, however, is that none of this activity could have taken place without a living language to hand. This is what makes my original notion of a purely literary revival absurd.

The next step was political. In its initial phases the industrial bourgeoisie treated the renaissance simply as a cultural sideshow. When increasing disillusion with both liberal and conservative governments in Madrid spurred the growth of Catalan nationalism, the language was adopted as a political instrument and thus acquired a powerful new dimension. The most famous text of this period is *La nacionalitat catalana* (1906) by the politician Enric Prat de la Riba, who was later to become the first president of the Mancomunitat (see 'Political Life and Institutions'). Promoted to centre stage, the language now required standardization. The moving spirit behind this was Pompeu Fabra, whose efforts led to the foundation of the Institut d'Estudis Catalans in 1906, and the publication of the institute's *Normes ortogràfiques* in 1913, the *Gramàtica normativa* in 1918 and the *Diccionari general de la llengua catalana* in 1932. The institute, incidentally, still enjoys such prestige that it yields only in popular esteem to the Generalitat.

The use of Catalan was further enhanced when the Mancomunitat (1914–25) introduced it into local government and made it obligatory in schools, from which it naturally flowed into the media. The Generalitat (1931–9) continued this process and Catalan moved from the schools to the university, thus completing the century-long process of recatalanization of the region. But no sooner was this achieved than the reborn language was subjected to the most savage proscription ever unleashed on it. After General Franco's victory its public use was prohibited and severely punished. It was banned from public administration, schools, the universities, the press, the radio and even from signposts, advertisements, announcements, warnings and tombstones. All public institutions, including the Church, were forced to collaborate with this deliberate process of decatalanization, which continued in its full rigour until the late 1950s.

The onslaught eased off very slightly in 1959 when the abbey of Montserrat began to publish a Catalan journal called *Serra d'Or* (*Golden Mountain*). There had been only 12 Catalan book titles published in 1946; by 1965 this had risen to 453 and by 1968 to 520. Most of these were of a specialist or learned variety. The odd weekly was also permitted, mainly for children, and the radio stations were allowed a few broadcasts of a sporting and popular nature during the 1960s. At the time of Franco's death in 1975 the Catalan language was in a delicate state of health. On the one hand it had regained some of the territory lost in the cultural field, but on the other the process of decatalanization had been much assisted by the immigration of more than a million workers from other parts of Spain with no knowledge of Catalan and little interest in learning it. Also, Castilian predominated overwhelmingly in the new popular medium of television, as it still does today. However, the Catalan publishing industry has picked up enormously and now produces some 3,000 titles a year; the language is fully restored as the main vehicle of teaching at all levels of education; most church services are celebrated in Catalan; and the Generalitat runs a radio station and one television channel. It is pretty clear the language will now survive and probably flourish indefinitely. But given the events I have outlined it is hardly surprising that the Catalans should be passionately attached to their language, almost to the point of obsession. Occasionally the visitor may find this tiresome but it simply has to be accepted and respected.

As far as practical guidance goes, I will simply mention a few of the language's fundamental characteristics. Whereas Portuguese is difficult at first to understand for lack of consonants to latch on to (e.g. São Paolo for San Pablo), Catalan suffers if anything from an excess of consonants and few open vowel sounds (though eventually and with practice it is of some advantage to the English palate that every unaccented *o* and *e* has the same weak 'uh' sound as in English 'sing*er*' or 'begg*ar*' and those English who learn Catalan properly tend to speak it better than Castilians). Another feature of Catalan is that there are a great many common monosyllabic words ending in a variety of consonants thus (with Castilian and English equivalents in brackets):

boig (*loco* – mad)	*fill* (*hijo* – son)
cap (*cabeza* – head)	*gran* (*gran/grande* – great/large)
cec (*ciego* – blind)	*ham* (*anzuelo* – fish-hook)
crec (*creo* – I believe)	*text* (*texto* – text)
cuc (*gusano* – worm)	*verd* (*verde* – green)
fil (*hilo* – thread)	*vull* (*quiero* – I want)

Also, most past participles end in *t*, eg. *passat* (*pasado* – passed), *recordat* (*recordado* – remembered). Thus it is hardly surprising that Catalan should make a rather clipped staccato impression on the ear. A noticeable difference from Castilian is the absence of words of Arabic origin (except for the names of a few scientific and navigational instruments) in contrast with the early permeation of Castilian by Arabic words from the *algarabía* of the marketplace used by the Christian subjects of the Moors.

Despite the problems that confront the would-be *catalano-parlant* Ford's stricture – 'They speak a local, and to most an unintelligible language – a harsh Limousin, spoken with a gruff enunciation' – is hardly fair. He was prejudiced by his love of Castilian and of the south. Though Catalan is lexically concise (100 lines of French or Spanish will reduce to 90 or 95 lines respectively of Catalan) it is nonetheless well endowed with vocabulary. The *Diccionari general* of Pompeu Fabra lists 53,250 words following the most restricted criterion, while the Alcover-Moll dictionary, using a more exhaustive method and including local variants and archaic forms, gives more than 160,000 words.

Finally, just a few tips. *Plaça, carrer, passeig* and *passatge* replace Castilian *plaza, calle* (street), *paseo* (avenue) and *pasaje* (passage) almost everywhere. *Ajuntament* supersedes *Ayuntamiento* (Corporation). In the older cities the signs *Conjunt Històric* (Historic Ensemble), *Casc Antic* (Historic Quarter), *Barri Gòtic* (Gothic Quarter) and *Oficina de Turisme* (Tourist Office) are all useful pointers to where you probably want to get to. Once on your rounds, you will find *església* for *iglesia* (church), *museu* for *museo*, *palau* for *palacio, castell* for *castillo, monestir* for *monasterio, banys* for *baños* (baths) and *call* for *aljama* or *judería* (Jewish Quarter).

As regards the basic civilities you have *Bon dia* and *Adéu* for *Buenos días* and *Adiós* and *si us plau* for *por favor* or *s'il vous plaît*. *Mas* and *masia* both mean farm and sometimes appear in restaurant names; *can* and *cal* are both forms of *casa de* or *maison de* and are also frequent in shop and restaurant names. *Cuina* is the word for *cocina* or cuisine. *Don* is not used in forms of address – if you write to someone it is plain *Senyor*. To end a friendly note *Ben cordialment* is appropriate. If you want to wish someone Happy Christmas it is *Bon Nadal* and Happy New Year *Bon Any*. If you advance to intimacy *abraçades* (*abrazos* – embraces) and *petons* (*besos* – kisses) may be in order. But space does not allow me to continue. Over to Alan Yates's excellent *Teach Yourself Catalan*.

12

Catalan Literature

The Catalan language was well established by the ninth century. Popular songs and legends were spread by wandering minstrels but nothing was written down. Latin ruled in the Church and monasteries and such literature as there was, was confined to the poetry of the troubadours, who composed in a conventionalized form of Provençal. Within the troubadour tradition the Catalans formed a school of their own, in which kings and courtiers vied with one another, as in the case of Alfons the Chaste (1162–96) and Guillem de Berguedà. Though by the eleventh century Catalan had begun to penetrate Latin works, the first known written text in homespun Catalan is a twelfth-century marginal commentary to a collection of Latin sermons known as the *Homilies d'Organyà*. By the time it graduated to the written word the Catalan tongue was fully formed and articulate – a direct, earthy, pithy vernacular with three centuries of usage behind it.

At the end of the thirteenth century the troubadour tradition declined. The golden age of Catalan literature began in 1272 with Ramon Llull's *Llibre de contemplació* (*Book of Contemplation*). A Franciscan missionary and great traveller, Llull (1232–1315) was one of the most remarkable polymaths of his time. He was familiar with Islamic philosophy and science and was one of the first European thinkers to write learned works in the common tongue. He understood the sphericity of the earth and wrote an *Art de navegar* (*Art of Navigation*) in 1295, which remained in use until the time of Columbus. His *Blanquerna* was the first novel to feature a protagonist who was not a knight but a bourgeois; and the *Llibre d'amic i d'amat* (*Book of the Lover and the Beloved*) is one of the outstanding contributions to the mystical literature of Christendom.

If Llull was an energetic traveller, so too were the splendid chroniclers who developed and enriched the language in this period of political expansion. The colourful chronicle of James the Conqueror (1213–76) is by various hands, but the reign of Peter the Great (1276–85) was recorded by the single and more sober hand of Bernard Desclot. The greatest chronicler of the age was Ramon Muntaner, who accompanied the extraordinary expedition of the Almogàvers under Roger de Flor to Byzantium and Greece (1302–11); a born story-teller inclined towards hyperbole, he has been called the Catalan Froissart. The chronicle of Peter the Ceremonious (1336–87), written by scribes and revised carefully by the king, is better documented than the rest.

Another active promoter of the language was Saint Vincent Ferrer (1350–1419), who preached his demagogic Catalan sermons not only in the peninsula but also in France and Italy (it should be remembered that Catalan writ or influence ran over large parts of those territories at the time). In the field of higher learning Francesc Eiximenis (1340–1409) was as prolific as Llull, if less inspired. His encyclopaedic *Llibre del crestià* (*Book of the Christian*) – of which only four out of thirteen volumes survived – looks back to the Middle Ages for its religious inspiration, but his *Regiment de prínceps* (*Precepts for Princes*) is remarkably egalitarian and democratic. His works were revived a century later with the arrival of printing and were influential in the Spanish Renaissance period.

The classical age is generally held to have been ushered in by the suave, ironical sceptic Bernat Metge (1340–1413), whose novel *Valter e Griselda* appeared in about 1388. A leading light of Catalan humanism, Metge was deeply influenced by Cicero and Petrarch. His *Lo somni* (*The Dream*) written in prison in about 1397 shows Catalan in its maturity, on a par with the Italian of the time and closer to its modern form than either English or French. In 1323 the *Jocs Florals*, literary festivals designed to keep the *langue d'oc* alive and preserve the disappearing poetry of the troubadours, were founded by the aristocrats of Toulouse. In 1395 the Catalans founded their own *Jocs Florals* in Barcelona. These gave rise to no great poetry, but acted as a forum for the ideas and fashions of the Renaissance. The Catalan school of lyric poetry was heavily

influenced by Petrarch and Dante; Seneca and Ovid were trans-
lated. Andreu Febrer's version of *The Divine Comedy* appeared in
1428 – it was eulogized by that fastidious Castilian poet the
Marquis of Santillana, as was Jordi de Sant Jordi's *Pasió d'amor*
(*Passion of Love*), a charming collection of earlier Provençal and
Catalan love poetry enriched by a score of his own works.

These are all signs of a flourishing literature. But the greatest
name in Catalan poetry of the classical period is undoubtedly that
of Ausiàs March (b. 1397). With Febrer and Jordi de Sant Jordi he
joined the successful expedition to Sardinia in 1420 and with
them was captured at Ponza off Naples in 1435 in the first defeat
of the Catalan navy for two hundred years. His hundred or so
philosophical poems probe deeply into the predicament of man
tormented by doubt and fear of death; his *Pregària a Déu* (*Prayer to
God*) ranks high in the mediaeval literature of the peninsula and
there is wide agreement with the assessment of Torras i Bages,
author of *La tradició catalana*, that he is the 'prince of poets' of
Catalonia. The last of the poets of this period was Jaume Roig of
Valencia, whose *Llibre de les dones* is a satirical work of 12,000
lines on the condition of women and much else besides; his
vigorous style has been likened to Boccaccio's.

The works of Llull and March apart, the best-known Catalan
text is almost certainly *Tirant lo Blanc* by another Valencian,
Joanot Martorell (1413–68). This belongs to the literature of
chivalry and Martorell actually went to the real-life source
provided by the adventures of the Almogàvers, drawing extensively on Muntaner's chronicle for his material. So successful was
he in infusing a new realism into his tale that Cervantes, through
the curate in *Don Quijote,* calls it 'the best book in the world'.
Tirant, however, is not entirely wrapped in chivalric dreams and
the story takes account of the attitudes of the bourgeoisie; it
antedates the Castilian picaresque genre and is thought by many
to be the first modern novel.

It is worth noting briefly that the Renaissance brought Latin
back into vogue for works of higher learning. The Catalan Ramon
Sibiuda taught philosophy and medicine at Toulouse and became
rector of the university from 1424 to 1436. His *Theologia Naturalis
sive Liber Creaturarum* was one of the most famous books of its
time and had a great effect on Montaigne, who translated it into
French two centuries later and devoted to its author one of the
most elaborate of his essays. Sibiuda's rational Christianity also
had a profound effect on the greatest Catalan intellectual of the
Renaissance, Joan Lluís Vives (1492–1540); a friend of Erasmus

and counsellor of Catherine of Aragon, he spent much of his life abroad, principally at Bruges but also at Corpus Christi College, Oxford, where he wrote *De Subventione Pauperum*, which concerns the relief of the poor and is considered to mark the beginning of modern social science. In his other works, also in Latin, he made outstanding contributions to the ideas of internationalism and public welfare and to the psychology of education. His self-imposed exile was due in large part to the long shadow of Castile, which had by then eclipsed the Catalan enlightenment.

This brings me to the long night – nearly three centuries – of Catalan letters. The court moved to the centre of the peninsula; the upper nobility followed; the Atlantic replaced the Mediterranean as the centre of economic activity; the Catalan bourgeoisie relapsed into conservatism; there were two protracted but ultimately unsuccessful wars against Castile leading to stern reprisals. All these factors contributed to the paralysis of Catalan literature. The baroque, neo-classical and *costumbrista* periods in Catalonia were simply pale reflections of these movements in Castile.

Yet the language did not die; it continued as the daily means of communication in homes and businesses. Also, a crude local narrative poetry and a popular theatre based on adaptations of mediaeval mystery plays survived (see also 'Catalan Language'). There was thus an instrument ready to hand when the *Renaixença* came, heralded by the publication in 1833 of Bonaventura Carles Aribau's poem *La pàtria*. The romantic movement then seized eagerly on the Catalan tongue, forming two camps: conservative-historicist and liberal-revolutionary – and minor writers flourished in both. The first important poet of the movement was the priest Jacint Verdaguer (1845–1902), whose lyrics draw on rural images to create a nostalgic dreamworld of some potency; his two epic poems *Atlàntida* (*Atlantis*) and *Canigó* (*Canigou*) attempted to fuse the worlds of Christianity and pagan mythology. Angel Guimerà was another influential poet who turned from historical tragedies to realist prose drama. The novel, the theatre, comedies and one-act sketches crowded thick and fast on to the literary scene. The novels of Narcís Oller in particular reflected the new industrial society and the revived dynamism of the bourgeoisie.

Out of the Catalan renaissance sprange Modernisme, a movement of great importance in architecture and painting, whose literary facet combined aggressive individualism and Nietzschean exaltation of the will with *fin de siècle* decadence. The leading poet of the time, Joan Maragall (1860–1911), was inspired by German romanticism spanning Nietzsche, Novalis, Heine and Goethe; his writing gave status to the everyday language of Barcelona and his theory of the *paraula viva* (living word) put a premium on spontaneity and sincerity in contrast with the earlier rhetorical posturing of the renaissance. Santiago Rusiñol, painter and man of letters (see 'Modern Art'), drew on the most decadent aspects of Modernisme in his works for the theatre.

Modernisme was overturned by the more severe, more classical and more ascetic Noucentisme, whose leading light was Eugeni d'Ors. The new movement was intended to attract a culturally responsible Catalan intelligentsia who would command respect abroad – folksy vapourings went out of vogue. Josep Carner, a sensitive, detached, ironical writer, embodied Noucentisme's ideal of the poet as citizen. Joan Salvat-Papasseit and Josep Viçens Foix became heavily involved in European avant-garde experiments but by the mid-twenties the novel at any rate had responded to a demand for a more classical format, as in the work of Mercè Rodoreda, hailed by some as the best Catalan novelist of the twentieth century.

Under Franco the Catalan novel and theatre virtually disappeared. The breach was partly filled by the revival on a larger scale of the great Catalan puppet tradition by the Teatre de la Claca, which toured not only Catalonia but the United States and Australia; its most famous production (which came to London) was the silent burlesque of the Franco régime called *Mori el Merma*, whose satirical masks and monsters were designed and painted by Joan Miró. Painting and poetry, judged to be of little popular appeal, fared slightly better than plays and prose. The great poem of the Franco years is *La pell de brau* (*The Bull's Pelt*, 1960) by Salvador Espriu, in which the bitter resignation of the land of 'Sepharad' is bitingly conveyed. The great poem of the post-Franco years is *L'espai desert* (*The Empty Space*, 1976) by Pere Gimferrer, which reflects the hollowness of the long interregnum under the dictatorship. But Gimferrer rejects *poesia social*: the surface of his early work was eclectic and aestheticist; his current style is richly baroque, exhibiting unabashed enjoyment of the language. He is a leading figure of the general movement of contemporary Spanish poetry away from social anguish towards the expression of refined aesthetic experience. More recently Carles Riba, translator of Aristophanes and other classical texts, has emerged as a major poet, while Josep Pla's atmospheric travel books have earned him a similar reputation in prose. The latest literary star is Quim Monzó, whose innovative streak and impatience with established literary modes have invited comparison with Martin Amis.

Lines by Joan Maragall carved on a rock on the hillside above Montserrat:

Throw yourself into your task
as if on every detail of your thought,
on every word you speak,
on every piece you set in place,
on each and every of your hammer blows
hangs the salvation of the human race
because – believe this – so it does.

13

Modernisme

The Modernist movement is somewhat difficult to define suc-
cinctly. In its wider context it was theological, philosophical and
literary and was indebted to Bergson, Nietzsche and Wagner. In
Catalonia it also permeated and deeply coloured architecture,
the fine arts, crafts and even politics. According to Alan Yates in
'Catalan Literature between Modernism and Noucentism' (*Homage to Barcelona*, 1985), its 'essential motivation . . . was to modernize all aspects of Catalan culture, to open it up to Europe and
enhance the autonomous character and cosmopolitan qualifi-
cations of Catalan society'.

Despite its all-embracing nature the traveller's interest will
almost inevitably centre on architecture and its associated
decorative arts and crafts, for these are the most accessible
aspects of the movement and can be experienced and enjoyed
without too much knowledge of the other threads. That will be
the focus of this short study. (Modernist painters, notably Casas
and Rusiñol, are discussed in 'Modern Art' and writers in
'Catalan Literature'.) In its architectural expression Modernisme
is often thought to be synonymous with Art Nouveau, but this
fails to do justice either to its exceptional élan and vitality or to
its idealistic revolt against industrial squalor. As David Mackay
writes in *Modern Architecture in Barcelona*, 'The whole process of
assimilation was itself energized by an ideological force that
went much deeper. Art Nouveau arrived in Catalonia with

appropriate connotations of modernity in a moment of cultural explosion.' The dates of Modernisme are generally held to run from the early 1880s to the outbreak of the First World War. It was given a tremendous boost by the Universal Exhibition of 1888 – at once an affirmation of Barcelona's identity and a powerful bid for a recognized place in the modern world.

In the nineteenth century a fundamental architectural schism developed internationally with strong ideological affinities on each side of the divide. Ruskin, Morris, Pugin and Viollet-le-Duc all believed it possible to recapture the democratic spirit of the Middle Ages through neo-Gothic buildings and design. The basic division, as they saw it, was between classical architecture – cold, official, oppressive and authoritarian – and Gothic architecture – flexible, adaptable, authentic, co-operative and popular. In political terms Gothic was the language of local self-determination, while the classical style represented academic centralism. It is interesting that at about this time the battle was won for a Gothic reconstruction of the British Houses of Parliament, which had burned down in 1834; Pugin hailed 'the erection of the Parliament Houses in the national style' as a great triumph, while condemning neo-classical Euston station because the Gothic style was more suitable for a centre of public (i.e. popular) transport. Palmerston, on the other hand, refused to have a Gothic design foisted on him for the foreign office: the classical style was more appropriate for imperial grandeur.

The Catalan revival, being anti-centralist, not unnaturally started from a neo-Gothic base, but it was more eclectic than the English equivalent, as it could draw on more diverse sources including the Arab world. And there is an additional twist: the distaste for pompous centralist classicism with its bland, boring, dressed stone buildings led to an exaltation of the humbler brick diversified by tiles. Brick had been widely used in Old Castile during the Romanesque and Mudéjar periods owing to the lack of stone quarries in the flat lands of the meseta. In Catalonia, however, the use of brick became ideological, a badge of regional regeneration. It is significant that the Arc de Triomf for the 1888 Exhibition was built not of 'noble' stone but of brick, as was Domènech's café-restaurant (now the zoological museum). And this ideological use of brick extends to many of the major works of the Modernist movement (though ultimately the haute bourgeoisie appears to have recoiled from brick surfaces and insisted on a stucco finish).

Modernisme moved from transitional eclecticism towards a

national style which blossomed, albeit with variegated blooms, in the last years of the nineteenth and early years of the twentieth centuries; it then withered as the cooler neo-classical wind of Noucentisme began to blow. There are three architects who not only worked through all these stages but also between them designed most of the celebrated Modernist buildings: Domènech i Montaner; Puig i Cadafalch and Gaudí. They do not form an entirely homogeneous group. Both Domènech and Puig were not only architects but active politicians; their concerns were mainly secular and civic (see 'Political Life and Institutions'). Gaudí, the most famous internationally, is really an exception to the main thrust of the movement. He was a founder member of the ultra-conservative circle of Sant Lluc, which was modelled on a mediaeval guild. Under the patronage of Eusebi Güell, an ennobled manufacturer and a key figure in the industrial revival at the end of the century, Gaudí designed several remarkable buildings. But for all the originality of his forms, his view of the world remained rooted in religiosity and some of his work displays a strange and even sinister neo-feudalism.

Lluís Domènech i Montaner (1850–1923) was a central figure in almost all aspects of Catalan life. He was president of the revived *Jocs Florals* (see 'Catalan Literature'), president of the Lliga de Catalunya and a signatory of the *Bases de Manresa*, a project for an autonomous state presented without success to the king. He was elected twice to the national parliament in Madrid. He also wrote a *General History of Art* (1886–97) in collaboration with Puig i Cadafalch. Domènech practised his profession in a period when the expansion of the city was in full spate along the lines of Cerdà's plan (see pp.32-3) and the commercial bourgeoisie was eagerly rehousing itself along the boulevards, providing rich pickings for architects who themselves bought and developed land at a handsome profit. From 1901 he directed the school of architecture, founded in Barcelona in 1875.

Domènech's principal buildings include the Editorial Montaner i Simon offices (1880) in the Carrer d'Aragó; the café-restaurant for the Universal Exhibition of 1888; the Hospital de Sant Pau (1902–12) and the Palau de la Música Catalana (1905–8). These important commissions are all clad in brick. Domènech, like his main contemporaries, preferred highly articulated street fronts in striking contrast to bland classical façades; external ceramic decoration was revived and new life breathed into the ceramic factories of Manises; his widespreading and highly decorated capitals have a Renaissance exuberance reminiscent of a number of sixteenth-century buildings in Salamanca; his domestic façades on the Passeig de Gràcia (No. 35 and notably No. 132, the Casa Fuster of 1908–10) use semi-circular tribune windows on the corners above the entrance, flanked by tribune galleries on either side.

Domènech's greatest and most characteristic building is the Palau de la Música. I have attempted an impressionistic account of this exhilarating building on pp.66–7, but in a wider sense it also achieves an exceptional synthesis of the various ingredients of Modernisme. Outside, the narrow façade is highly accentu-

Palau de la Música: the façade combining colourful mosaic tile pictures (note the fangs of Montserrat behind the choir in the central panel) with grave busts of great composers.

ated with cantilevered columnettes, mosaics, the busts of great composers and so forth. Inside, the sumptuous auditorium is hung within a steel-frame glass box, which permits stained-glass walls and an amazing luminous glass ceiling. All the decorative arts and materials are thrown in – stucco, brick, iron, woodwork, ceramics, mosaic tiles, stained glass – and the eye can make its own tour of these riches without impeding the ear. The Palau de la Música trembles on the brink of vulgarity but is saved from this by the architect's powerful vision, through which all the potentially warring elements are made to serve the functional and symbolic purposes of the whole. This is one of the most remarkable concert halls in Europe – and the acoustics are superb.

Josep Puig i Cadafalch (1867–1957), Domènech's collaborator and seventeen years his junior, also had a distinguished political career, culminating in the presidency of the Mancomunitat from 1917 to 1924, when it was suspended by General Primo de Rivera. One of his early works was the Casa Martí, home of the famous Modernist café Els Quatre Gats (1895–6); but he is most remembered for two buildings: the Casa Terrades (1903–5), popularly known from its spires as Casa de les Punxes, on a triangular site between the Avinguda Diagonal and the Carrer Rosselló; and the Casa Amatller (1898–1900). The former is a large mediaeval-

Els Quatre Gats, the famous Modernist café by Puig i Cadafalch, scene of many artistic, literary and musical events at the turn of the century.

inspired block of mansion flats with a gabled roof line, mullioned windows and cylindrical towers rounding off the sharp corners; Puig's bulky floral capitals on short columns at ground level closely resemble Domènech's. But Puig was the arch-eclecticist, a sort of Catalan Lutyens. In his early work, as Ignasi de Solà-Morales points out in 'Modernista Architecture' (*Homage to Barcelona*, 1985), 'The influence of the domestic architecture of Mackintosh and the Viennese secessionists is modified by reminiscences of Catalan and central European baroque, combined with mediaeval civic architecture.' Puig later built the Casarramona yarn factory whose two minaret-towers give it the appearance from a distance of a large mosque. In David Mackay's view he was closer to the spirit of William Morris than any of his compatriots and attempted to establish the Catalan equivalent of English free architecture of the turn of the century. With the advent of Noucentisme he turned to modified institutional classicism. In 1915 he made a grandiose design for an aborted exhibition to celebrate the great new life force, electricity, and he was responsible for some of the pavilions at the 1929 Exhibition: in one of these Corinthian columns and capitals sustained an iron and glass roof over Packard and Rolls-Royce.

Casa Amatller in the Passeig de Gràcia, next door to Gaudí's Casa Batlló, belongs to Puig's early period. It has a stepped Dutch gable with ceramic panels and bosses crowning the pargeted stucco façade. In this building the architect collaborated extensively with decorative artists, notably Antoni Maria Gallissà (likewise a politician and president of the Unió Catalanista), who with Domènech had set up an arts and crafts workshop in the café-restaurant after the great Exhibition was over. Now known as the Castell dels Tres Dragons, the building was given over to the production of furniture, ceramics, tiles, glass and banners. It might be thought that the combination of stylistic electicism with a wide range of craft materials would lead to fussiness, but it is remarkable how far most Modernist buildings hold together – possibly through the inner conviction of their designers that the desire and pursuit of the whole, the search for total art employing all crafts, was not a vain endeavour. As Bruce Tate of Nottingham University suggested in a recent lecture, these buildings need careful reading; the print is small. There is also a gestural or symbolic content to many of them and this is particularly the case with Antoni Gaudí.

Antoni Gaudí i Cornet (1852–1926) was Domènech's almost exact contemporary but his career developed along very different lines. Gaudí was a very private individual who attracted a few faithful followers, notably the architects Josep Maria Jujol, Francesc Berenguer and Joan Rubió. He was a strong Catalanist who refused to speak Castilian though he had no ambition for a public life in nationalist politics like that led by Domènech and Puig. He was an ardent Catholic and indeed he and his circle would have been horrified by the term Modernist, which they would have associated with *fin de siècle* artists and writers of whose anarchistic view of life, philosophical nihilism and libertarian lifestyles they strongly disapproved. Among the younger generation Gaudí was considered a religious fanatic. When Picasso went to Paris in 1900 he and his companion Casagemas wrote back to their friend Reventós: 'If you see Opisso [an artist who occasionally worked on the Sagrada Família] tell him to come here as it is good for saving the soul – tell him to send Gaudí and the Sagrada Família to hell . . . Here are the real teachers everywhere.'

However, if Gaudí was ultra-conservative in his private and spiritual life, this was emphatically not the case in his approach to structure, form and decoration. 'After experimenting in youthful works', writes Ignasi de Solà-Morales, 'with stylistic repertories derived from the Gothic, Moorish, baroque and classical traditions, Gaudí arrived with maturity at the formulation of a strongly personal language, essential and free, in which any reference to historical styles was obliterated in a fluid magma where the principal tectonic elements acquired new significance.' That is perhaps what differentiates him most from his major contemporaries, in whose work historical references are usually quite apparent.

An early work, the Casa Vicens (1883–5) in the Carrer de les Carolines, off the Carrer Gran de Gràcia, is a modest-sized brick house built for a tile manufacturer in humbler surroundings than the lower and wider Passeig de Gràcia favoured by the haute bourgeoisie. The surface is variegated with strongly marked indentations and the disparate elements are drawn together by the use of green and yellow tiles of Mudéjar inspiration and pinned down by a strong flattened-W roof line. The screen-like façade with the main windows recessed behind a perforated outer wall was to be a feature of several of his buildings.

It was in 1878 that Gaudí first met Count Eusebi Güell, the textile manufacturer who became his principal patron. Their symbiotic relationship produced some unusual results. In 1885

The authoritarian façade of Gaudí's Palau Güell rising above menacing iron gates giving on to a narrow street.

Gaudí began a townhouse for Güell on a rather cramped site in the narrow Carrer Nou de las Ramblas (formerly Calle Conde del Asalto). The façade has two elliptical arches opening into the porte-cochère and protected by menacing iron gates. Gaudí's ironwork, though always interesting and inventive, is extremely aggressive here, and throughout the building he seems to have reverted to the model of an urban fortress-dwelling favoured by prominent and frequently feuding families in mediaeval times. Güell is reputed to have said as the construction progressed that he liked it less and less and Gaudí to have replied that he liked it more and more – the architect seems to have prevailed. The interior arcades are also elliptical on highly original spear-shaped columns. There is a central well under a cupola with sly little shuttered windows at the gallery stage, and the whole flavour is stern, authoritarian and paternalistic. This brilliantly executed but frankly sinister building is an extraordinary statement of the architect's view of the role of the industrial magnate. Gaudí also built a palace for the bishop of Astorga, near León, which incorporates some not dissimilar features, but this is a free-standing building outside the old city walls and is not nearly so oppressive.

Palau Güell: gallery overlooking the central well of the house.

Gaudí's view of a suitable town residence for his patron is very much in line with the so-called industrial feudalism of the *colonies industrials.* These grew up mainly along the river Llobregat, where water power was available for the looms, and took the form of enclosed compounds, complete with factory buildings, workers' housing estate, owner's mansion, church and village school. Such was the Colònia Güell at Santa Coloma de Cervelló, where Gaudí and his assistants worked from 1898 to 1915. Berenguer built the school. Gaudí's most important contribution was the crypt chapel, in which his stress-defying predilection for tilted columns with brick arches and radial ribs was given its greatest scope. David Mackay writes that the crypt took shape 'like a full-scale model, which needed almost daily supervision'. This required a high degree of teamwork and the project ended in effect with the death of Berenguer in 1914.

The lighter side of Gaudí is to be found in the Parc Güell (1900–

14) described on pp.57–8. The abandoned project for a hillside garden city has left Barcelona with a public park graced by various grottoes and walks supported on the pervasive tilted columns, the whole culminating in the great *mirador* with its famous serpentine bench-cum-parapet surfaced entirely with broken tiles and pottery (usually attributed to Jujol). Of the intended sixty or so villas only two were ever built – the bourgeoisie was evidently not ready to climb so far up the hill. This leads me back to their preferred district, the Passeig de Gràcia, which boasts two of Gaudí's best-known buildings. The smaller Casa Batlló (1905–7) is a remodelling of an existing family house on the inside while the outside has been most delightfully reclothed: the façade shimmers with broken tiles and plates – white, silver, grey, blue, pink; if David Mackay is right the scaly sinuous roof line represents the spine of Saint George's dragon, while the metal balconies recall the skulls the beast devoured before its death at the hands of Catalonia's patron saint. Fantasy, symbolism and humour are all conjured up by Gaudí the magician. Immediately adjacent is Puig's Casa Amatller: the two together are said to form the centrepiece of the *manzana de la discordia* – there is a play on words here as the Castilian word *manzana* means both 'city block' and 'apple' – but in fact they make rather an instructive contrast, Gaudí's undulating and glimmering façade offering a sly comment on the earnest historicism of its neighbour.

Across the street and a little higher up on the right, the Casa Milà (1905–11) – popularly referred to as La Pedrera – is a much larger block of flats incorporating a number of technical and spatial innovations. The eye is first caught by the flowing seaweed forms of the wrought-iron balconies by Jujol, but the real originality is structural. The fluid concrete surface is hung on a steel frame; the lifts are not contained in the stairwell as Gaudí apparently wanted to 'relegate the stairs to use by servants. . . large apartment dwellings could thus be designed according to the traditional hierarchy of the detached house, without problems of cross-circulation between owners and servants.' This is David Mackay's interpretation and (again, if he is right) it suggests that Catalan Modernisme was not exactly democratic. But in other respects it was in tune with the times: here Gaudí's porte-cochère gives access to underground parking by means of a ramp, the first amenity of its kind in the city.

Though these were all startling achievements, Gaudí is best known to the vast majority of people as the architect of the uncompleted Sagrada Família church. He took over the work on the death of the first architect Villar in 1883. For more than a hundred years the rising spires (initially four, now eight) have been as much a symbol of Barcelona as the Eiffel Tower is of Paris or Big Ben is of London. In the early years Gaudí took it in his stride along with his other commissions. But in 1914 his chief assistant Berenguer died, followed by his patron Güell in 1918, and taste turned against Modernist extravagance. Gaudí was thus thrown back on this overambitious project, which obsessed him until his death in 1926. Yet his method of work has made it virtually impossible for it to be completed posthumously. The almost day-to-day creative approach adopted in the crypt chapel at the Colònia Güell is inconceivable as a working basis for a temple whose main spire was intended to be five hundred feet high (the present 350-foot rockets belong merely to the transepts) particularly when the energy and the vision have drained away. Mackay has suggested (with some justice, I think) that 'Gaudí in his prime seems to have delighted in creating problems in order to demonstrate how he could solve them'. That is perhaps rather splendid while you are alive but obviously not feasible when you are dead. One solution, as I have suggested, would be to stop the work, remove the great brooding crane, take down the ugly hoardings, wind up the stonemasons' yard with all its litter and put the whole area inside the shell down to lawn and fountains, allowing people to enjoy one of the greatest pieces of open-air sculpture ever made. This would be the most fitting monument of all to Gaudí's genius.

Modernisme was a spent force well before Gaudí's death, despite the dogged determination of first its designer and subsequently his followers and admirers to press on with the Sagrada Família regardless of the change of taste. Modernisme was not, however, wiped out at one fell swoop. *Fin de siècle* bohemianism and anarchism continued well into the new century, and Modernist architecture after 1900 still had some of its most successful works ahead. It was then fairly swiftly eroded by Noucentisme, which preached a new classicism, a new puritanism, a new asceticism and a new search for order, stamping down hard on the flamboyance of Modernist decoration. Ironically one of Gaudí's most valued assistants, Josep Maria Jujol, emerged as a leading practitioner of the new order. The First World War saw an influx of foreign artists and the establishment in Barcelona of an influential group of European avant-garde painters. Noucentisme was overtaken in its turn by Surrealism, Functionalism, Dada and

253

Art Deco. In architecture the neo-classicism of glass, steel and concrete became the dominant mode. The new mentors were Le Corbusier, Mies van der Rohe and Josep Lluís Sert. The 1929 Exhibition was a very different kettle of fish from that of 1888, but the earlier of the two, in the first flush of Modernisme, was more abundantly Catalan.

14

Modern Art

Catalonia produced remarkable Romanesque art and good craftsmanlike painting in the Middle Ages; it then entered a long
decline and did not resurface with any sort of major contribution
to the visual arts until the late nineteenth century. There are a
number of historical reasons for this eclipse: Castile absorbed
Aragon-Catalonia; patronage came mainly from Madrid; Velázquez and Zurbarán were sucked into the centre from Andalusia,
as was Goya later from Aragon. Political discrimination against
Catalonia under the Habsburgs and to a greater extent under the
Bourbons did little to encourage Catalan artists. How is it, then,
that this not very promising soil gave birth to native artists such
as Miró, Dalí and Tàpies and became such an important staging
post for that brilliant bird of passage, Picasso?

The answer lies, I think, in the Catalan *Renaixença* of the mid-
nineteenth century and subsequently the Modernist movement.
In Catalonia this found expression primarily in architecture and
the decorative arts (see 'Modernisme') but it also had a stimulating effect on other branches of the arts, such as graphics and
ultimately painting. Yet a visit to the Museu d'Art Modern in
Barcelona is not on the whole tremendously encouraging. The
museum is replete with history paintings, anecdotal realism, pre-
Raphaelite damsels and the like, and it is not until the last two
decades of the century that any painting worthy of closer
attention emerges. This period coincides with the advent of

Modernisme but the impact of that movement is less pronounced than in architecture. The Olot painters led by Joaquim Vayreda are reminiscent of the French Barbizon school; the luminists such as Arcadi Mas i Fontdevila are often referred to as Impressionists, though their work is in reality closer to the brilliant staccato colouring of Marià Fortuny. The two leading painters of the time were undoubtedly Ramon Casas (1866–1932) and Santiago Rusiñol (1861–1931). The latter first went to Paris in 1889 and both enjoyed sufficient private means to allow them to spend long spells in the mecca of the artistic world. In 1891 Rusiñol bought and converted an old house in the seaside town of Sitges, where he inaugurated a series of *Festes Modernistes*. These were designed to promote a new openness towards Europe, widen the horizons of Catalan culture and end provincialism. Rusiñol also had literary and theatrical interests and acted in the first performance of

This poster designed by Santiago Rusiñol for his own play
L'alegria que passa *(1898) shows North European influence.*

Ramon Casas: portrait of the painter Isidre Nonell, c.1899.

the Catalan translation of Maeterlinck's *L'Intruse* during the second *Festa Modernista* in 1893. In the realm of painting the *Festes* brought together the Olot painters, the luminists and practitioners of other styles. If there was any artistic common denominator, it was an intense preoccupation with light, but in general the work was more muted, more dependent on Paris and less aggressive than was the case with architecture and the decorative arts.

In 1900 Casas and Rusiñol held an important joint show of paintings whose esfumato line and modern subject matter – mainly café and street life – were described as Catalan Impressionist, though their work is actually closer to Degas and

Whistler. Later the two men followed increasingly divergent paths. At his best Rusiñol has an elegance reminiscent of Sir William Nicholson, but his work was to drift into symbolism, allegorical murals and finally a sugary series on the great gardens of Spain. Casas, however, focused throughout his career on contemporary personalities and events. His series of charcoal portrait drawings is an important record of the leading artistic figures of the time; in this respect he outshines Sir William Rothenstein. His portrait of Erik Satie as a bohemian in Montpar-

Ramon Casas: two of the founders of Els Quatre Gats, Casas himself and Pere Romeu, on a tandem, 1897.

nasse is delightful; he did not, however, restrict himself to the artistic milieu; he was also politically aware and in 1894 painted *Garrote vil* (Museo Español de Arte Contemporaneo, Madrid), the scene of the public garrotting of an anarchist who had tried and failed to kill General Martínez Campos the previous year (the painting caused a lady to faint when it was exhibited). *La Carga* (1899 – Museu d'Art Modern, Olot), in which a mounted Civil Guard drives back a crowd of demonstrators, is another work in the same vein.

In 1897 Casas and Rusiñol together with Miquel Utrillo and the entertainer Pere Romeu had founded Els Quatre Gats (The Four Cats café), which became the venue for a variety of literary and artistic events. Joan Maragall read his poems there; Isaac Albéniz and Enric Granados gave concerts. The café also provided a second generation of Modernist painters with wall space. Joaquim Mir (1873–1940) and Isidre Nonell (1873–1911) were the leading figures and it was here that the young Picasso made his Barcelona début. He had arrived with his family at the age of fourteen in 1895 and in 1900 exhibited a series of portraits of those who frequented the café, in the same vein as that by the doyen of the circle Casas, who added the young Andalusian to his own series in 1901. The Casas portrait of Picasso is worth dwelling on: a whiff of the fairground or popular theatre seems to attach to the

Ramon Casas: portrait of Pablo Picasso, 1901.

youth in wide-brimmed hat, baggy trousers and spats, who looks something of an outsider in the world of eyeglasses and beards which were the badges of the bourgeois bohemian; it is clear from this moment that Picasso was different. He was influenced, it is true, by Nonell's gypsies and other characters on the fringe of society, which he drew on during his blue period, but it was not long before Barcelona's art world became too cosy and introspective for him. In 1900 he began to alternate between Barcelona and Paris and in 1904 he settled in France for good.

Some mention must be made of Noucentisme here. The term was coined by Eugeni d'Ors, who aimed to awaken artists to their mission in the new century, which was to form a 'cultural brigade' in support of Catalonia's political aspirations. But the work did not measure up to this high purpose. The sculptors Josep Clarà

Pau Gargallo: stone head of Pablo Picasso, c.1913.

and Enric Casanovas reverted to a rather banal classicism; the restless Gargallo produced the most impressive work including an amusing stone head of Picasso looking like a bantam-weight boxer (Museu d'Art Modern, Barcelona). Among painters, Joaquim Sunyer's classic Mediterranean landscapes were strongly influenced by Cézanne.

Then in 1912 a major event in the artistic life of Barcelona took place, an exhibition of Cubist art at the Dalmau gallery. Picasso, who did not attend, was represented only by blue-period drawings, but the Catalan public experienced its first encounter with Albert Gleizes, Metzinger, Marie Laurençin, Marcel Duchamp, Fernand Léger and Juan Gris. Incidentally Gris is sometimes thought of as a Catalan (which he was not), possibly because he contributed illustrations to the Catalan magazine *Papitu* from 1908 to 1911, when his name was probably printed in Catalan as 'Joan'. In fact he was born and studied in Madrid, moving to France in 1906, where Kahnweiler became his dealer. Gris was so immersed in France that he preferred to be known as 'Jean' and spent virtually all his working life in his adopted country until his early death at the age of forty.

Nineteen twelve also saw the arrival of Joan Miró (1893–1983) in Barcelona. Miró joined the anti-academic art school founded by Francesc d'Assís Galí, whose teaching was directed towards a universal and active education of the sensibilities, one that included music, literature and country excursions. According to the critic Sebastià Gasch (*Joan Miró*, 1963), Miró at that time only 'saw coloured designs and lines. Form slipped through his fingers.' Galí set out to remedy this by obliging him to make pottery, and this tension between the calligraphic and the plastic seems to have remained an important feature of his work throughout his life.

The influence of the foreign avant-garde was to become even more important in Barcelona with the outbreak of the First World War as Spain's neutrality attracted a whole galaxy of foreign artists. Robert and Sonia Delaunay came; likewise the pacifists Albert and Juliette Gleizes and the Russians Olga Sackaroff and Serge Charcoune. Most were shown by Dalmau in 1916; their arrival created a reaction against the local patriotism and Mediterranean classicism of the Noucentiste artists. In 1917 a great exhibition of French art comprising 1,450 works was held. All the trends developed in France since the second half of the nineteenth century were on view: Impressionism, Post-Impressionism, Fauvism, Cubism. Again according to Gasch, when Miró saw Fauve paintings for the first time, they struck him like a thunderbolt. In the same year Diaghilev's Ballets Russes brought *Parade* to the Liceu theatre with music by Satie, script by Cocteau and costumes and décor by Picasso, who returned in triumph (though not to stay). Among *Parade*'s admirers was Miró, who met Picasso and was invited to visit him in Paris. In 1918 Dalmau gave Miró his first one-man exhibition.

This cosmopolitan milieu meant that young Barcelona artists could draw on a very wide range of stimuli for their experiments and innovations, and the impact of foreign influences on local trends turned Barcelona into an important centre of the visual arts. Without these influences it is likely that Noucentisme would simply have drifted into a new academicism. But even so Paris continued to exercise its magnetic attraction, to such an extent that in 1919 almost all the members of the Agrupació Courbet, to which Miró belonged, left for the French capital. Paris, on this occasion, had such a disturbing effect on Miró that he was unable to paint; he returned to Mont-roig near Tarragona in 1920. After this he alternated summers in Mont-roig with sojourns in Paris, where his international reputation began to grow. Yet Mont-roig remained the fount of his creativity.

As well as promoting Miró, Dalmau gave Salvador Dalí (b. 1904) his first one-man show in 1925, his second in 1926–7 and a third in 1928–9. Dalí was brought up in Cadaqués and Figueres and in 1921 went to study in Madrid, where he met Federico García Lorca and Luis Buñuel, with whom he worked on the film *Un Chien Andalou* (1929). Dalí and Lorca were close between 1925 and 1927, when the poet stayed in Cadaqués and Barcelona, where Dalmau put on an exhibition of Lorca's drawings. Dalí was extremely impressionable, absorbing a great many influences: in 1924 he wrote that he was interested in Juan Gris and André Derain and described how he had returned to Raphael, Poussin and Ingres; he then became fascinated by Vermeer. At about this time the Sitges journal *L'Amic de les Arts* gave currency to Dalí's ideas on Surrealism. In 1928, with Lluís Montanyà and Sebastià Gasch, Dalí signed the *Yellow Manifesto*, which attacked the current state of Catalan culture and argued that sportsmen, music-halls, the cinema, jazz, the automobile and the aeroplane were the proper subject matter of art in the new machine age. The establishment was hostile – and Dalí's career as public exhibitionist was launched. Despite his self-portrait with *L'Humanité* (1923) and his brief friendship with Lorca, Dalí supported General Franco during and after the Civil War. He will never be forgiven for this by the great majority of passionately anti-Franco Catalans, but his linear felicity, inventiveness and humour will always ensure him devoted admirers.

The great post-war success story of Catalan art is that of Antoni Tàpies (b. 1923). This is unusual in a number of respects. First, it is hardly reflected at all in the public galleries of Barcelona – there are only two Tàpies in the Museu d'Art Modern – though a Tàpies museum is said to be under consideration. Second, after his brilliant début in 1950, Tàpies's numerous one-man and retrospective shows worldwide have disseminated his work to an extent that can hardly be matched even by Picasso, Miró or Dalí. Barcelona, Madrid, Málaga, Chicago, Venice, Stockholm, Paris, Dusseldorf, Milan, Washington, Berne, Munich, New York, Bilbao, Essen, Buenos Aires, Hanover, Zurich, Cannes, Toulouse, Tokyo – there appears to be no art centre in the world that has not seen Tàpies live. Third, and most important, he is an extraordinarily different artist from his famous predecessors. Though influenced in his formative stages by Miró and Klee, Ernst and Magritte, with all their linear, spatial and symbolic brilliance, his fascination with physical objects has led him to attach overwhelming importance to the surface and texture of paint, in which he makes his marks as with a stick or thumb in sand, and to lean towards collage not as one among many art forms but as the most fundamental and powerful of all. Given the expressive restrictions of his material, the results are often amazingly monumental. Finally, Tàpies's abstraction has not made him a political neutralist or caused him to avoid Catalan acts of protest. In 1966 he participated in a meeting of intellectuals in the Capuchin convent of Sarrià in Barcelona, for which he was arrested and fined; in 1971 he painted *L'Esprit Catalan*, in which the four red bars of the national flag, dragged as if by bloody fingers over a yellow background, are overscrawled with slogans: *Catalunya, Veritat, Cultura, Democràcia, Espontaneïtat, Igualtat Social, Dret Nacional, Estat Constitutional*, etc. – this at a time of great political sensitivity in the dying years of the Franco régime when most painters resorted to a hermetic abstractionism which gave no handle to the authorities. There can be no doubt that Tàpies is a very Catalan painter.

So why – to sum up – did Barcelona acquire this pre-eminence in painting within the peninsula and a major reputation in the rest of the world? The same concentration of talent and achievement had not been seen since the Andalusians Murillo, Velázquez and Zurbarán captured Spanish painting in the seventeenth century. The answer, I suggest, lies in the interaction of a number of elements, notably the Catalan mid-nineteenth century renaissance; Modernisme and Noucentisme; the dealer Dalmau and his exhibitions of European art in 1912, 1916, 1917 and 1920; the First World War and the influx of the European avant-garde; and the two-way traffic that developed between Barcelona and Paris. But cosmopolitanism on its own, though stimulating, carries with it the danger of slavery to fashion, so these influences would not necessarily have borne such fruit as they did had they not been nourished by the deep respect in which Catalans hold their own cultural traditions. Picasso is the exception here: he refused to be trammelled by regionalism or nationalism – and he was not in any case a Catalan – so he moved on. Miró, Dalí and Tàpies, on the other hand, acquired language from abroad but built their reputations out of the bones, stones and traumas of Catalonia. That is why they are so potent.

15

Popular Culture

Feast Days and Fairs

These play an extremely important part in Catalan national life.
In this respect Catalonia is no different from other Mediterranean
countries, but there are interesting points of divergence in the
relative importance attached to the main days and events. Within
the peninsula this divergence is particularly marked between
Catalonia and Andalusia, though in both regions a distinction is
made between feast days and fairs. On the former commerce and
industry are closed, people dress up and the main rituals usually
take place on fixed sites indoors (whether church, monastery or
the home). On the other hand, fairs – especially the more
traditional ones – are normally held in the open air on working
days and commercial activity is by definition increased. The
Church calendar, which in turn bears a close relationship to the
older solar cycle, has historically provided the framework for
both types of festivity. The revival of commerce in the early
Middle Ages was stimulated by royal grants of tax exemption to
favoured towns for specific periods during which fairs might be
held and the dates chosen tended to cluster around the great feast
days of the Church. Thus in Seville *Feria* follows hard on *Semana
Santa* (Holy Week) while in Barcelona Christmas is preceded by
the two-week fair of Santa Llúcia.

However, what might be called the axis of the year varies from
north to south. The Catalan axis is solstitial, running from

Christmas (much more important than in the south) to Saint John's Day (24 June), while further south the axis follows an equinoctial cycle from Easter (much more important than in Catalonia) to the Assumption (15 August). Though the reasons for this divergence are no doubt partly climatic – Easter processions cannot count on clement weather in Barcelona – they are much more deeply based on Andalusian mariolatry with its emphasis on the agony of the Virgin and her eventual apotheosis. Also, the Assumption reflects much older celebrations in honour of Astarte which were held in Cádiz in pre-Christian times.

In Catalonia religious faith is not so extravagantly expressed nor is there the same idolatry of saints as in Andalusia, where religious fervour reaches fever pitch in the cults of the Macarena and the Virgin of Rocío. Undoubtedly in the Middle Ages there were pilgrimages or *romerías*, such as still exist in the south, but in Catalonia these have largely died away: the sober veneration the Catalans feel for the Virgin of Montserrat, for example, can be expressed on a coach trip; they do not parade her through the streets or form gypsy caravans to her shrine.

Throughout Catalonia there is evidence of a lively renaissance of almost anything that can be considered popular or traditional. There is undoubtedly a political dimension to this: as public holidays provide a natural outlet for local nationalist sentiment, some of the more important ones were banned under Franco, notably the February carnival. With the end of that régime in 1975 it is not perhaps surprising that these celebrations should have been resumed with new energy and as an affirmation of independence. This renaissance has also received considerable impetus from teachers and neighbourhood associations, many of whom are in touch with political parties anxious to promote national identity. Thus old festivals have been refurbished for new ends.

Commercial fairs are also experiencing something of a boom. To those of traditional stamp devoted to the sale of livestock and produce there has been added a whole new range of contemporary activities and goods – the cinema, holidays and leisure, fashion, agricultural machinery and so forth. Ever since the Universal Exhibition of 1888 Barcelona has been famed as a centre of trade fairs and today occupies the leading position in the peninsula in this regard. Just as the desire for national self-expression and differentiation has breathed new life into ancient observances, so industrialization, aided by the media in a publicity-conscious age, has led to a crowded calendar of commercial fairs.

In a book of this length it is impossible to provide a comprehensive guide to all the feasts and fairs in Catalonia, but some fundamental dates are worth noting down. First, the Catalan equivalents of bank holidays are as follows:

Cap d'Any – New Year's Day (1 January)
Els Reis – Epiphany (6 January)
Divendres Sant – Good Friday (March–April)
Festa del Treball – May Day
Sant Joan – Saint John's Day (24 June)
L'Assumpció – Assumption (15 August)
La Diada – National Day (11 September)
Festa de la Hispanitat – Feast of the Hispanic Race (12 October)
Tots Sants – All Saints' Day (1 November)
La Inmaculada – the Immaculate Conception (8 December)
Nadal – Christmas (25 December)
Sant Esteve – Saint Stephen's Day (26 December)

Some of these are imposed by the Spanish state and are celebrated with less commitment than others. Those that really count are celebrated with special panache in certain towns as I indicate below, but for the host of local festivities you will have to acquire the relevant comarcal leaflet (see 'Maps, Plans, Leaflets and Guides').

Fira de Santa Llúcia (13 December) Originally the fair of students and dressmakers, today it inaugurates the Christmas and New Year season. In Barcelona stalls specializing in earthenware figurines for the crib and handicrafts aimed at the Christmas market are set up on 8–24 December.
Fira de Gall (21 December) Street markets specialize in turkeys, game birds and Christmas fare in general and the Catalans stock up for the celebratory meals of the following three weeks. The display is especially remarkable at Vilafranca del Penedès, where there are also games and competitions.
Nit de Nadal (24 December) Christmas Eve is celebrated particularly in the mountain towns and villages; in Corbera de Llobregat scenes from the birth of Christ are acted out by villagers in a play called *El pessebre vivent* (*The Living Crib*).
Nadal (25 December) The traditional Christmas menu is *escudella* and *carn d'olla* (see 'Food and Drink'), stuffed turkey, nougat, biscuits, dried fruit and champagne. The crib is finally completed by the addition of the figure of the infant Jesus. Carols and choral concerts are held within the family.

Cap d'Any (31 December/1 January) Twelve grapes are eaten, one each on the twelve strokes of midnight, as in the rest of Spain. This celebration is faintly licentious and takes place more among friends than relatives. It is difficult for foreigners to break into intimate circles bent on mild debauch.

Els Reis (6 January) Father Christmas has no jurisdiction in Catalonia; instead, ever since Christmas Day, the Three Kings' page has been slipping down chimneys to see if children are behaving well enough to deserve a gift. He goes by different names: he is Xiu-xiu in Terrassa, Quatre-Ulls (Four Eyes) in other places and so on. In Barcelona, the Three Kings arrive by sea and are received in the port by the mayor; they then set off on a great cavalcade through the city which brings traffic to a halt for a good three hours. That night the children put a shoe out on their balconies and the following morning find it surrounded by presents.

Sant Antoni (17 January) The abbot Saint Anthony had special healing powers over animals so this is the feast of domestic animals and is celebrated particularly in Barcelona, Castell-tercol, Caldes de Montbui and Balsareny. The heroes of the day are oxen, horses and mules, which are blessed and paraded garlanded through the streets; at Balsareny there are horse races

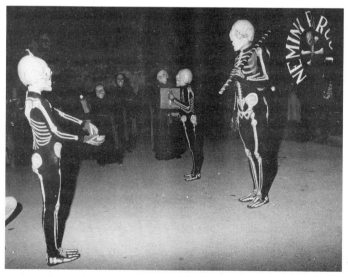

The macabre Dansa de la mort, *preserved from mediaeval times at Verges.*

and in some places tractors are now admitted as draught animals.

Carnaval (February–March)   This 'feast of the mad' is remarkable for masks and disguises and is especially lively at Vilanova i la Geltrú, where the townspeople go out to welcome Carnestoltes, king of all vices; after sporting with him for three days, the throng condemn him to death and burn or bury him. This festival is comparable to Mardi Gras elsewhere.

Fira de Ramos (March–April)   In Vic the traditional Mercat del Ram (Palm Market) is held during the three days preceding Palm Sunday; here people buy palm leaves that will grace their balconies and protect their houses from evil throughout the year.

Divendres Sant (March–April)   Good Friday is confined to church and cloister; there are no processions. However, Verges in l'Empordà is almost the only place in Europe that has preserved intact the mediaeval *Dansa de la mort*: some of the townspeople dressed as corpses and skeletons dance to the beat of a drum under a flag bearing the legend *Lo temps es breu* (Time is brief).

Diumenge de Pasqua (March–April)   Easter Sunday is very low-key except where *La Passió*, a twelve-hour passion play, is enacted, notably in Olesa de Montserrat, Esparragera and El Vendrell.

Sant Jordi (23 April)   Saint George's Day is also the day of roses and lovers – the ideal rose should be a deep crimson. As Cervantes died on this day, it is also the National Day of the Book; this is taken more seriously by the Catalans than anyone else, especially in Barcelona where young lovers exchange both roses and books.

Corpus (June)   Curiously enough, this grave Church feast day on which the host is brought out into the street in a great silver monstrance is treated with less *gravitas* in Catalonia than in the south. At Sitges there is a procession through the flower-festooned streets; at the *Festa de la Patum* at Berga, which lasts three days and is one of the greatest Catalan festivals, processions consisting of giants, dwarves and *capgrossos* (grotesque cardboard creatures with enormous heads) derived from mediaeval farces, are accompanied by the music of the *gralla* (or hornpipe), the most characteristic of all Catalan musical instruments. On the Saturday night after Corpus there is an extraordinary dance called *Els plens* which is performed by masked men covered in fresh grass; the whole extravaganza ends in an orgy of smoke, light, uproar and drunkenness.

Sant Joan (24 June)   On Saint John's Day tremendous bonfires are lit on the threshing floors and circles of dancers sway round them to the accompaniment of fireworks. It is said that this is the night that witches are born, and that remedial herbs brought to the boil on the stroke of midnight are especially efficacious. It is also a propitious night for illicit encounters. Shepherds form relays to carry sparks from the bonfire on Mount Canigó to light other fires all over Catalonia. This is the feast par excellence of the Catalan countryman and of *catalanitat*.

Smoke and frenzy in the Festa de la Patum, *the three-day orgy that accompanies Corpus Christi at Berga.*

Festa Major d'Estiu (September) This great summer festival varies from town to town. Barcelona lives at fever pitch for several days preceding the feast of its patroness, the Mare de Déu de la *Mercè* on 24 September. The city vibrates with song and dance, both formal and informal; with open-air theatre; with proclamations and bands and bells; with galas; with *sardanas*; and with processions of carnival giants and historical figures. It is not quite as exhausting as the *Feria* in Seville, but requires stamina in the steamy late summer heat before the first rainfall.

Some readers may be struck by the omission so far of any mention of bullfights in this account of popular festivals, but the *corrida de toros* has never occupied as important a place in the popular culture of Catalonia as in other parts of the peninsula. Such following as it once had has been further eroded by the decline of the *corrida* in the eyes of serious aficionados, to such an extent that there is now no regular bullfighting column in any Catalan

The team of castellers *from Valls builds its aspiring human column, buttressed by the arms of fellow townsmen, in the Plaça de Sant Jaume, Barcelona.*

271

newspaper. Of the two rings in Barcelona one, Las Arenas, is used mainly for pop festivals; the other, the Monumental, still runs a season but this is confined to a few major feast days and is largely patronized by tourists and immigrant Andalusian workers. There is, however, one genuinely popular taurine festival during the September fair at Cardona; the main event is *la Cargolera*, in which the bull attacks a man in a sort of laundry basket to the great delight of the crowd.

There is, finally, a Catalan festival speciality that cannot be left without mention and that is the competition between rival *castells* or human towers formed by *castellers* who balance on each other's shoulders to form up to seven or eight human tiers, crowned sometimes by a single child, some forty feet above the ground. This unforgettable expression of strength, balance and agility is best seen in the towns near Tarragona such as Montblanc and Valls or in Vilafranca del Penedès on the day of Saint Ursula.

Dance, Music and Song

These are at the heart of popular Catalan culture. The traditional national dance is the *sardana*. I first came across it in Móra d'Ebre on a Sunday morning: twenty-odd citizens in their Sunday best, who may well have come together after church, had formed a circle and were swaying gently to the left and then to the right to the accompaniment of a small band on a raised platform. The *sardana* is a very refined popular dance like a delicate reel without whoops and capers or solo performances. The footwork is neat and delicate and taken very seriously by the participants. A communal spirit is maintained by the joining of hands at shoulder level throughout the dance. It is so different from the dances of the rest of Spain – whether Aragon, Galicia, the Castiles or Andalusia – that you may well wonder where on earth it came from.

The current orchestration is a nineteenth-century adaptation of a much older dance called the *contrapas* and it may have originally been a harvest dance performed by reapers and their wives in Homeric times with sheaves or other produce in the centre, where contemporary participants deposit sportsbags, handbags and the like. In the 1920s General Primo de Rivera rather petulantly wanted to ban it unless the Spanish flag was held solemnly in the centre. Though bourgeois and somewhat prim the *sardana* gives a tremendous impression of solidarity.

Today it is danced throughout Catalonia on 11 September and on national and local feast days. Its most renowned centres of excellence are La Bisbal, Torroella and Peralada, all close to Girona.

Sardana *in front of Barcelona cathedral: this Homeric harvest dance has survived official persecution to become the national dance of Catalonia.*

Properly danced, the *sardana* is more intricate than it looks, as the steps have to be counted in order to pause correctly for the break from the short into the long sequences; individual embroidery is allowed, though this must never interrupt the uniform rhythm of the circle as a whole. It is rather fascinating to watch the earnest faces and neatly shod footwork of bourgeois dancers in this ancient rite in town and village squares on Sunday mornings. But the *sardana* is never exclusive: especially on feast days, circles expand, multiply, contract and swell again as they sway gently one way and then back on the promenade or quayside or under the cathedral façade in Barcelona during the *Mercè*. In 1929 John Langdon-Davies wrote:

> Anyone can break into any circle: it is altogether democratic this dance; peasants in rope-soled canvas shoes and bank clerks in patent leathers, a manufacturer's daughter, in whose face art is helping nature, and the goat-girl and the factory-girl, the young Jewish doctor with a jewel in his necktie and the blue-shirted fisherman with neither tie nor collar; all submit together to the will of the dance, and move in the same direction, all equal though variegated beads of the communal necklace. (*Dancing Catalans*)

273

The social classes and their sartorial distinctions have changed radically since those days, yet the general proposition remains the same. But pick your circle: don't break into an obviously serious and semi-professional group on a normal Sunday. On any of the feast days described above, however, lack of expertise will be forgiven.

The curious eleven-man band that accompanies the *sardana* is called *la cobla*. When James Erskine Murray commented on the dance in *A Summer in the Pyrenees* (1837), he added: 'These dances are executed to music which at first sounds somewhat strange. The flageolet, the tambourine, two oboes, the borassa, and the bagpipes form an orchestra more agreeable than, from the motley character of the instruments, might have been expected.' That

La cobla, *the special band of mainly wind instruments that is* de rigueur *for the* sardana.

motley was taken over and developed by Pep Ventura, father of the contemporary *sardana*, who abolished the bagpipe, added three more wind instruments and a double bass and introduced the *tenora* (tenor), which is now the lead instrument and which, in John Langdon-Davies's words, 'above every instrument is responsible for the peculiar beauty of the Sardana Cobla'.

Other traditional dances are best seen performed by *esbarts*, amateur dancers' associations devoted to folklore research and the projection of their findings to the public. In this field L'Esbart Dansaire de Rubí has achieved international recognition. Among the dances that should be seen if the opportunity arises are *La dansa de la mort*; *El ball de l'àliga* on the Thursday of the Corpus festivities at Berga; *La dansa de Castelltercol*, in the village of that name; *El ball de l'Amorratxa*, a reformulation of an ancient Arab dance; *El ball de la morisca*, also of Arab origin and particularly graceful; and the more recent *El ball de l'hereu Riera*, and *El ball de gitanes*.

The song that most stirs the Catalan blood is *Els Segadors* ('The Reapers'), which dates back to the War of the Reapers when Catalonia rose against taxes and conscription imposed by the Count-Duke of Olivares, minister of Philip IV. Led by Pau Claris, a canon of Urgell who became president of the Generalitat and was supported by the minor Pyrenean nobility, the people attacked royal officials and murdered the viceroy, the count of Santa Coloma, in 1640. A republic was proclaimed under the protection of Louis XIII of France and a long and sporadic war dragged on until 1652, when the rebellion was finally suppressed. In its early stages urban artisans were joined immediately after the harvest by reapers from the countryside; their marching song was basically a litany of grievances with the refrain '*Bon cop de falc, defensors de la terra*' ('Power to your good sickles, defenders of the soil'). This was adopted as a national anthem during the nineteenth-century renaissance and was proclaimed officially as such by the Generalitat in 1931. After the Civil War it was banned until 1976, when it was restored to its official position. *Els Segadors* can be heard on 11 September and at rallies and political demonstrations.

There are also other traditional songs that are perhaps better known abroad such as *El cant dels ocells*, which has been performed by both Pau Casals and Joan Baez. Some are lullabies such as *Non, nin, non;* others simple refrains for children like *Arri, arri, tatanet;* yet others are workplace songs – *Pica, pica, sabater.* Popular ballads include *Els fadrins de Sant Boi, Amèlia, L'hostal de la perdiu, La filla del marxant, Rossinyol, Quan jo tenia quatre ans* and *Muntanyes del Canigó.* Many of these now figure in the recordings of choral groups and such outstanding singers as Maria del Mar Bonet, Joan Manuel Serrat and Els Pavesos.

The two best-known Catalan composers, Isaac Albéniz (1860–1909) and Enric Granados (1867–1916), both prominent pianists, are generally associated with pan-Hispanic nationalism but both had a certain feeling for Catalan popular music as well. Albéniz's main contribution to Catalan music was his *Suite Ibèria* in which traces of Catalan folklore are evident.

In the popularization of classical music the choral movement in Catalonia was extremely important. The Cors de Clavè founded during the *Renaixença* were followed in the Modernist period by the Asociació Wagneriana and the Orfeo Català, both launched in 1891. These had largely conservative and bourgeois memberships but Enric Morera's Societat Coral Catalunya Nova (1895) was a genuine workers' choir. It participated in the *Festes Modernistes* at Sitges (see 'Modern Art'), where Morera tried to replace the traditional Spanish *zarzuela* with a repertory of Catalan light opera.

The other great name in Catalan music, Pau Casals (1876–1973), also made his début in the Modernist period. In 1920 he formed his own orchestra, which brought Stravinsky to Barcelona in 1924–5. Yet Casals was not only concerned with grand occasions for the bourgeoisie: in 1926 he founded the Asociació Obrera de Concerts which brought low-priced concerts to working people and published its own magazine. By these means the barriers between the highbrow and the popular, the avant-garde and the traditional, were lifted and the foundations laid of the lively Catalan interest in music of all kinds which you find today.

Saints and Sinners

Behind the outward manifestations of popular culture there is a ghostly gathering of legendary characters – some with more and some with less foundation in fact – who are the progenitors and guardians of the national psyche. Often they are represented in processions and the popular theatre.

The poles between which these figures perform their respective roles in the Catalan national consciousness are expressed by the two untranslatable words *seny* and *rauxa*. The former, as I suggested in the Introduction, 'lies somewhere in the area of good sense, judgement, wisdom, a sense of proportion'. The dictionary adds prudence, discretion, soundness of mind. Those possessed of *seny* are the guides to the development of sound character and correct philosophy. At the other end of the spectrum are those imbued with *rauxa*, which the dictionary defines as 'impulse, outburst, rage, fury, fit'. This tends to take the form of unpremeditated action, often of a violent kind in defiance of all the established norms, thus threatening the whole political, moral and juridical landscape.

One of the most quoted examples of *seny* is the story of Councillor Fiveller, whose statue stands just to the right of the entrance to Barcelona's city hall, facing across the Plaça de Sant Jaume towards the Generalitat. When the city fathers imposed a tax on meat the chef of King Ferdinand I (1412–16) refused to pay it. Fiveller was then sent by the Consell de Cent to claim the tax from the king, who had threatened to hang anyone who demanded the money of him. Dressed in mourning, Fiveller proclaimed from the steps of the Saló de Tinell that he would defend the rights of the city to his death. History does not relate what happened when this representative of Barcelona's bourgeoisie was admitted to the presence of the arrogant king from Castile – there were no witnesses to the interview. But when Fiveller emerged, it was to let the people know that the king had agreed to pay the tax and if he did not keep his word they would hang the king. It is clear, then, that *seny* cannot be equated with mere utilitarian good sense, which might have led the councillors to knuckle under to their monarch. It also contains an element of obstinacy and attachment to principle.

The most potent figure in Catalan mythology is Sant Jordi, portrayed in the charming stone medallion on the flank of the Generalitat, in the chapel and main salon of that building and in countless retables and sculptures up and down the country. His cult reached its apogee in the later Middle Ages, by which time he had been adopted as patron not only by the English and the Catalans but also by the Venetians, Genoese and Portuguese; he was important also to the Greeks and the Piedmontese. As the protector of soldiers, knights, armourers and archers, his stature inevitably diminished with the advent of gunpowder. Historically, he is most insubstantial. If he existed at all, he was probably a soldier and may have been martyred in about 303. On these grounds he was deselected by the Vatican in 1969 and relegated to the rank of local cult. But he will never be abandoned by the Catalans – or by the English, I daresay – because he represents a human ideal for which he had to be invented: he is the personification of all the virtues and noble arts and what is purest and most elevated in our natures – as opposed to all that is mean and low and perfidious, as embodied in the dragon.

Another prominent hero is James I (the Conqueror), who reigned for more than sixty glorious years (1213–76) and recaptured Majorca and Valencia from the infidel. The legend runs that so many were his admirers and followers that the cloud of dust raised by them turned into the Milky Way, otherwise known as the *camí del Rei en Jaume* or King James's Highway. His long reign and the positive balance of his successes over his failures probably site him well towards the *seny* end of the spectrum. The needle pointing to other prominent but lesser figures flickers somewhere

277

near the centre of the scale, as with the great naval captains Roger de Llúria, who played an important part in the capture of Sicily under Peter the Great, and Roger de Flor, conqueror of the counties of Athens and Neopatria, who inspired the famous novel *Tirant lo Blanc* (see 'Catalan Literature'). At once pirates and patriots, both qualify as national heroes with statues in public places.

There are other personages who are admired, but not unreservedly. The position of Christopher Columbus in the Catalan pantheon is ambiguous. He was received by Ferdinand and Isabel in the Saló de Tinell on his return from his first voyage and is honoured by an imposing statue on a Corinthian column at the lower end of Las Ramblas. But his discovery of the New World put an end to the predominance of Mediterranean trade which had been the lifeblood of Barcelona. An attempt to merge his identity with that of his contemporary, the Catalan corsair Joan Colom, has not succeeded in endearing him to the Catalans. His ration of *seny* favoured Castile rather than Catalonia.

Much more popular is Serralonga, a seventeenth-century bandit and villain who was put to death at the orders of the Castilian viceroy; he is now seen as a defender of the rights of the Catalan people against the oppression of Castile. Any tendency to *rauxa* in such popular brigands is forgiven them. Then there is the bad-tempered Saint Eulalia, in whom *rauxa* may predominate despite her sainthood. Martyred in Mérida in 304 and later adopted by Barcelona as patroness, her remains are contained in the cathedral in a crypt completed in 1339. But in more recent times Barcelona deserted her and elevated the Mare de Déu de la Mercè to joint (and in effect senior) status. Saint Eulalia takes her revenge by endeavouring to release heavy rains on the feast of her rival in late September. She failed while I was there but the resulting heat and unreleased humidity were pretty unpleasant.

The champion of *rauxa*, however, is undoubtedly Comte l'Arnau, protagonist of a fine lyric ballad by Joan Maragall. Of the many legends concerning this Catalan Don Juan, the most revealing is the account of his rape of the abbess of Sant Joan de les Abadesses, whom he kills after her reproaches for his unknightly behaviour; he then goes to the church to confess not only this but all the other sins of his life. Refused absolution, Arnau stabs the chaplain to death with the words, 'He who cannot absolve his lord and master is equally useless for absolving the lower orders!' Admired by women, feared by men, the count makes pacts with fairies, witches and, most importantly, the devil; stands godfather to all the male children in his domains so that they can never turn against him; wins a hundred battles against the Moors but refuses to pay his debts; and converses with his virtuous wife on the stroke of midnight, having himself become a soul in torment roaming the terrain of Ripoll and the Garrotxa, where he still today terrifies countrymen and shepherds. Even campers and tourists are not immune.

In search of the essence of Catalonia the keen eye and the attentive ear will find many clues in popular culture and legend. Kings and heroes, demons and dragons and comic characters all sway along in the festival processions or figure in mime and song. None of them represents any single incontrovertible truth about the Catalans. But it is a sign of maturity that the grave *sardana*, an expression of *seny*, and the licentious *Patum de Berga* with its strong dose of *rauxa*, can both flourish at one and the same time: it is a wise nation that devises an appropriate outlet for all its impulses.

16

Museums

Barcelona is one of the European cities most richly endowed with museums, of which not a single one is administered by a central state museum service: all exist thanks to municipal, provincial, diocesan or private initiative. There are also some notable museums in other Catalan cities and towns, and hardly one of the thirty-eight *comarques* is without a museum of some sort, while many boast five or six. In short, there are several hundred museums within the boundaries of Catalonia. If you are a museum enthusiast like me you can have a field day, but remember that many museums are closed on Mondays. Cathedrals and abbey churches are in many cases open throughout the day, but their dependencies – some of which contain important works of art – tend to have opening hours similar to those of museums; these are normally posted at the entrance. Parish churches present more of a problem: as a general rule of thumb you are most likely to get in during the first half of the morning or during the evening, but very seldom in the afternoon.

The main museums with their opening hours are listed in the Michelin *Tourist Guide*, which is updated from year to year. The rest are listed in the comarcal leaflets issued by the Generalitat and in municipal handouts. It is worth looking through these if you have a special interest: ceramics, for example, are well represented in a number of towns as are agricultural tools, musical instruments, ironwork and viniculture. If you spot one you would like to visit, it is worth checking at your hotel desk to see if and when it is open; some museums are more aspirations than realities. Others with significant collections can only be seen after elaborate negotiations with the curator. For reasons of space I shall confine myself here to the principal Barcelona museums and the dozen or so more substantial ones outside the capital.

Barcelona's thirty most important museums are administered by the municipality and they are all listed and described (both the buildings and a very general account of their contents) in the *Guia dels museus de Barcelona* published by the Ajuntament of the city. Those most likely to be of interest are all situated in one of the following six zones:

LAS RAMBLAS   There are several museums in or near Las Ramblas. Moving towards the port from the Plaça de Catalunya, on the right, is the Palau de la Virreina, housing the not tremendously interesting Museu d'Arts Decoratives (a field in which Barcelona loses out to the Madrid museum of the same name) and also the Cambó collection of paintings. Continuing downwards and taking the right-hand turn into the Carrer Nou de la Rambla (formerly Calle Conde del Asalto) is the theatre museum or Museu de les Arts de l'Espectacle, which features rotating exhibitions on theatrical subjects. This is housed in the strange and rather sinister Palau Güell, built by Gaudí for his patron. At the bottom of Las Ramblas and to the right of the monument to Columbus is the Museu Marítim, which spreads itself in the old shipyards or Drassanes: the models, large and small, are particularly noteworthy.

BARRI GÒTIC   This is the area in the vicinity of the cathedral. There is a small diocesan museum in the chapter house off the cloister, but of greater importance are the Museu Frederic Marès, with its collections of Romanesque and Gothic art and ceramics, and the Museu d'Història de la Ciutat in the Carrer Veguer, which features interesting maps, models, plans and an unusual subterranean archaeological section.

CARRER MONTCADA   The main attraction is the Museu Picasso in an old and rather unsuitable Gothic palace. Almost facing this is the Museu Tèxtil i de la Indumentària. At the far end of Montcada rises the great church Santa Maria del Mar, built with the subscriptions of the merchant class, already powerful in the fourteenth century.

MONTJUÏC   Top of the league is the superb Museu d'Art de Catalunya. Housed in the Palau Nacional put up for the 1929 Exhibition, it is undoubtedly, as the city council claims, 'the finest artistic legacy in Catalonia': it contains splendid collections of Romanesque and Gothic art and a fine ceramics museum. Also on the Montjuïc hill are the beautifully designed Fundació Miró; the Museu Etnològic; the Museu d'Arts, Indústries i Tradicions Populars, distributed among various buildings in the Poble Espanyol; and the Museu Arqueològic, containing a number of important pieces of sculpture from Empúries. Higher up in the fortress crowning the hill is the Museu Militar.

PARC DE LA CIUTADELLA   After Montjuïc the greatest concentration of museums is to be found in this park. The Museu d'Art Modern at present shares the same building with the Catalan parliament; it will be moved gradually to the Palau Nacional on Montjuïc hill. You have to be very much interested in local themes and the nineteenth century in particular to enjoy it. The park also contains the Museu de Zoologia in the café-restaurant built by Domènech i Montaner for the 1888 Exhibition, the Museu de Geologia and the small zoo.

PERIPHERY   The Sagrada Família, though well within the nineteenth-century extension of the city, is quite far from the centre and is best reached by the metro station of the same name; it contains a subterranean museum devoted to the building's history and featuring some Gaudiana; the Parc Güell on the upper rim of the city also contains a small museum run by the Friends of Gaudí. Right on the fringe of the city is the district of Pedralbes. In the upper part, near the old village of Sarrià, is the Monestir de Pedralbes museum; the church is open throughout the day but the museum in the cloister, which is well worth visiting, is only open on Sundays. Lower down, almost on the Diagonal, the museum at the Palau de Pedralbes offers standard Bourbon palace furniture; there is also a carriage museum in the grounds.

Outside Barcelona the museums which should not be missed are as follows in alphabetical order of placenames. Though some are diocesan they are not always part of the normal tourist visit to the cathedral and should not be confused with the collection of church plate and liturgical utensils known as the 'treasure'; the most important of these are housed in separate buildings outside the church.

FIGUERES   Museu Dalí – for the fun of it.
GIRONA   Museu d'Art: Romanesque, Gothic and Renaissance art excellently displayed.
LLÍVIA   Pharmacy museum.
RIPOLL   Municipal museum: local industries.
SANT JOAN DE LES ABADESSES   Small abbey museum: very fine embroidery.
SEU D'URGELL, LA   Diocesan museum: small but choice.
SITGES   Cau Ferrat museum: ironwork, mediaeval alabaster and *fin de siècle* mementoes collected by Santiago Rusiñol.
SOLSONA   Diocesan museum: wins the award for presentation; strong on local archaeology, Romanesque and Gothic art.
TARRAGONA   Archaeological (Roman) museum; also absorbing paleo-Christian museum.
TERRASSA   The Visigothic Esglésies de Sant Pere are fascinating: small collection of Gothic art; the textile museum is also excellent.
VIC   Diocesan museum: the most important collections of Romanesque and Gothic art outside Barcelona; also ceramics.
VILAFRANCA DEL PENEDÈS   Museu del Vi: the art and craft of viniculture from Roman times to the nineteenth century; also geological and archaeological sections.

17

Food and Drink

The Catalan cuisine or *cuina* ranks high in the peninsular league.
The best restaurants in Spain, including some of the best regional
restaurants, are in Madrid, but in general the food on offer to the
traveller in the centre and south is monotonous with the exception of that available at highly priced establishments or specialities such as seafood. Catalan cooking, on the other hand, shares
the general characteristics of northern cuisine, which means that
it is more substantial, more varied and more elaborate in
restaurants of all categories – though meals are not as gargantuan
as in the Basque provinces.

Breakfast in a hotel is a terrible bore: soggy toast, packaged
butter, glutinous jam. Tea is not to be recommended – it is badly
prepared and insipid everywhere. The only exception is camomile
tea, *manzanilla*, with which I always asked to be called before
going out to the nearest café-bar. The brioches and croissants are
universally good and the coffee is excellent (the only problem is
getting enough of it but it is better to have two or three *tasses* than
a cold pot in a hotel). On a sortie of this kind you will no doubt
catch sight of the heavy breakfasts favoured by manual workers
and indeed by some of more sedentary occupation: *esmorzar de
forquilla* (fork breakfast), as it is called, requires both a knife and
fork and may include slices of dried cod, a six-egg omelette or
lamb chops with vegetables, accompanied by beer or wine and
followed by a coffee and a brandy. Shop assistants and office
workers tend to stick to *pastissos*.

284

The next thing to note is that there are no *tapas* in the Andalusian fashion, which encourages a dozen drinks and a dozen tidbits before you sit down to a meal or even in lieu of it. There is much to be said for this in southern climes, but it is not to be found in the north except in bars catering for Andalusian immigrants. Catalonia is the land of the proper course or dish. Beware of *plats combinats* (or 'combination platters' – these can be ordered by number from illustrated menus) aimed at the tourist, unless you are in a great hurry. Even then, it is much better to ask for *pa amb tomàquet*, which is the real national snack. It is made by rubbing a doorstep of bread with half a fresh tomato and adding a pinch of salt and a good dollop of the best olive oil. In its simple form it can accompany any meal but is often used as the foundation of a sort of open sandwich of ham, tuna, cheese or anything else you fancy.

As in other Mediterranean regions, the Catalan kitchen relies to a great extent on aromatic herbs and aims at a robust but not particularly piquant flavour. Dried fruits and dried fish are frequently mixed with fresh produce. Thus you find aubergines with hazelnuts or *bacallà* (dried cod) with *samfaina* (a sort of ratatouille), while sweet and sour dishes are a speciality of the coastal plain of Empordà, amongst them squid with garden peas, lobster with chocolate sauce, duck with pears, pork with prunes, chicken with apple and so forth. Outside Empordà the districts which have most successfully preserved and developed their rural culinary traditions are those of Lleida and the Ebro valley.

It may be helpful to review briefly the main categories of dishes.

STARTERS   The Catalans are keen on heavy salads along the lines of salade niçoise which to my mind are almost a meal in themselves. The *xató* or *xatonada* of Sitges, for example, combines endives and olives with *bacallà* and *anxoves* (anchovies). *L'amanida catalana* incorporates preserved pork products. (*Amanida*, incidentally, is the generic word for salad; *salat* or *salada* means salted.) *Escalivada* consists mainly of peppers and aubergines; *esqueixada* is a salad of *bacallà* and tomatoes – very popular in summer. Vegetable dishes, also usually served as a first course, include *espinacs a la catalana*, which combines raisins and nuts with spinach, and *faves estofades* or broad beans cooked with pork and wine.

SOUPS   Almost everywhere there is a variant of *escudella*, a vegetable stew or stockpot enriched by a bone of ham or veal. This is popular in the mountains and throughout Catalonia in winter. *Carn d'olla* is the most substantial soup of all, obligatory at Christmas: it combines meatballs with chicken, pork, black and white sausages, lamb, cabbage and potatoes. Fish soups are of the usual Mediterranean type. On the Costa Brava ask for *suquet de peix*. The Hostal del Sol in Barcelona serves a particularly luscious clam soup called *sopa de cloïsses estil Cadaqués*.

RICE   The success of paella with tourists has in general had an unfortunate effect on that Valencian dish, which is now served all over Spain, not least in Barcelona. But the Catalans really prefer their own rice dishes, among which *arròs a banda* and *arròs negre* are unusual and memorable. In the former the rice is served separately from the other ingredients, thus avoiding the glutinous mix of so many poor paellas; in the latter the rice is darkened and enriched by the ink of squid.

PASTA   It appears that the first Catalan restaurants were run by Italians which explains how pasta or *pastes* entered the native cuisine. However, the Catalan variants have a quite distinctive flavour. Try *fideus a la cassola* (baked vermicelli), *macarrons* and especially *canelons* – even Italians are impressed.

EGGS   *Ous* is nearer lexically to French *oeufs* than to Spanish *huevos* but there are no outstanding or original egg dishes. Also, be warned that by a curious quirk of the language the words for omelette and trout are identical: *truita*. Thus *truita d'alls tendres* is not, as you might think, trout cooked in garlic but an omelette with a garlic filling. For trout dishes turn to the appropriate section of the menu.

FISH   *El peix* is the touchstone of Catalan gastronomy. Soups have already been mentioned. They are followed by grilled fish – *a la brasa* or *a la planxa* or *graellada* (barbecued), which many prefer to more elaborate concoctions. The most popular boiled dish is the *sarsuela*, an assortment of fish with peppers, peas and tomatoes, and there are a number of local variants of this called *calderetes*. *Rapé a l'all cremat* (*rapé* with creamed garlic) is the speciality of Vilanova i la Geltrú (near Sitges). The best seafood is available on the Ebro delta and the best lobster dishes are to be had on the Costa Brava. The richest of these is *llagosta amb pollastre* which combines slices of chicken with lobster in a sauce that includes, among other ingredients, dry anis, almonds and a little chocolate. *Bacallà* is virtually a chapter apart and is almost as important in the Catalan cuisine as *bacalao* is in the Basque or Portuguese. Once the staple of the poor man's diet, it has now moved up in price and status. *Bacallà a l'all, bacallà amb samfaina* and *bacallà amb panses* (with raisins) are all well worth trying. *Truita*, which is indeed trout in the fish section of the menu, is at its best in the Pyrenees. *Truita de riu a l'agredolc* is a sweet and sour dish using vinegar and honey.

MEAT   In Catalonia *la carn* is of much better quality than the stringy cuts available on the central meseta and in Andalusia. Lamb, veal, pork, beef, poultry and game are abundant. Charcoal grilling is the preferred method of cooking with excellent results, especially in the mountains. Though oil or butter would be used for basting in other parts of Spain, pork lard is preferred in Catalonia. Stews of meat and vegetables, *estofats*, are found everywhere. The classic dish for family lunch on Sunday is *vedella amb pèsols* (veal with peas). Try also *fricandó amb moixernons* (a veal casserole with local fungi). For quick meals at bar counters both *mandonguilles* (meat balls in a sauce with peas) and *croquetes* (small rissoles) can be recommended. Rabbit, or *conill*, and game dishes such as *civet de llebre* (jugged hare), *civet de senglar* (jugged boar) and *civet de cérvol* (jugged venison) appear on many menus in the interior.

SWEETS   These almost deserve a chapter on their own because of the Catalan addiction to pastries, of which there are a very large variety. Statistically Terrassa just outside Barcelona has the largest number of patisseries per thousand of the population but it must be run pretty close by many other places, not least by Barcelona itself. These pastries and tarts are on the whole lighter than in the rest of the peninsula – as is the bread. Each town or village has its own speciality such as the almond-based *menjar blanc* of Reus, the *borregos* of Cardedeu and so on. The pastry cook has not only to cater for local tastes but must keep an eye on the national saints' calendar; thus there are *crema de Sant Josep*, a flan referred to as *crema catalana* the rest of the year; *mones de Pasqua* (Easter); *panellets de Tots Sants* (All Saints); *torrons de Nadal* (Christmas); *neules de Cap d'Any* (New Year's Eve); *tortells de Reis* (Epiphany); *martells de Sant Eloi, coques de Sant Joan*, etc.

CHEESE   The word is *formatge*, another instance of the lexical affinity of Catalan with French. Local cheeses are not found much on restaurant menus but don't miss an opportunity to try *mel i mató,* an old favourite of shepherds consisting of cottage cheese and honey.

FRUIT AND NUTS Catalonia is an important fruit producer, especially of apples, peaches, pears and strawberries – of the latter (*maduixots*) the Catalans are extremely fond. There is a considerable external trade in dried fruits, almonds and hazelnuts, all of which make an important contribution to the domestic table.

WATER Good fresh water abounds everywhere except in Barcelona. Never drink tap water in the capital or ask for natural water at table. It is perfectly safe but is so chlorinated as to be undrinkable. There are several good brands of mineral water, both sparkling and still, including Vichy Catalan and Font Vella.

WINES Catalonia's vineyards are extensive and their wine, though less renowned than La Rioja's, is of higher quality than neighbouring Aragon's. There are plenty of light refreshing white wines such as *blanc d'Alella.* Most regions produce a rosé – those from the Ebro valley are very drinkable. The wines from Gandesa, the Priorat, the Conca de Barberà and the Penedès all now have their properly regulated denominations of origin. Gandesa and the Priorat produce some reds that are rightly called black; both reds and whites are high in alcoholic content. Vilafranca del Penedès is the capital of the whole district of that name but neighbouring Sant Sadurní d'Anoia is the headquarters of the Catalan sparkling wine industry, which developed when Catalonia began supplying corks to the French for their expanding champagne trade. Officially the Catalan version is called *vi de cava*; the word 'champagne' or any local variant of it has been banned from the label by law after a successful lawsuit by the French producers. However, the wine undergoes the same double fermentation process as champagne and is universally known as *xampany.* It is the essential accompaniment of sweets at any celebratory meal; bottles are available from most pastisseries and it is sold by the glass in numerous *xampanyeries.* Having sampled a good *vi de cava*, I doubt you will miss your Moët, and in fact across the whole vinous spectrum you can live happily off the land.

Finally, here are some suggested eating places in Barcelona, none of which is expensive – all fall within upper medium (UM), medium (M) and economical (E) categories.

OLD CITY
Agut d'Avignon, Trinitat 3, 302 6034 – Catalan (UM)
Brasserie Flo, Junqueras 10, 317 8037 – Catalan/French (UM)
Caracoles, Los, Escudillers 14, 302 3185 – Catalan/regional (M)
Casa Agustin, Vergara 5, 301 9745 – Catalan (E)
Cuineta, La, Paradis 4, 315 0111 – Catalan: fish a speciality (UM)
Egipte, Jerusalem 3, 317 7480 – home cooking (E)
Gran Café, El, Avinyó 9, 318 7986 – sweets a speciality (UM)
Quatre Gats, Els, Montsion 5 – snacks only (E)
Siete Puertas, Isabel II 14, 319 3046 – Catalan (M)
Sogas, Avinyó 56, 301 1647 – Catalan (E)

EIXAMPLE
Balcons, Provença 203, 254 6083 – pasta and fish (M)
Ca' L'Agustí, Verdi 28, 218 5396 – Catalan (E)
Clara d'Ou, La, Gran Vía 442, 223 6280 – Catalan (M)
Flash-Flash, Granada 25, 237 0990 – omelettes a speciality (M)
Gargantua i Pantagruel, Aragó 214, 253 2020 – Lleidan (M)

SARRIÀ AND UPPER TOWN
Botafumeiro, Major de Gràcia 81, 218 4230 – fish (UM)
Dorado Petit, El, Monserdà 51, 204 5153 – Ampurdan (UM)
Fonda de Sarrià, La, Clos de Sant Francesc 34bis, 204 0153 –
   home cooking (M)
Tula, Sant Hermenegild 3, 200 4515 – meats a speciality (M)

POBLE NOU
Café dels Pescadors, Plaça Prim 1, 309 2018 – Catalan (M)

18

Accommodation

It is neither appropriate nor feasible here to give comprehensive hotel listings and prices. Only an annual publication can do this properly and the red Michelin handbook to Spain and Portugal does the job excellently. Spain has a five-star system which applies even in autonomous Catalonia. There is not an exact equivalence between the Michelin gables and the Spanish stars. Michelin's three gables (I am assuming that few travellers will want to be more than *très confortable*) are normally equivalent to four stars in the Spanish system and two gables to three stars – the latter also guarantees a good standard of comfort. The Michelin single gable is usually equivalent to two stars and is very adequate. The Spanish stars are preceded by letters: H stands for Hotel with a full range of services; HR for *Hostal Residencia* with no restaurant (but breakfast is available and very often a cafeteria is attached); HsR provides the same services as HR but occupies only a floor or floors of a larger building; HA refers to *Hotel Apartmento* with limited self-catering facilities; P is for *Pensión* and F for *Fonda*, the simplest of all. This national system of gradation maintains a high standard of cleanliness at all levels, particularly in Catalan establishments.

Within the borders of Catalonia there are seven National Paradors (*Paradores Nacionales*) belonging to the world-famous state-run network and one collaborating Parador that can be recommended. These are situated in or outside the following places:

AIGUABLAVE	Parador Nacional Costa Brava
ARTIES	Parador Nacional Don Gaspar de Portolá
BALAGUER	Parador Conde Jaime de Urgel
CARDONA	Parador Nacional Duques de Cardona
SEU D'URGELL, LA	Parador Nacional
TORTOSA	Parador Nacional Castillo de la Zuda
VIC	Parador Nacional
VIELLA	Parador Nacional Valle de Aran

A good source of information about accommodation is the series of thirty-eight leaflets issued by the Generalitat under the title *Comarques de Catalunya* (available from local tourist offices but not in London). Most of these have a list of all the lodgings and campsites within the *comarca* and include telephone numbers. In the case of coastal *comarques* with large tourist capacities such as Maresme or Tarragona you are referred to the National Tourist Office publications *Catalunya Hotels* and *Catalunya Camping* (available from the Spanish National Tourist Office, St James's Street, London SW1 and local offices).

Barcelona itself has every conceivable type of establishment. In the upper price range the Majestic in the Passeig de Gràcia is very agreeable, while the Colón is the best situated in this category for the Barri Gòtic. The Gótico, Suizo and Rialto are also well placed for the old quarter. Hotels in Las Ramblas should, I suggest, be avoided on grounds of noise, though I have a sneaking affection for the Oriente, which may attract those intent on squeezing the last drop of night-life out of that remarkable promenade.

I have mentioned by name in the text nearly thirty lodgings where I stayed and which I list here in alphabetical order of placenames. The towns and villages in bold face are, in my view, exceptionally pleasant and well placed, if you are attracted to the surrounding area and want to explore it more thoroughly. They are the base camps of the Legend (p.vi), which are shown within a box on the maps.

BALAGUER	Parador Conde Jaime de Urgel
BANYOLES	Hostal L'Ast
BOÍ	Hostal Fondevila
CADAQUÉS	Hotel Playa Sol
	Hostal S'Aguarda
CAMPRODON	Hotel Güell
CARDONA	Parador Duques de Cardona

291

CERVERA	Hotel Canciller
ESPLUGA DE FRANCOLÍ, L'	Hostal del Senglar
ESPOT	Hotel Saurat
FIGUERES	Hotel Duran
GANDESA	Hotel Piqué
LLEIDA	Residencia Principal
LLÍVIA	Hotel Llívia
MANRESA	Hotel Pedro III
OLOT	Hostal La Perla
PALAMÓS	Hotel Trías
PORT DE LA SELVA, EL	Hostal Amberes (in La Selva de Mar)
RIPOLL	Hotel Solana de Ter
SALARDÚ	Hotel Garona
SANTES CREUS	Hostal Grau
SEU D'URGELL, LA	Parador Nacional
SITGES	Hotel Los Pinos
SOLSONA	Hotel Gran Sol
TARRAGONA	Hotel Residencia Lauria
TORTOSA	Parador Nacional
TREMP	Hotel Siglo XX
VIC	Hostal Ausa
VILAFRANCA DEL PENEDÈS	Hotel Pedro III el Grande

19

Maps, Plans, Leaflets and Guides

By whatever means of transport the traveller arrives in Catalonia and however he or she intends to proceed, it is vital for the motorist to be provided with up-to-date road maps and satisfying for the user of public transport to be able to follow the various routes; the pedestrian also requires good street plans in order to pinpoint his position without constantly asking for directions, while the trekker needs a reliable map or maps showing country tracks and trails.

Though Chapters 2 to 5 have been largely written with the motorist in mind, a private or hired car is by no means the only way of getting about in Catalonia. There are 1,437 kilometres of railway track, linking Barcelona with Girona, Lleida and Tarragona; there is also a picturesque, nature-defying railway from Lleida up to Tremp and La Pobla de Segur in the foothills of the Pyrenees – these lines are all part of the national rail grid. In addition, there is a very efficient local network linking the capital with the industrial towns of Terrassa and Sabadell; this provides a useful method of excursion to intermediate stations such as Sant Cugat. The 532 kilometres of motorway link the main cities with Barcelona, from where there are frequent coach services, and there are also local bus services from all the small towns – for details consult your hotel or the local tourist office.

Michelin road map 990 covers the whole of Spain and Portugal at a scale of 1:1,000,000 and is a basic tool for anyone planning to proceed further into the peninsula. The Firestone opposite number is 1:1,100,000. But such scales are useful only for the grand strategy and you are immediately confronted by the choice of the next size up. Michelin 1:400,000 (sheet 43) shows railways and roads of scenic beauty (the latter are highlighted by a green line); it is more accurate than Firestone on Catalan placenames and links up with the town plans in the indispensable Michelin hotel and restaurant handbook. But this sheet is sometimes not obtainable, in which case Firestone 1:500,000 (sheet 3) is an adequate substitute; it runs a little further into France than Michelin and includes Perpignan. But neither Michelin 43 nor Firestone 3 stretches far enough south to cover all of New Catalonia – for journeys south of Tortosa Michelin sheet 445 or Firestone sheet 6 is required. There is also a useful German 1:500,000 map by Kümmerly and Frey which covers all Catalonia and includes enlarged insets of the Costa Brava and Costa Daurada.

Moving up the scale, you have a choice between two 1:300,000 maps, both of which extend from the Pyrenees well south of the Ebro delta and into the autonomous region of Valencia. The first is 'Costa Brava, Costa Dorada', a large-scale regional map (it is in fact German but has been packaged between British covers by Roger Lascelles). This map has a number of virtues: it is very conscientiously Catalan, preferring *monestir* to *monasterio*, *serra* to *sierra*, etc. and the marking of monuments and churches, some of them quite obscure, is commendably thorough. The second, Firestone's more accurately named 'Catalonia', mixes Castilian and Catalan placenames on no clear principle, eg. San Pedro de Roda and Ruinas de Ampurias (Castilian) but Sant Vicenç de Montalt and Sant Martí Sarroca (Catalan). On the reverse side it has a very large-scale plan (1:12,500) of Barcelona, which is fine indoors but difficult to handle in the street. On balance I think the Lascelles is the better of the two but either is acceptable.

The next size up includes the Firestone 1:200,000 area maps 'Pirineo Oriental' (sheet T24) and 'Costa Brava' (sheet T25), which attempt stereoscopic presentations of the main geographical features; the rather crude little pictures of a few principal monuments detract from cartographic seriousness and do not produce a good-looking map. The reverse sides of both, however, carry useful information. T25 has town plans of Perpignan, Figueres, Girona, Sant Feliu de Guíxols and Sitges. T24 is prolific with panoramic skylines naming the Pyrenean peaks from different viewpoints; stereoscopic presentations of some of the main ski slopes; lists of the main ski stations and mountain refuges; and a smallish inset map of the national park of Aigües Tortes which features the main jeep tracks and some of the paths.

This brings me to *excursionisme* or cross-country trekking, which has been a national passion for more than a century. Much of the countryside is superb for this purpose but care should be taken to set off properly equipped. Although T24 gives a general impression of the national park with its lakes and main routes, it does not provide compass points or accurate contours, so it is inadequate for serious walkers, who should get themselves to Stanford's in Long Acre, where they will find some if not all of the *Guías cartográficas* published by the Editorial Alpina in Granollers near Barcelona. These rather charming little handbooks come complete with loose maps, in most cases at a scale of 1:25,000 or 1:40,000; they also suggest walks and timings for the various legs. They do not provide total coverage of the Spanish Pyrenees but for those areas they do cover – the Vall d'Aran and the lake district of Sant Maurici, Andorra and the Serra del Cadí – they are an essential part of the walker's equipment. They also cover other areas of Catalonia such as the Serra de Montseny and Montserrat.

As far as the towns are concerned, both the Michelin red hotel handbook and the green *Tourist Guide* include plans of Barcelona with enlargements of the centre. The Falk street plan at a scale of 1:15,000 has a virtually windproof folding system, which you attempt to undo at your peril (it is not intended to be opened out). It shows the underground and local railway stations, which Michelin does not. All the same, it is nice to be able to unfold a plan of the whole city before zoning in on a particular district. The reverse side of the Firestone 'Catalonia' 1:300,000 provides for this, but it is a bit flimsy; on the other hand the Hallweg Barcelona city map performs the same service at more or less the same scale (1:12,500) on tougher paper – it also has an inset of the metro system (lacking in Firestone). Both use mainly Castilian versions of the names of buildings and streets.

I have so far mentioned only commercial publications but it is worth noting the quite voluminous free literature available. Before leaving for Catalonia a trawl through the shelves of the Spanish National Tourist Office in St James's Street is worth while. In addition to the usual booklets, leaflets and folders on cities, monuments and the Paradors there is a whole range of information about sports. This is in fact the best place to obtain details of ski stations and slopes, of deep-sea fishing facilities and licences, of aquatic sports, of yacht basins and marinas, or to pick up the appropriate volume or volumes of the *Guía náutico-turística de España* – invaluable for sailors. This office does not carry much locally produced Catalan literature but once on the ground you will find that every place of any distinction, especially those with a *barri gòtic* or *casc antic* has a municipal leaflet with a town plan and index of monuments. Some – notably those of Tarragona and Vic – are very thorough, others more cursory. In most cases they are available from hotels or local tourist offices.

As well as municipal literature there is also the series *Comarques de Catalunya* produced by the Generalitat, which can be handy particularly for the smaller towns and villages and the remoter regions. There is a leaflet for each of the thirty-eight *comarques*. These leaflets include *un peu d'histoire*, lists of lodgings and museums, short sections on gastronomy and sport (and where appropriate, addresses for any necessary permits), and information on local folklore and fairs. There is a map too, showing all the main monuments and attractions of the area, but it is always worth checking whether the roads are all as passable as they appear. Inevitably some of the *comarques* slightly oversell their charms or overquote their assets. But on the whole this series provides useful information and pointers to enjoyable excursions.

Finally, the question of other guidebooks. This book is not meant to be exhaustive. For details of admission charges and the opening times of museums, churches and other public buildings it is advisable to take with you the slimline green Michelin *Tourist Guide*, while for categories and prices of hotels and restaurants there is no better source than the red Michelin handbook. The latter is updated annually. Among the British arts-based guidebooks Benn's *Blue Guide* to Spain, edited by Brian Robertson, is extremely sound and particularly useful if you are proceeding further into the peninsula; the last edition is some ten years old but the information is not of the sort that dates much except where museums have been reorganized. I may also perhaps be forgiven for mentioning my own Collins *Companion Guide to Madrid and Central Spain* for anyone continuing from Catalonia into the Castiles; the general bibliography suggests material for background reading as well as a number of art books which give more complete accounts of the various periods and styles as they took shape in Catalonia.

In any event, whatever you read or do not read, you simply cannot do without maps: even in an age of efficient road networks you need to know how and when to get off or under or over the

motorway to escape into the hills, and you will often be faced with
tortuous terrain once you are off the beaten track. Small-scale
maps for the big strides and large-scale ones for the minutiae:
both are indispensable and provide a remarkably cheap source of
interest and enjoyment. Certainly they are essential companions
for anyone who wants to do something more than merely scratch
the surface of Catalonia. With this book, the basic annuals and a
wise selection of maps you are in business.

Chronological Table

DATES	RULERS AND DYNASTIES	POLITICAL AND ECONOMIC LIFE	ARCHITECTURE AND THE ARTS
5000 – 2000 BC	Neolithic culture	Balearic islands and Celtic mainland occupied by herdsmen; small unfortified settlements in plains; ceramics, wheel, glass, crude textiles, rudimentary navigation	Megalithic monuments
2000 – 1500 BC		Introduction of copper; first large population centres	
1500 – 1000 BC	Bronze Age	Agriculture and commerce prosper, particularly around Valencia	
1000 – 500 BC	Iron Age Indo-European invasion of Ter and Llobregat valleys (c.700) Celtic herdsmen and agri-		

	culturalists penetrate Cerdagne and the Segre valley (700–500) Iberian culture spreads up from south and east of peninsula (600–500)	Iron in widespread use; economy based on agriculture, stock breeding, mining, metallurgy, jewellery, ceramics	Iberian votive statues: *Dama de Elche*, *Dama de Baza*; cyclopean walls of Tarragona; Iberian alphabet in use until Romans arrive
	Greeks found Empúries (550)		
500 – 200 BC	Carthaginians wrest Mediterranean from Tartessians and Greeks	Fortified Iberian settlements at Ullastret, Olerdola, etc; absorption of Celts into native population produces Celtiberian culture; monetary economy develops	
239 – 206 BC	Carthaginian occupation of Spain	First Punic War: Hamilcar lands in Spain (237); treaty of Ebro (226) establishes frontier between Romans and Carthaginians; second Punic War (218–201) leads to Carthaginian expulsion from peninsula (206)	

DATES	RULERS AND DYNASTIES	POLITICAL AND ECONOMIC LIFE	ARCHITECTURE AND THE ARTS
200 – 27 BC	Spain under Roman republic	Romanization proceeds rapidly in cities; commerce and industry overtake agriculture; Greater Catalonia included in province of Hispania Citerior except north-eastern sector which is ruled from Narbonne (197)	
29 BC	Augustus, Emperor	Augustus spends eighteen months at Tarraco; city elevated to capital of imperial province of Tarraconensis	
27 BC – AD 410	Spain under Roman empire	Penetration of Roman law; Christian communities develop throughout Catalonia; Roman citizenship conferred on all Spaniards (212); Fructuós and two deacons martyred (259); rise of professional corporations and gradual replacement of slavery by clientship and serfdom; division of empire (395); Visigoths	Bridge and road building; temples at Vic, Barcelona, Tarragona; baths at Caldes de Montbui and Malavella; arch at Bera; Barcelona and Tarragona main centres for Roman sculpture; paleo-Christian art develops; construction of Barcelona city walls after Frankish invasion (258)

412–531	Visigothic occupation of Spain	under Alaric sack Rome (410); Visigothic capital still at Toulouse; code of laws issued by Euric in Latin (475)	
531–711	Visigothic kingdom in Spain	First capital Barcelona (531–48); Toledo capital from 554; Arianism abandoned and Catholicism adopted as state religion; common law under *Lex Visigotorum* (654); reversion to agricultural economy; death of last Visigothic King Witiza (710)	Seventh-century revival of religious and cultural activity; Visigothic basilica at Barcelona and cathedral at Terrassa
711–17	Muslim invasion of Spain, followed by occupation lasting nearly eight centuries	Catalonia overrun with exception of Pyrenees (717)	
732		Muslims halted at Poitiers; Franks push south	
771–814	Charlemagne, king of the Franks (Holy Roman Emperor, 800)	Revival of commerce in grain, salt, cloth, spices, silk; slaves and arms exported; reform of weights, measures and coinage; frontier with Moors from Lleida to Penedès established	Carolingian renaissance finds expression in pre-Romanesque churches and revival of frescoed walls: first Benedictine monasteries established from early ninth century

DATES	RULERS AND DYNASTIES	POLITICAL AND ECONOMIC LIFE	ARCHITECTURE AND THE ARTS
814–50	Disintegration of empire begins followed by development of feudal system; empire divided among sons of Louis the Pious		
850–900	Charles the Bald and Louis the Stammerer cede virtual autonomy to Catalan nobility		
	House of Barcelona		
878–97	Guifré el Pilos (Wilfred the Hairy), count of Cerdanya-Urgell, asserts independence	Wilfred secures control of Barcelona, Vic, Girona and Besalú; bishopric of Vic restored (887); repopulation of Solsona, Bages, Vic and Ripoll districts	Second wave of Benedictine foundations in late ninth and throughout tenth centuries
897–911 *897–946	Guifré II Borrell Sunyer	Balearics captured by Moors (902–3); foundation of caliphate of Córdoba (929)	Catalonia becomes scientific and philosophical intermediary between Islam and Carolingian world; introduction of astrolabe, Arabic numerals

Dates	Ruler	Events	Culture
946–66	Miró		
*946–92	Borrell II	Growth of artisan, mercantile and financial class; prosperous slave trade between Barcelona and Valencia; raids by Al-Mansur devastate county of Barcelona; Borrell breaks Frankish link after Louis V refuses help (986) but becomes tributary of caliph	
992–1017	Ramon Borrell	Borrell sacks Córdoba; disintegration of caliphate begins (1010)	Abbot Oliba builds church of Ripoll (1008–46) – library famed throughout Europe for history, poetry, astronomy, mathematics
1017–35	Berenguer Ramon, el Corbat (the Hunchback)	Caliphate of Córdoba divided into *taifas*	
1035–76	Ramon Berenguer I, el Vell (the Old)	*Usatges de Barcelona*, judicial code on feudal lines, drawn up (1064–8); growth of shipbuilding in Barcelona and maritime trade	
1076–82	Ramon Berenguer II, Cap d'Estopa (Towhead)	'Assemblies of peace and truce' lay foundations for future *corts*	Terms *Catalunya* and *catalans* first appear in early eleventh-century documents

*indicates joint or concurrent rule

DATES	RULERS AND DYNASTIES	POLITICAL AND ECONOMIC LIFE	ARCHITECTURE AND THE ARTS
*1076–97	Ramon Berenguer II, el Fratricida		
1093–1131	Ramon Berenguer III, el Gran (the Great)	Provence acquired by marriage; Majorca and Ibiza gained from and lost to Moors; *taifas* fall to Almorávides	Mature Romanesque style; beginnings of written Catalan; *langue d'oc* kept alive by troubadours
1131–62	Ramon Berenguer IV	Berenguer marries Petronella, heiress of Aragon (1137); Tortosa and Lleida reconquered; frontier with Islam established along Ebro (1148–9); repopulation of New Catalonia; Cistercian order becomes influential	Templar fortresses established at Tortosa and Miravet (1153)
	Count-kings of the Catalan-Aragonese Confederation		
1162–96	Alfons I, el Cast (the Chaste)	By treaty of Cazorla, federation secures right to reconquer Valencia but cedes rights to Murcia and Andalusia to Castile (1179); federation seeks expansion in France and the Mediterranean	Transition to Gothic architecture initiated in Cistercian monasteries; 'pointed' style develops

Date	Ruler	Events	Cultural notes
1196–1213	Pere I, el Català	Battle of Las Navas de Tolosa (1212); Peter killed at Muret (1213)	
1213–76	Jaume I, el Conqueridor (the Conquerer)	Catalan navy conquers Majorca and Ibiza (1229), retakes Formentera (1235) and captures Valencia (1238); by treaty of Corbeil (1258) Catalans renounce claims north of Pyrenees with exception of Cerdagne and Roussillon; *Consolat de Mar* (1258–72), code of trading practice, applied thoughout Mediterranean	Gothic style supersedes Romanesque
1276–85	Pere II, el Gran (the Great)	Revolt of Sicilian Vespers against Angevins; Peter takes Sicily (1282)	Development of Catalan prose with Desclot's chronicle of the reign of Peter the Great
1285–91	Alfons II, el Franc	Conquest of Minorca (1287)	
1291–1327	Jaume II, el Just	Almogàvers sent to lend support to Byzantine empire; Roger de Flor takes Athens and Neopatria (1302–11); Sardinia captured (1324)	Muntaner records exploits of the mercenaries
1327–36	Alfons III, el Benigne		

DATES	RULERS AND DYNASTIES	POLITICAL AND ECONOMIC LIFE	ARCHITECTURE AND THE ARTS
1336–87	Pere III, el Ceremoniós	Black death kills off quarter of population (1347–8); Generalitat founded (1359); plagues and famine recur (1362, 1370–1), population falls	Flowering of Catalan Gothic painting; foundation of *Jocs Florals* in Barcelona (1395)
1387–96	Joan I, el Caçador (the Hunter)	Saint Vincent Ferrer preaches against heretics and Jews; outbreaks of anti-Judaism begin in large cities (1391)	
1396–1410	Martí I, l'Humà (the Humane)	Unrest among rural population due to poor condition of land	
1410 –12	Interregnum		
	House of Trastamara		
1412–16	Ferran I (Ferdinand of Antequera)	Ferdinand, brother of Henry III of Castile, chosen king by electoral college at Caspe (1412)	
1416–58	Alfons IV, el Magnànime	Conquest of Naples (1423); economic crisis leads to tensions between upper bourgeoisie and small traders in towns and land-	Sant Jordi and March emerge as important poets

Date	Ruler	Political events	Cultural events
		lords and tenants in countryside	
1458–79	Joan II, Sense Fe (the Faithless)	Peasant revolt and rebellion of Generalitat against John II (1462); John's heir Ferdinand marries Isabel of Castile (1469); Barcelona submits to John (1472)	Martorell writes his chivalric romance, *Tirant lo Blanc*
1479–1516	Ferran II, el Catòlic	Effective union of Aragon with Castile, though Ferdinand only king-consort and later regent in Castile; second peasant revolt (1482–5); imposition of Castilian Inquisition on Catalonia (1484–7); Jews expelled, America discovered (1492); Castile secures monopoly of American trade; creation of Supreme Council of Aragon puts Catalan affairs under Castilian control (1494)	
House of Austria			
1516–56	Carles I (Charles I of Spain; Charles V of Holy Roman Empire)	Barcelona still debarred from trade with New World; Mediterranean trade restricted by	Spread of Castilian culture in Catalonia; decline of Catalan literature

DATES	RULERS AND DYNASTIES	POLITICAL AND ECONOMIC LIFE	ARCHITECTURE AND THE ARTS
		piracy and Church prohibition of trafficking with infidels	Catalan culture enters long decline
1556–98	Felip I (Philip II of Spain)	Imposition of Castilian viceroys in Catalonia; battle of Lepanto achieves relative peace in Mediterranean (1571); French Huguenots take refuge in Catalonia; Inquisition and censorship applied with rigour	
1598–1621	Felip II (Philip III of Spain)	Moriscos expelled (1609); Thirty Years' War begins (1618)	
1621–65	Felip III (Philip IV of Spain)	Portugal throws off Castilian yoke (1640); War of the Reapers (1640–52) sees Catalans revolt against taxes and conscription for Thirty Years' War, and republic declared under protection of Louis XIII of France; Barcelona capitulates to royal army (1652); by treaty of Pyre-	

		...nees Spain cedes Roussillon and part of Cerdagne to France (1659)
1665–1700	Carles II (Charles II of Spain)	Ceded territories seek to rejoin Catalonia; Charles's death without issue leads to War of Spanish Succession

House of Bourbon

1700–46	Felip IV (Philip V of Spain)	Catalonia supports Archduke Charles of Austria against Philip of Bourbon, but Peace of Utrecht (1713) confirms Philip on throne and cedes Minorca to English; after 13-month siege Barcelona surrenders to Philip (1714); Majorca follows suit (1715); *Nova Planta* abolishes laws, privileges, institutions and constitution; severe repression and economic decline. Suppression of Catalan universities and opening of Cervera university (1718); Catalan language banned from official use
1746–59	Ferran III (Ferdinand VI of Spain)	Creation of Barcelona chamber of commerce (1758); numerous private foundations in fields of agriculture, commerce and navigation develop

DATES	RULERS AND DYNASTIES	POLITICAL AND ECONOMIC LIFE	ARCHITECTURE AND THE ARTS
1759–88	Carles IV (Charles III of Spain)	Deputies from Barcelona, Valencia, Zaragoza and Majorca unsuccessfully demand restoration of Aragonese and Catalan rights (1760) though economic progress continues; Charles founds port of Sant Carles de la Ràpita; Catalonia finally licensed to trade with American colonies (1778); Minorca recovered by Spain (1782)	Cathedral in neo-classical style replaces old Seu de Lleida (1760–81)
1788–1808	Carles V (Charles IV of Spain)	French revolution (1789); war against French Convention sees French revolutionaries woo Catalans with promises of restored liberties (1793–5); Charles abdicates in favour of son Ferdinand (1808)	
1808–14	Josep Bonaparte (nominal king during Ferdinand's exile)	Ferdinand held in France for six years; Peninsular War (1808–14): French sack Montserrat,	

1814–33	Ferran IV (Ferdinand VII of Spain)	Girona falls after heroic defence (1809); re-emergence of Catalan federalism (1810–14); liberal-dominated parliament in Cádiz enacts constitution specifying unitary state; Catalan delegates fail to reclaim autonomy	Castilian becomes official language in schools (1825); Aribau's *La pàtria* published (1833) and becomes clarion call of *Renaixença*
		Ferdinand re-established on throne by Congress of Vienna (1814), tears up Cádiz constitution, restores Bourbon rule; liberal rebellion (1820–3) suppressed by French invasion of 'the hundred thousand sons of Saint Louis'; absolutism restored;	
		French occupation of Catalonia (1823–6); entry of French manufactures provokes economic crisis – Catalan industrialists espouse protectionism; advent of steam power (1830)	

DATES	RULERS AND DYNASTIES	POLITICAL AND ECONOMIC LIFE	ARCHITECTURE AND THE ARTS
1833–68	Isabel I (Isabel II of Spain); her mother regent (1833–40); Espartero regent (1841–3)	First Carlist War (1833–9); disentailment of church lands by Mendizábal (1837); Catalan industry suffers under Espartero's free-trade policy; decade of repression under Narvaez (1844–54); foundation of Civil Guard; revolutionary movements in Barcelona and Valencia frustrated (1848); 'progressive biennium' (1854–6); first general strike (1855); further period of repression and illegal workers' associations (1856–68)	*Renaixença* divides into liberal-progressive and conservative-historicist streams (1840); *Jocs Florals* revived in Barcelona, Cerdà's plan for Barcelona chosen (1859)
1868–70	Revolutionary period	General Prim overthrows Isabel (1868) and introduces universal suffrage, right of association, religious and press freedom; Prim dies (1870)	
1870–3	Amadeu de Savoia		

1873–4	First Spanish Republic	
1874–85	Alfons V (Alfonso XII of Spain)	Coup d'état by General Martínez Campos inaugurates second Bourbon restoration; second Carlist War (1874–6); protection-ism restored (1875–81) followed by economic boom	
1885–1931	Alfons VI (Alfonso XIII of Spain); his mother regent (1885–1902)	Labour movement develops; foundation of UGT and PSOE in Barcelona (1888); *Bases de Manresa*, project for autonomy, devised (1892); anarchist bombings and executions (1892–7); loss of Cuba, Puerto Rico and Philippines (1898); foundation of Lliga Regionalista, first Catalan party (1901); protest against conscription for Moroccan war leads to *Setmana Tràgica* (1909); Mancomunitat, first regional government for two centuries, established with Prat de la Riba as president (1914–23); Spanish neutrality in First World War (1914–18) leads to export boom;	Almirall's seminal work *Lo Catalanisme* published (1886); last decade of nineteenth century sees foundation of choirs, dance groups, athenaeums; Modernist architects and artists flourish but at turn of century Noucentisme reverts to classical austerity after previous extravagance; Institut d'Estudis Catalans founded (1906); Prat de la Riba's *La nacionalitat catalana* published (1910); Picasso and Miró emerge as significant artists; foreign avant-garde becomes influential during First World War

DATES	RULERS AND DYNASTIES	POLITICAL AND ECONOMIC LIFE	ARCHITECTURE AND THE ARTS
		labour unrest and wave of assassinations (1917–23); coup d'état by Primo de Rivera endorsed by Alfonso (1923)	
1923–30	Primo de Rivera, dictator	Formal abolition of Mancomunitat (1925); Macià's invasion of Catalonia fails (1926); Primo falls (1930)	Dalí holds first one-man show (1925)
1931–6	Second Spanish Republic	Alfonso XIII abdicates; Generalitat restored; new statute of autonomy for Catalonia (1932); right-wing victory in national elections (1933); death of Macià – Companys succeeds him as president of Generalitat (1934); Catalan revolt against national government; statute of autonomy suspended (1935); popular front wins elections, autonomy restored (1936)	

1936–9	Spanish Civil War	Military revolt against the Republic (July 1936); Majorca, Ibiza, Formentera join rebels but Minorca and Catalan mainland loyal to Republic; failure of Republican offensive in Aragon (1937) and across Ebro (1938); Catalonia invaded (1938); Barcelona falls (1939); mass exodus of refugees to France	Civil War produces spate of foreign literature: Orwel, Borkenau, Peers
1939–75	General Franco, caudillo and regent of Spain	All Catalan institutions abolished; severe post-war reprisals and repression; Spanish 'economic miracle' (1960s) draws million Spanish immigrants to Catalonia; tourist boom; death of Franco (1975)	Post-war Catalan painting achieves world-wide acclaim with work of Tàpies; literary resistance to Franco led by Espriu; Gimferrer leading poet of 'generation of '68'
1975	Joan Carles I (Juan Carlos I of Spain)	Bourbon monarchy restored; Josep Tarradellas, exiled president of Generalitat, returns (1977); new Spanish constitution provides for semi-autonomous regions (1978); statute of autonomy creates autonomous community of Catalonia (1979)	Riba, Pla and Monzó emerge as literary figures

Bibliography

Art and Architecture

Arts Council of Great Britain, *Homage to Barcelona: the city and its art (1888–1936)*. London: 1985.

*Barral i Altet, Xavier and Gumí, Jordi, *L'art pre-romànic a Catalunya, segles IX–X*. Barcelona: Edicions 62, 1981.

Bevan, Bernard, *History of Spanish Architecture*. London: Batsford, 1928.

Bohigas, Oriol, *Reseña y catálogo de la arquitectura modernista*. 3rd ed. Barcelona: Editorial Lumen, 1983.

*Carbonell, Eduard and Gumí, Jordi, *L'art romànic a Catalunya, segle XII*. 2 vols. Barcelona: Edicions 62, 1974–5.

Cirici i Pellicer, Alexandre, *El art modernista catalán*. Barcelona: Ayma, 1951.

*Cirici i Pellicer, Alexandre and Gumí, Jordi, *L'art gòtic català, segles XIII i XIV*. Barcelona: Edicions 62, 1977.

— *L'art gòtic català, segles XV i XVI*. Barcelona: Edicions 62, 1979.

Collins, G.R. and Bassegoda, J., *The Designs and Drawings of Antonio Gaudí*. Princeton University Press, 1983.

Conant, Kenneth J., *Carolingian and Romanesque Architecture (800–1200)*. London: Pelican, 1959.

Durliat, Marcel, *Art Catalan*. Paris: Collection Zodiaque, 1963.

Fundació Enciclopèdia Catalana, *Catalunya romànica*. Vols. I–IV to date. Barcelona: 1984. (Each volume of this series is devoted to a single *comarca*; eventually it will cover the whole of Catalonia.)

Gudiol i Gunill, Josep and Sanpere i Miquel, Salvador, *La pintura medieval catalana: els primitius* (3 vols.); *Els trescentistes* (2 vols.); *Los cuatrocentistas catalanes: historia de la pintura en el siglo XV* (2 vols.). Barcelona: printed privately, 1909–55.

Harvey, John, *The Cathedrals of Spain*. London: Batsford, 1957.

Junyent, Eduard, *Catalogne romane*. 2 vols. Paris: Collection Zodiaque/La-Pierre-Qui-Vire, 1968–70.

Mackay, David, *Modern Architecture in Barcelona (1854–1939)*. London: The Anglo-Catalan Society, 1985.

Martinell, César, *Gaudí. His Life. His Theories. His Work*. Cambridge, Mass.: MIT Press, 1975.

Puig i Cadafalch, Josep, *L'arquitectura romànica a Catalunya*. 3 vols. Barcelona: Institut d'Estudis Catalans, 1909–18 and reprinted 1983.

Whitehill, Walter M. and Gumí, Jordi, *L'art romànic a Catalunya, segle XI*. Barcelona: Edicions 62, 1973.

Worringer, Wilhelm, *Form in Gothic*. London: Putnam, 1927.

Asterisked volumes belong to the same series.

History, Politics and Economics

Almirall, Valentí, *Lo catalanisme*. Re-issued Barcelona: Edicions 62/La Caixa, 1979.

Borkenau, Franz, *The Spanish Cockpit*. London: Faber & Faber, 1937.

Brenan, Gerald, *The Spanish Labyrinth*. Cambridge University Press, 1943.

Gibbs, Jack, *The Spanish Civil War*. London: Ernest Benn, 1973.

Kaminski, H.E., *Ceux de Barcelone*. Paris: Editions Denoël, 1937.

Langdon-Davies, John, *Behind the Spanish Barricades*. London: Secker & Warburg, 1936.

Moreno, Eduardo and Martí, Francisco, *Catalunya para españoles*. Barcelona: Gráficas Alfonso, 1979.

Muntaner i Pascual, Josep Maria, *Cap a una economia dels països catalans*, Barcelona: Edicions La Magrana, 1979.

Orwell, George, *Homage to Catalonia*. London: Secker & Warburg, 1938.

Peers, E. Allison, *The Spanish Tragedy, 1930–36*. London: Methuen, 1936.
— *Catalonia Infelix*. London: Methuen, 1937.
— *Spain in Eclipse*, 1937–43. London: Methuen, 1943.

Prat de la Riba, Enric, *La nacionalitat catalana*. Re-issued Barcelona: Editorial Barcino, 1977.

Thomas, Hugh, *The Spanish Civil War*. London: Pelican, 1968.

Travel, Topography and Culture

Alford, Violet, *Pyrenean Festivals*. London: Chatto & Windus, 1937.

Baedeker, Karl, *Spain and Portugal*. London: T. Fisher Unwin, 1898 and subsequent editions.

Belloc, Hilaire, *The Pyrenees*. London: Methuen, 1909.

Brenan, Gerald, *The Literature of the Spanish People*. Cambridge University Press, 1943.

Casassas i Simó, Lluís and Gumí, Jordi, *Fires i mercats a Catalunya*. Barcelona: Edicions 62, 1978.

Cirici i Pellicer, Alexandre (ed.), *Relaciones de las culturas castellana y catalana*. Barcelona: Generalitat de Catalunya, 1983.

Fàbregas, Xavier and Gumí, Jordi, *Tradicions, mites i creences dels catalans*. Barcelona: Edicions 62, 1979.

Fedden, Robin, *The Enchanted Mountains*. London: John Murray, 1962.

Ford, Richard, *Handbook for Travellers in Spain*. London: John Murray, 1845 and subsequent editions.

Langdon-Davies, John, *Dancing Catalans*. London: Jonathan Cape, 1929.
— *Gatherings from Catalonia*. London: Cassell, 1953.

Locker, Edward Hawke, *Views in Spain*. London: John Murray, 1824.

Macaulay, Rose, *Fabled Shore: from the Pyrenees to Portugal*. London: Oxford University Press, 1949.

Michener, James, *Iberia*. London: Secker & Warburg, 1969.

Murray, James Erskine, *A Summer in the Pyrenees*. 2 vols. London: John Macrone, 1837.

Myhill, Henry, *The Spanish Pyrenees*. London: Faber & Faber, 1966.

Robertson, Ian, *Spain, the Mainland*. London: Ernest Benn, 1975.

Townsend, Joseph, *A Journey through Spain, 1786–87*. 3 vols. London: C. Dilly, 1792.

Trueta, Josep, *The Spirit of Catalonia*. London: Oxford University Press, 1946.

Vázquez, Montalbán, and Manuel and Gumí Jordi, *L'art de menjar a Catalunya*. Barcelona: Edicions 62, 1977.

Vila, Marc-Aurel and Sagarra, Montserrat, *La casa rural a Catalunya*. Barcelona: Edicions 62, 1980.

Violant Somorra, Ramon and Gumí, Jordi, *L'art popular a Catalunya*. Barcelona: Edicions 62, 1980.

Workman, Fanny Bullock and Hunter, William, *Sketches Awheel in Fin de Siècle Iberia*. London: T. Fisher Unwin, 1897.

Index

accommodation 290–2
Agramunt 151, 152, 153, 199
Aguiló 154–5
Aiguablave 291
Aigües Tortes 136–7
Albéniz, Isaac (1860–1909) 117, 258–9, 275
Alfons I, el Cast (the Chaste) (1162–96) 6, 177, 180, 185, 237, 304
Alfons II, el Franc (1285–91) 305
Alfons III, el Benigne (1327–36) 305
Alfons IV, el Magnànime (1416–58) 9, 306
Alfons V (XII of Spain)(1874–85) 12, 221, 312
Alfons VI (XIII of Spain)(1885–1931) 17, 54–5, 61, 142, 225, 313, 314
Alforja 177
Al-Mansur 187, 196, 303
Almirall, Valentí 12, 222, 233
   Lo catalanisme 233, 313
Almogàvers 7–8, 238–9, 305
Alp 126
Amer 105–6
Amposta 169
Andorra 130–1
Andorra la Vella 131
Aneto, Mt 139
architecture
   Gothic 193, 197, 200–2, 244
   Modernisme 15, 55–60, 243–54
   Romanesque 193–8
   transitional 199–200
Aribau, B.C.: *L'oda a la pàtria* 233, 311
Arnau, Comte l' 278–9
art
   Gothic 202–6
   modern 255–64
   Romanesque 198
Arties 140, 141, 142, 291
Augustus, Emperor 4, 300
Avellanes, Les 134

Balaguer 133–4, 156, 291
Banyoles 108–9, 208, 291
Barcelona 1–4, 10, 17, 18, 23–67
   accommodation 291
   Ajuntament de Barcelona 37–8

Arc de Triomf 40, 55, 244
Barceloneta 11, 162
Barri Gòtic 29–40, 281
Biblioteca de Catalunya, 32, 47
Born Market 55
Casa Amatller 56, 247–8, 252
Casa Batlló 56, 248, 252
Casa Fuster 56
Casa Milà (La Pedrera) 56, 252
Casa Terrades (de les Punxes) 57, 247–8
Casa Viçens 57, 249
churches
   cathedral 30–1, 201
   Monestir de Pedralbes 60–1, 282
   Sagrada Família 15, 58–60, 252–3, 282
   Santa Agata chapel 30, 33
   Santa Anna 44
   Santa Maria del Mar 42–4, 201, 281–2
   Santa Maria del Pi 40, 202
   Sant Pau del Camp 46, 47
   Sant Pere de les Puelles 44
   Sants Just i Pastor 38, 202
Ciutadella, Parc de la 10, 54–5, 147, 282
Eixample 32–3, 55–60, 65
environs 60–4, 282–3
feasts and fairs 162, 267–71
Hospital de Sant Pau 57
Institut d'Estudis Catalans 47, 233–4
maps and guides 24–5, 41, 281, 295
Montjuïc 29, 48–54, 282
museums
   Arqueològic 52, 282
   d'Art de Catalunya 15–16, 34, 36, 48–51, 198, 282
   d'Art Modern 54–5, 255–6, 282
   d'Arts Decoratives 47, 281
   d'Arts, Indústries i Tradicions Populars 282
   de les Arts de l'Espectacle 46, 281
   Etnològic 52, 282
   Frederic Marès 34–6, 281
   Fundació Miró 51–2, 282
   de Geologia 55, 282

d'Història de la Ciutat 31–3, 281
Marítim 45–6, 281
Militar 53, 282
Monestir de Pedralbes 282
Picasso 44–5, 281
Tèxtil i de la Indumentaria 62, 281
de Zoologia 55, 282
Palau de la Generalitat 38–40
Palau de la Música 66–7, 246–7
Palau Nacional 15, 48, 53, 282
Palau de Pedralbes 61, 282
Parc Güell 57–8, 251–2, 282
Parlament de Catalunya 55, 228, 282
Passeig de Gràcia viii, 15, 33, 56–7, 246
Plaça del Rei 33, 35
Poble Espanyol 53–4, 282
Ramblas, Las viii, 23–8, 64–5, 281
restaurants 289
Tibidabo 29
transport 29, 52–3, 61, 65, 293
Bases de Manresa 223, 313
Beatus of Liébana 129
Beget 119
Bellpuig 151, 156
Bellver de Cerdanya 126
Benavarri 145
Benedict XIII, Pope (Pedro Martínez de Luna)(1328–1422) 173, 210
Benedictines 19, 79, 92, 111, 193, 207–8, 302
benvengi 139–40
Berenguer, F. 249, 251, 253
Berenguer Ramon, el Corbat (the Hunchback)(1017–35) 219, 303
Berga 79, 269
Berguedà, Guillem de 237
Bermejo, Bartolomé 31
Besalú 109–11
Binéfar 145
Bisbal, La 87, 275
Black Friars *see* Benedictines
Blai, Pere 38
Bofill, Guillermo 98
Boí 144, 291
Borén 138
Borges Blanques, Les 150–1
Borràs, Vicenç 89
Borrassà, Lluís (1380–1424) 78, 85, 103, 204
bourgeoisie, nineteenth-century role 13–15, 221–3
Brenan, Gerald: *The Spanish*

Labyrinth 1, 16, 105, 215
Burgunya, Joan de (1470–1555) 103

Cadaqués 91, 94, 291
Cadí, Mt 128
Calaf 154
Calafell 161
Caldes de Boí 145
Camarasa 134
Cambó, Francesc 16, 48, 226
Camprodon 116–19, 291
Cardet 144
Cardona 75–6, 197, 291
Carles I (V of Holy Roman Empire) (1516–56) 30, 179, 307
Carles II (1665–1700) 10, 308
Carles IV (III of Spain) (1759–88) 11, 170, 220, 233, 309
Carles V (IV of Spain) (1788–1808) 310
Carmelites 210
Carner, Josep 241
Casa dels Cornellà 109, 110
Casals, Pau (1876–1973) 72, 275, 276
Casas, Ramon (1866–1932) 54–5, 256–9
Casserres 81
castellers 155–6, 271, 272
Castelló d'Empúries 89, 202
catalanisme 13, 16–17, 222
catalanitat 16–17, 19, 170, 271
Cava, La 169–70
Cerdà, Ildefons 33
Cervera 152–4, 156, 292
Charles (kings) *see* Carles
Cistercians 62, 169, 177–88, 200–2, 209–10, 304
Coll 144
Coll de Nargó 132
Colom, Joan 278
colonies industrials 81–2, 222–3, 251
Columbus, Christopher 9, 23, 162, 278
comarques 3, 228
Companys, Lluís 18, 53, 225–6, 314
Conant, Kenneth: *Carolingian and Romanesque Architecture (800–1200)* 144
Consell de Cent (Council of One Hundred) 219–20, 277
Consolat de Mar 219, 305
Corbera 176, 267
corrida de toros 271–2
Costa Brava 73, 94
Cruïlles 87, 94
Cubells 133
Cuixà (Sant Miquel de Cuixà) 121, 124, 194, 208–9

Dalí, Salvador (b. 1904) 15, 89–91, 255, 262–4, 313
Dalmau, Lluís 50, 204
dances, traditional 272–5
Desclot, Bernard 238, 305
Diada 10, 267
Domènech i Montaner, Lluís (1850–1923) 55–7, 66, 223, 244–8, 282
Dominicans 9, 210
drinks 26–7, 65, 288
see also wines

Ebro river viii, 4, 18, 169, 174–7
Eiximenis, Francesc (1340–1409) 238
Empúries 4, 88–9, 202, 299
Erill-la-Vall 144–5, 196, 198
Escala, L' 88, 94
Escaló 136
Espluga de Francolí, L' 177, 292
Espot 136–8, 142, 292
Espriu, Salvador: *La pell de brau* (*The Bull's Pelt*) 26, 79, 241, 315
Estartit 88
Esterri d'Àneu 138
Eulalia, Saint 30, 278

Fabra, Pompeu 233, 235
fairs 265–72
Falset 178
feast days 265–72
Febrer, Andreu 239
Felip I (II of Spain)(1556–98) 77, 307
Felip II (III of Spain)(1598–1621) 232, 308
Felip III (IV of Spain)(1621–65) 10, 146, 232, 308
Felip IV (V of Spain)(1700–46) 10–11, 89, 95, 146, 220, 232, 309
Ferran I (Ferdinand of Antequera) (1412–16) 6, 8–9, 38, 180, 220, 277, 306
Ferran II (el Catòlic) and Isabel (1479–1516) 9, 38, 180, 210, 220, 278, 307
Ferran III (VI of Spain)(1746–59) 309
Ferran IV (VII of Spain)(1814–33) 11–12, 221, 311
Ferrer Bassa (active 1324–48) 85, 204–6
Ferrer, Jaume II (active 1434–57) 78, 85–6, 204
Ferrer, Saint Vincent (1350–1419) 104–5, 216, 238, 306
Figols 131–2
Figueres 89–91, 292

Museu Dalí 89–91, 283
Fiveller, Councillor 276–7
Flix 175
Flor, Roger de 7–8, 37–8, 238, 278, 305
Fluvià monastery 208
Fluvià river 83, 95, 110
Foix, Josep Viçens 241
Fonoll, Reinard (Raynard Fonoyll) 182, 184, 202
food and drink 65, 284–9
Ford, Richard: *Handbook for Travellers in Spain* 2, 13–14, 22, 30–1, 64–77 *passim*, 88, 95, 97, 114, 125, 145, 164, 179–81, 235
Franciscans 75, 210
Franco, General (1939–75) 315
Franco years 18–20, 72, 226, 234, 241, 263, 266
Franja, La (the Fringe) 145–6, 150

Gali, Francesc d'Assis 261
Gallissà, A.M. 248
Gandesa 175–6, 292
Garona river 140
Gasch, Sebastià: *Joan Miró* 261, 262
Gascó, Joan (late 15th–early 16th century) 86, 103
Gaudí i Cornet, Antoni (1852–1926) 15, 56–9, 223, 248–53
Generalitat (founded 1359) 9, 17, 20, 38–40, 218, 220, 225–7, 305–6, 314
and Catalan language 234, 275
Gerri de la Sal 135–6, 208
Gimferrer, Pere: *L'espai desert* (*The Empty Space*) 19, 26, 241
Girona 3, 12, 95–105
Banys Àrabs (Arab Baths) 101–2
cathedral 97–9, 201
diocesan museum 99, 204, 206
Jewish quarter 104–5
Museu d'Art 103–4, 283
Museu d'Història de la Ciutat 102–3
Sant Feliu church 99–100
Sant Pere de Galligants 100–1, 194, 197–8
Goya, Francisco (1746–1828) 11, 104
Granados, Enric (1867–1916) 259, 275
Great Exhibitions (1888 and 1929) 13, 15, 17, 53–4, 225, 244, 254
Greater Catalonia 2, 228–9, 232
Gris, Juan 261
Güell, Count Eusebi 245, 249–50, 253
guides and maps vii, 73, 88, 112, 137–8, 174, 282, 290, 293–7
guild system 31
Guimerà, Angel 240

history of Catalonia 2, 4–20, 187–9, 218–29
  see also Chronological Table
Homilies d'Organyà 131, 232, 237
Horta de Sant Joan 175–6, 210
Hostalets d'en Bas 106
hotels
  grading system 290
  Paradors 290–1
  suggestions 291–2
Huguet, Jaume (*c*.1415–92) 31, 33, 50–1, 63, 86, 203, 204

Ibáñez, Blasco: *El Papa del Mar* 173
Igualada 155
Illes Medes 88
Inquisition 9, 105, 210, 307
Institut d'Estudis Catalans 47, 49, 233–4, 313
Isaac el Cec (the Blind)(1165–1235) 214–15
  Museu d'Isaac el Cec 104
Isabel I (II of Spain)(1833–68) 12, 221, 311
Isil 138–9

Jaume I, el Conqueridor (1213–76) 7, 111, 180, 213–14, 216, 238, 277, 304
Jaume II, el Just (1291–1327) 94, 186, 305
Jesuits 74–5
Jews 13, 50, 111, 212–17
  attacks on 9, 104–5, 215–16, 306–7
Joan I, el Caçador (the Hunter) (1387–96) 306
Joan II, Sense Fe (the Faithless) (1458–79) 9, 180, 306
Joan Carles I (1975–) 19, 315
Jocs Florals 222, 231, 233, 238, 306, 311
Jordi de Sant Jordi 239, 306
Jujol, J.M. 249, 252–3

Langdon-Davies, John:
  Dancing Catalans 1, 273–4
  Gatherings from Catalonia 1
language viii, 10–13, 19, 139–40, 145–6, 164, 170, 218, 226, 230–6, 309
  useful tips 235–6
legends 5, 276–9
Lés 144
literature 237–42
Llagostera 86
Llanars 119
Llavorsí 136
Lleida viii, 3, 146–50, 206, 292

La Seu Vella cathedral 146–9, 198–9, 201
Lliga Regionalista 16–17, 48, 223–4
Llívia 125, 283, 292
Llobregat river 72–3, 75, 81
Llull, Ramon 237–8
Llúria (Lauria) Roger de 8, 162, 186, 278
Locker, E.H. and Russell, Lord John: *Views in Spain* 1–2

Machado, Antonio 18, 156
Mackay, David: *Modern Architecture in Barcelona (1854–1939)* 56, 58–9, 243–4, 248, 251–3
Maladeta, Mt 139
Mancomunitat (1914–25) 17, 188, 224–5, 234, 313
Manresa 73–5, 292
Maragall, Joan (1860–1911) 12, 26, 233, 241–2, 258, 278
March, Ausiàs (b. 1397) 239, 306
Mare de Déu de la Mercè 270, 278
Marès, Frederic 34–6, 180–1
Martí I, l'Humà (the Humane) (1396–1410) 8, 33, 181, 220, 306
Martinet 126
Martorell, Bernat (active 1427–52) 86, 103, 204
Martorell, Joanot: *Tirant lo Blanc* 239, 306
Mas de Barberans 171
Masella 126
Mates, Pere (d. 1558) 103–4, 205
Mendizábal 12, 180, 311
Mestre de la Seu d'Urgell 51
Metge, Bernard (1340–1413) 238
Mir, Joaquim (1873–1940) 259
Miravet 175, 210, 304
Miró, Joan (1893–1983) 15–16, 51–2, 176–7, 241, 255, 261–4, 313
Modernisme 14–15, 55–60, 240–56, 313
Molina, La 126
Molló 119
monasticism 200, 207–11
  see also individual orders
Montagut 111
Montanyà, Lluís 262
Montblanc 169, 181–2, 272
Mont-roig 178, 262
Montserrat 11, 19, 68–9, 72–3, 155, 195, 208, 210–11, 234
Monzó, Quim 242, 315
Moreno, Eduardo and Martí,

Francisco: *Catalunya para españoles* 14, 16
Morera, Enric 276
municipis 3, 228
Muntaner, Ramon (1265–1336) 94, 238, 305
Mur, Ramon de (1402–35) 85, 204
Mura 75
Murray, J.E.: *A Summer in the Pyrenees* 274
museums 280–3
see also individual cities/towns
music 66–7, 275–6
mythology 5, 276–9

Negre river 142
Noguera Pallaresa river 135, 138
Noguera Ribagorçana river 134, 177
Nonell, Isidre (1873–1911) 259
Noucentisme 15–16, 241, 245, 253, 260–2, 313
Nova Planta 220–1, 309

Obiols 81, 198
Oliba, Abbot 92, 111–12, 121, 124, 208, 210
Olius 79, 195
Oller, Narcís 240
Oller, Pere 84
Olot 106–7, 292
Organyà 131
Ors, Eugeni d' 241, 260
Orwell, George: *Homage to Catalonia* 1, 16–18, 225

painting *see* art
Palafrugell 87
Palamós 87, 292
Palau-Sator 88
Paradors (Paradores Nacionales) 130, 290–1
Peers, Prof. E. A.: *Catalonia Infelix* 1
Peninsular War (1808–14) 1, 11–12, 95, 97, 119, 146, 221
Peralada 93–4, 273
Peratallada 88
Pere I, el Catòlic (1196–1213) 7, 304
Pere II, el Gran (the Great)(1276–85) 7–8, 186, 238, 305
Pere III, el Ceremoniós (1336–87) 38, 155, 178, 180–1, 185, 220, 238, 305
Philip, Kings *see* Felip
Picasso, Pablo (1881–1973) 15, 44–5, 175–6, 249, 255, 259–61, 263–4, 313
Pla, Josep 242, 315
Platja d'Aro 87

Poblet 169, 177–87, 200–1, 209
political life and institutions 218–29, 36
Porqueres 109
Port de la Selva, El 91–2, 94, 292
Portella, La 208
Prades 177
Prat de la Riba, Enric 17, 223–5, 313
La nationalitat catalana 224, 233, 313
Primo de Rivera, Miguel 17, 225, 272, 313
Puig i Cadafalch, Josep (1867–1957) 17, 23, 56–7, 64, 198, 223, 245, 247–8
Puigcerdà 124–5

Quatre Gats, Els (Four Cats tavern) 247, 258–9
Queralt 79

Ramon Berenguer I, el Vell (the Old) (1035–76) 30, 303
Ramon Berenguer II, Cap d'Estopa (Towhead)(1076–82) 99, 303
Ramon Berenguer II, el Fratricida (1076–97) 303
Ramon Berenguer III, el Gran (the Great)(1093–1131) 6, 36, 112, 157, 166, 303
Ramon Berenguer IV (1131–62) 6, 146, 157, 171, 209–10, 304
rauxa 276, 278–9
Renaixença (Renaissance) 12–15, 221–2, 231, 233–4, 255, 275, 311
Riba, Carles 241–2, 315
Ribagorçano dialect 145
Riba-roja d'Ebre 176
Ricart, Gudiol: *Museo Episcopal de Vich* 84
Ripoll 6, 111–13, 194–7, 208–9, 283, 292
Rocabruna 119
Rodoreda, Mercè 26, 241
Roig, Jaume 239
Romeu, Pere 258
Roses 4, 91, 94
routes into Catalonia 119, 121, 131, 142, 293
Rovira, Antoni 33
Rubió, Joan 155, 249
Rusiñol, Santiago (1861–1931) 55, 160, 241, 256–8, 283

Sabadell 64
Salardú 140, 141, 292

Salou 169
Salvat-Papasseit, Joan 241
Sant Carles de la Ràpita 11, 170
Sant Climent de Taüll 143, 144, 198
Sant Cugat del Vallès 61–2, 208–9
Sant Esteve d'en Bas 106
Sant Feliu de Guíxols 87, 94
Sant Hilari Sacalm 86
Sant Joan de les Abadesses 6, 114–16, 194, 197, 206, 208, 283
Sant Jordi 38, 277
Sant Llorenç de Morunys 78–9, 208
Sant Martí del Canigó 124, 208
Sant Martí Sarroca 156
Sant Miquel de Cuixà *see* Cuixà
Sant Pere de Ponts 132, 133, 198
Sant Pere de Rodes 92–3, 197–8, 208
Sant Quirze de Pedret 79–81, 198
Sant Ramon de Portell 154
Santa Coloma de Queralt 154, 156
Santa Pau 108
Santes Creus 169, 183–9, 200–1, 209, 292
sardana 272–4, 279
Saulet, Bernat 85
Segadors, Els ('The Reapers') 10, 275
Segre river 125–6, 131–4, 177
Sénia, La 171
seny 20, 276–9
Serra, Pere (1357–1409) 74, 78–9, 85, 129, 204
Serralonga 278
Sert, Josep Lluís 15, 38, 52, 254
Sert, Josep Maria 37–8, 54, 84
Setcases 119
Setmana Tràgica (Tragic Week) (1909) 16, 224, 313
Seu d'Urgell, La 126–30, 194, 197, 283, 291
Sibiuda, Ramon: *Theologia Naturalis* 239
Sitges 157, 160–1, 269, 283, 292
Solà-Morales, Ignasi de: 'Modernista Architecture' 248–9
Solsona 4, 76–9, 156, 292
diocesan museum 77–8, 283
songs, traditional 275
Sort 136
Southey, Robert 1
Spanish Civil War (1936–9) 1, 17–19, 53, 69, 76, 174, 176, 225–6, 314
Subirachs, Josep Maria 20, 39–40
Superespot 137–8
Súria 75
Swinburne, Henry 1

Talamanca 75
Tamarit 168–9
Tamarit de Llitera 145
Tàpies, Antoni (b. 1923) 255, 262–4, 315
Tarradellas, Josep 10–11, 20, 226, 315
Tarragona 3–4, 89, 161–8, 292
archaeological museum 163–4, 283
cathedral 166–8, 206
Museu i Necròpolis Paleo-cristiana 165–6
Pont del Diable 165
Rambla Nova, La 162
Roman remains 163-6
Tàrrega 151–2, 156
Tate, Bruce 248
Templars 210, 304
Ter river 95, 116
Terrassa 5, 61–4, 166, 283
Tivenys 173
Torras i Bages: *La tradició catalana* 239
Torre dels Escipions 161
Tortosa 171–4, 201–2, 210, 291, 304
Townsend, Joseph 1
Tredòs 140, 198
trekking 295
Tremp 135, 292
Trueta, Josep: *The Spirit of Catalonia* 1, 4

Ullastret 87–8, 94
Ulldecona 170–1, 202
Usatges de Barcelona 219, 303
Utrillo, Miquel 258

València d'Àneu 139
Vall, Pere 85
Vall d'Aran 139–42
Vallbona de les Monges 169, 182–3, 199, 200–1, 209
Valls, 169, 272
Vaqueira 140, 142
Ventura, Pep 274
Verdaguer, Jacint (1845–1902) 12, 26, 233, 240
Verges 269
Vic 82–6, 269, 291–2
diocesan museum 84–6, 204, 206, 283
El Cloquer 83, 84, 197–8
Viella 142, 291
Vilabertran 94
Vilafranca del Penedès 155–6, 202, 267, 272, 292
Museu del Vi 155, 283

Vilanova i la Geltrú 269
Visigoths 5
Vives, Joan Lluís (1492–1540)
  239–40

War of the Reapers (1640–52) 9, 146,
  232, 275, 308
War of the Spanish Succession (1700–
  13) 10, 95, 146, 308
White Friars *see* Cistercians

Wilfred, Count (Guifré el Pilós) (878–
  97) 5–6, 102, 111–12, 114, 208, 302
wines 156, 175, 177, 288
Worringer, Wilhelm: *Form in
  Gothic* 200

Yates, Alan: 'Catalan Literature
  between Modernism and Noucentism' 243
  Teach Yourself Catalan 236